ICELAND SAGA

Magnus Magnusson

ICELAND SAGA

THE BODLEY HEAD
LONDON

For
ELSE PAULSEN

British Library Cataloguing
In Publication Data
Magnusson, Magnus
Iceland Saga
I. Iceland — History
I. Title
949.1'2 DL338

ISBN 0–370–31074 8 – Trade Paperback
ISBN 0–370–31065 9 – Hardback

© Magnus Magnusson 1987
Printed in Great Britain for
The Bodley Head Ltd
32 Bedford Square, London WC1B 3EL
Phototypeset by Wyvern Typesetting Ltd, Bristol
First published in 1987
First reprinted 1987

Contents

LIST OF PLATES

The Commonwealth Farm in Thjórsárdalur: back view of the modern reconstruction of the excavated farm of Stöng, showing the two side-chambers off the main long-house.

Between pages 182 and 183

Aerial view of Skálholt, and the modern memorial church that replaced the old cathedral. In the background, the hill of Mosfell where the first settler in the district, Ketilbjörn the Old, made his home.

Holar in Hjaltadalur: seat of the former northern diocese. The modern bell-tower stands beside the eighteenth-century church, flanked by the buildings of the modern school.

Between pages 214 and 215

Borg at Borgarnes: the home of Egill Skallagrímsson, eponymous hero of *Egils Saga*, and also, for a time, of his descendant, Snorri Sturluson, the historian and probable author of the saga.

Snorri's Pool at Reykholt: the open-air pool, filled from a natural hotspring, was built in the thirteenth century by Snorri Sturluson. In the background, the underground passage that led to the cellar of his home.

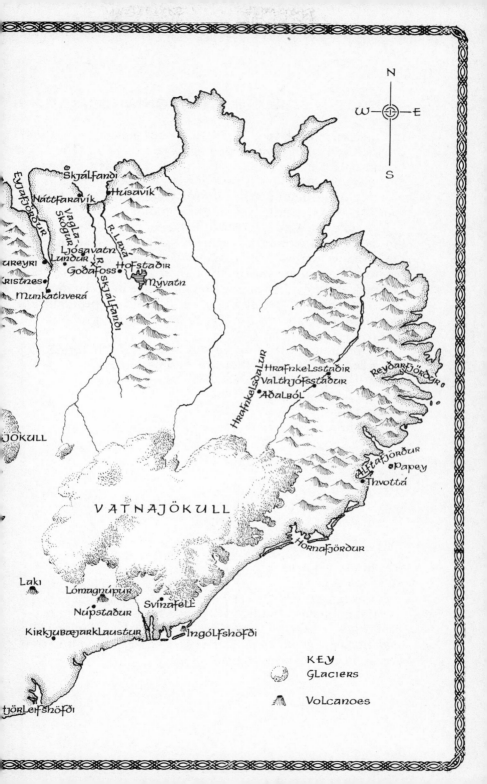

A NOTE ON PRONUNCIATION AND USAGE

In this book I have used Icelandic names and words in their original form and original spelling, accents and all. The only exception is the Icelandic letter þ (Þ), which is the Anglo-Saxon letter *thorn* and is pronounced as the unvoiced *th* in *thin*. To avoid undue difficulty for English readers, I have transliterated this letter into *th* throughout.

Icelandic words may look a little formidable at first glance, but the rules of pronunciation are basically simple and can be mastered very easily by readers who want to be able to pronounce the names correctly in their heads as they read.

Apart from þ, the only extra consonant in Icelandic is ð (Ð), the so-called 'crossed d' or 'eth', which is pronounced like the voiced *th* in *breathe*. The letter j is always pronounced like *y* in *yellow*.

The pronunciation of the vowels is strongly conditioned by the accents. This is how they are all pronounced:

a as in *father*
á as in *owl*
e as in *get*
é as *ye*, in *yet*
i as in *bid*
í as in *seen*
o as in *got*
ó as in *note*
u as in German *mütter*
ú as in *soon*
y, ý – like i, í.
æ, œ as in *life*
ö as in French *fleur*
au as in French *œil*
ei, ey as in *tray*

Personal names frequently change form in the genitive—Egill/Egils, Gunnar/Gunnars, Björn/Bjarnar, and so on. The saga titles are given in the Icelandic, like *Egils Saga*, to avoid the clumsiness of writing *Egill's Saga*.

CHAPTER 1

Saga Landscape

Landslag yrði
lítilsvirði,
ef það héti ekki neitt.

Landscape would have
little value
if the places had no names.

(Tómas Guðmundsson: *Fjallganga*)

There is a charming and witty little poem by the late Tómas
Guðmundsson (1901–84), 'the poet of Reykjavík', called
Fjallganga (Hill-walking). In it he describes the breathless
efforts of a suburban would-be climber on a day's outing in
the hills—the puffing and the panting, the scrabbling and the
scrambling, followed by the profound and self-conscious
satisfaction of reaching the top and gazing around with eagle
eyes like stout Cortez, silent, upon a peak in Darien, trying to
identify and name all the other peaks he can see in the far
distance; because, as the poet said, 'landscape would have
little value if the places had no names'.

It's an ironic and telling observation. And the converse is
just as true: that place-names would have little value if they
had no landscape, no physical perspectives to give them
identity and dramatic context. This is particularly true of
Iceland, for the story of Iceland—the Iceland Saga, as I like
to call it—is deeply rooted in the living landscape of the
country; this is what gives it a tremendous sense of place, an
alluring vividness of impact, for one can so readily relate it to
the natural landscape in which the historical events of the past
happened.

That landscape is very spectacular. Iceland has been called Nature's geological laboratory, for it is one of the most vigorously active volcanic regions on earth: Icelanders are now accustomed to expect an eruption to break out every five years or so. Geologically speaking, it is a very young country. It emerged in a series of convulsive volcanic effusions a mere twenty million years ago, in the Upper Tertiary period. Before that, Iceland did not exist. According to geologists, it came about because of the phenomenon known as continental drift. Some 200 million years ago, the major continents formed a super-continent called Pangaea; the pressure from below the earth's crust eventually cracked Pangaea into a number of tectonic plates that began drifting apart. As the American continental plate pulled away from the Afro-European plate, the basin of the Atlantic Ocean came into being; and where the original cracking occurred, incessant volcanic activity on the ocean floor created what is called the Mid-Atlantic Ridge—a long chain of submarine mountains that meanders from Antarctica to the Azores and on to Iceland. The molten rock, or magma, that underlies this rift system surfaces in a number of geological 'plumes'. Iceland is situated right on top of one such plume. As the sea-floor spreads, molten rock explodes through the vents to fill the gap and push the continental plates even farther apart. That is how the Icelandic plateau came into being, twenty million years ago; and that is what continues to make Iceland an active geological crucible.

The very first eruptions created a platform of laminated layers of basalt lava-flows. This is the basic bedrock of Iceland, about 10,000 metres thick. It can now only be seen in the east and north-west of the country, because so much of it has been overlaid by subsequent frenzied periods of volcanic activity. At the start of the Pleistocene period, about three million years ago, there were violent effusions of dolerite (grey basalt); and during the latter stages of the Ice Age, some 700,000 years ago, when Iceland lay submerged under the successive polar ice-sheets that invaded most of the northern hemisphere, the plume under Iceland erupted again and again. A thousand metres under the ice-fields furious conflicts raged, as volcano after volcano tried to force a way up through the ice. The mountains that were born under this chilly shroud were formed of compacted volcanic tuffs and breccias called palagonite (Icelandic *móberg*); this is a rather soft rock, rich in brownish hydrated glass, easily moulded into the individual and readily identifiable mountains that delineate the horizon at every turn.

When the covers came off at the end of the last Ice Age, some 10,000 years ago, Iceland began to emerge in something like the shape we know today: a brawling mass of mountains, young and dishevelled still, interspersed with fertile valleys gouged by the raking passage of the ice as it went grinding inexorably towards the coast. But the shaping has never ceased: no less than one-tenth of the surface of Iceland is covered by lava-flows that have spilled from more than 200 active volcanoes in geologically 'recent' time, in the post-glacial period. Some of the cover still remains, in a number of extravagantly beautiful glaciers and ice-caps covering another tenth of the country, including Europe's largest glacier, Vatnajökull (Waters Glacier) on the south coast.

At least thirty volcanoes are known to have been active in Iceland since the discovery and settlement of the country, only 1,100 years ago—and several of them many times over. Mount Hekla, which was renowned through Europe during the Middle Ages as one of the vents of Hell itself, has erupted on sixteen occasions, most recently in 1980/81. In earlier times it was hated and feared: a map of Iceland made in 1585 shows the volcano in full fury, captioned *HEKLA perpetuis damnata estib. er nivib. horrendo boatu lapides evomit* ('Hekla, cursed with eternal fires and snow, vomits rocks with a hideous sound'); but today's Icelanders are more concerned lest a new eruption destroys the classic beauty of its majestic shape!

Some volcanic eruptions have been catastrophically destructive. Two centuries ago, in 1783, the mountain Laki burst open in a fissure about twenty-five kilometres long. This fissure contained more than a hundred separate craters, the

Laki Craters (Lakagígar). From them poured the most extensive lava-flows on earth in historical times, covering 565
square kilometres of the southlands. But that was not the
worst of it. The long eruption (it lasted for ten months) was
accompanied by an enormous effusion of sulphur dioxide that
shrouded Iceland with a bluish haze, and the pastures were
poisoned by a mantle of volcanic ash that contained a fluorine
compound. Three-quarters of Iceland's livestock—horses,
cattle, sheep—died of starvation, and in the resultant
famine, known as the *Móðuharðindi* ('Haze Famine'), some
10,000 people perished, a fifth of the total population.

In the appalled aftermath of the Lakagígar eruption there
was talk of evacuating the surviving population of Iceland and
resettling them on some moorland in Denmark—all 40,000
of them. But no one took it very seriously, least of all the
Icelanders. They had grown used to their volcanoes, however
devastating. Today the Lakagígar area is regarded with awe
and even pride. It is spectacularly and eerily beautiful: the
sombre black ash-cones, the silent craters with their walls of
red-burned scoria, the lunar reaches of lava deeply carpeted
with soft grey moss that turns a brilliant green in the rain.
Visitors instinctively take care not to injure or despoil the
environment, as if it were a vast memorial to some ancient
cosmic war.

It is only within the last few years that the world at large has
come to realize how intensely volcanic Iceland actually is. In
November 1963 a submarine eruption off the south coast gave
birth to a new island, Surtsey (named after the fire-god of
Norse mythology, Surtur), and millions of television viewers
throughout the world were given a vivid action-replay of the
way in which the world itself was formed. Surtsey is now a
science reserve, a sanctuary in which scientists can study the
processes whereby newly-wrought land, isolated by the
ocean, is colonized by plant and animal life.

Ten years later, in 1973, another eruption off the south
coast brought the reality of volcanic activity much closer
home, to the very threshold of the little township on Heimaey
(Home Island) in the Westmann Islands (Vestmannaeyjar).

Much of the town was destroyed, but the population of 5,250 was evacuated overnight to the mainland without a single casualty; and when the eruption subsided, some five months later, the town and its prosperous fishing industry were rebuilt from the ashes, and Heimaey thrives again—a living example of the Iceland Saga of survival against all the odds.

Such is the dramatic, eventful landscape which provides the setting for the Iceland Saga. And historically as well as geologically Iceland is comparatively young; indeed, it is the only country that can actually remember its own beginnings, enshrined in the works of its early historians.

There is no evidence that Iceland was ever inhabited in prehistoric times: Iceland has history in abundance, but no prehistory at all, which makes it unique amongst the world's nations. However, it is clear that people in classical times had an inkling, at least, that Iceland existed, even if they knew little about it. As early as 330 BC—about the time when Alexander the Great was setting out on his attempt to conquer the known world—a resourceful Greek navigator called Pytheas of Marseilles (Massilia) was commissioned by his local city fathers to reconnoitre the relatively unknown world of northern Europe, to chart a new trade route by sea to the tin and amber markets there. His original report on his voyage has not survived, but it is possible to surmise some of its contents from references in later classical sources. He seems to have reached Britain, and even the Shetland Islands. There he heard of an island that lay six days' sail to the north, and this island he called Thule, or Ultima Thule. A day's further sail to the north lay 'the lung of the ocean', where the sea was said to be congealed into a sort of primeval jelly. There is no way of telling whether Pytheas meant Iceland or the arctic regions of Norway; but the name has since adhered to Iceland: Ultima Thule, the island at the end of the world.

There is a possibility—but no more than that—that a stray Roman ship may have reached Iceland, because four Roman copper coins from the period AD 270–305 have been found at three separate sites in the south of Iceland. They are certainly the oldest artefacts so far discovered in Iceland, and because they date from a period of peak Roman naval power under the command of the British governor Carausius (AD 286– 293), it has been suggested that they found their way there on board a Roman galley on long-range patrol, or perhaps storm-swept off its course, and were then hoarded as souvenirs by the early Viking settlers of Iceland several centuries later. But since coins of this kind have been widely found in Britain, it is considered much more probable that they were taken to Iceland during the Viking Age as curios, antique relics without monetary value.

In the Middle Ages it is clear that the name Thule had become attached to Iceland as an article of academic faith. The Venerable Bede, early in the eighth century, referred to Thule more than once in his *De temporibus* (AD 703) and the larger *De temporum ratione* (AD 725), and was cited as an authority by the early Icelandic historians:

> In his book *On Times*, the Venerable Priest Bede makes mention of an island called Thule, which in other books is said to lie six days' sail to the north of Britain. He says that there is neither daylight there in winter, nor darkness during summer when the day is at its longest. For that reason, learned men reckon that Thule must be Iceland, for there are many places in the land where the sun shines throughout the night during the longest days and where it cannot be seen during the day when the nights are longest.
>
> (*Landnámabók*: *Book of Settlements*)

A century later, in AD 825, an Irish cleric called Dicuil at the court of the Emperor Charlemagne wrote a geographical treatise, *De mensura orbis terrae*. His work had urgent topical relevance, for Europe was then wincing from the early impact of the Viking Age—hammer-blow raids on ecclesiastical and commercial centres by sea-borne pirates from Scandinavia. Ireland and England, and to a lesser extent France, had already felt the sting of attacks on Lindisfarne and other island monasteries, from AD 793 onwards; so any information about these new barbarians was eagerly welcomed. Dicuil was writing with all the authority of the Church of Ireland, whose disciplined learning had enriched the libraries of Europe and whose ardent monks had carried the gospel to hitherto heathen lands. Dicuil knew stories of distant countries from monks who had experienced them at first hand —including Thule:

> It is now thirty years since priests who lived in that island from the first of February to the first of August told me that not only at the summer solstice but on the days to either side of it the setting sun hides itself at the evening hour as if behind a little hill, so that no darkness occurs during that very brief period; but that whatever task a man wishes to perform, even to picking the lice from his shirt, he can manage as precisely as in broad daylight . . .

Scholars are in no doubt that by Thule Dicuil was referring to Iceland. Nor should it surprise us that the Irish could undertake such sea-voyages at this time. Irish hermit monks had established themselves on the then uninhabited Faroes around 700, bringing with them the sheep from which the islands derive their name. They sailed in large hide boats called currachs, made of ox-hides tanned in oak bark, stretched over a wooden framework and sewn together with leather strips, and then tautened with melted tallow. They could carry a crew of twenty men with ample provisions for long journeys, and carried sail as well as oars. They were excellent ocean craft, as was shown by the adventurer Tim Severin, who constructed just such a boat for a voyage he made from Ireland to the Faroes and Iceland in 1977, and from there to Greenland and North America.

The early Icelandic historians certainly believed that Irish monks had been present in Iceland before the arrival of the first Viking settlers in the second half of the ninth century. The first vernacular historian, Ari the Learned (see Ch 12), wrote about their presence, and hasty departure, at the time of the first settlers in his *Íslendingabók* (*Book of Icelanders*):

At that time there were Christians living here, whom the
Norsemen called *papar*, but they left the country because
they did not want to associate with pagan people; they
left Irish books and bells and croziers, from which one
could tell that they were Irishmen.

A scattering of place-names from the south-east of Iceland,
like Papey and Papós and Papýli, might seem to corroborate
this tradition by indicating where these *papar* ('little fathers')
had once lived. But despite diligent archaeological excavation (on the island of Papey in 1972, for instance), no material
evidence of Irish occupation has yet been found.

The Settlement of Iceland proper was carried out by
Norsemen in the second half of the ninth century, a few
decades after the onset of the so-called Viking Age (800–
1050). Tradition has it that the name of the first settler was
Ingólfur Arnarson, who made his home at Reykjavík in the
year 874 (see Ch 2). His was not the first visit by a Norseman,
however; an earlier explorer, Hrafna-Flóki (Ravens-Flóki),
had wintered there a few years previously and bestowed on it
the unflattering name of 'Iceland' (*Ísland*) in preference to
the more romantic-sounding Thule.

Ingólfur Arnarson was followed by a steady stream of
immigrants, mostly from western Norway but some from
Viking enclaves in the British Isles, particularly Shetland and
the Orkneys and Ireland. The reasons for this mass migration
were doubtless complex, as indeed were the 'causes' of the
Viking Age itself—a mixture of Scandinavian power-politics,
land-hunger, commercial expansionism, technological skill
(especially in ship-building), enterprise and sheer physical
vigour. Early Icelandic historical tradition tended to simplify,
indeed over-simplify, the position: the Settlement of Iceland
was the direct outcome of the tyrannical behaviour of the first
king to unite the scattered regions of Norway into a single
realm, King Harald Fine-Hair. According to the Icelandic
historians, Harald Fine-Hair succeeded to the petty kingdom
of Vestfold in south-eastern Norway around the year 870 at
the age of sixteen. Not only did he manage to hold on to his

inheritance, but soon he was engaged in a determined and ruthless campaign to make himself master of all Norway; eventually, around the year 890, he won a celebrated victory against a confederacy of recalcitrant chieftains and sea-kings at the naval battle of Hafrsfjord, just off the modern Norwegian oil-boom town of Stavanger. As a result of this victory, many of the defeated chieftains and independent-minded magnates who had opposed Harald's rise to power fled the country, some to Iceland and others to join kinsmen who had settled in Scotland and Ireland. Harald pursued the fugitives to the Orkneys and Shetland and conquered those Northern Isles, too, making them subject to the Norwegian crown— whereupon another exodus to Iceland began, of Norsemen who had by now intermarried into families of native Celtic stock and who took with them Scottish and Irish wives and kinsmen and slaves.

Such, in outline, was the political situation in Norway late in the ninth century. Iceland's historians tended to telescope the time involved, in order to explain the motives of the early settlers; but it is reasonable to assume that even if Harald Fine-Hair was not the prime cause of the first settlements, his forcible centralization of royal power in Norway added considerable impetus to the movement westwards to Iceland.

The earliest settlers came in small family groups, sailing in relatively small cargo vessels that could accommodate sufficient livestock with which to start farming—sheep, cattle, pigs, horses, goats and geese. The boats were not the celebrated longships used for coastal warfare, like the Gokstad and Oseberg ships that were excavated from burial mounds in Norway in 1880 and 1904, but the stubbier, swanbreasted deep-sea traders that were the all-purpose ships of the Viking Age. This maid-of-all-work was called a *knörr*. By great good fortune, a *knörr* was discovered in 1962 and salvaged, almost entire, from the waters of Roskilde Fjord in Denmark. Standing on display in the Roskilde Ship Museum, she looks astonishingly small: what a cramped, uncomfortable and perilous journey the passage to Iceland must have been!

These early immigrants found a vast island that was to all intents and purposes virgin territory. The central highlands were barren and uninhabitable, but round the coasts were plains and valleys well capable of supporting the kind of farming they had pursued in Norway. The climate was tolerable, despite the country's chilly new name—what meteorologists tactfully call 'cold-tempered oceanic' or even 'temperate sub-boreal', which means that it is considerably better than one has any right to expect at such a northern latitude. Furthermore, the mean temperature in the first centuries of settlement was a little warmer than it is today, by an average of about 1°C, and at that latitude a single degree makes a great deal of difference. In the second place, the pattern of vegetation was very different then. Iceland's first vernacular historian, Ari the Learned, wrote in his *Íslendingabók* around 1130 that 'in those days, Iceland was wooded between mountain and shore'. That statement may come as a surprise to those who know Iceland today as a country almost entirely bare of trees; but it shows that only 250 years after the first settlers had arrived, there were already far fewer trees than there had been: the severe denudation of Iceland's vegetative cover had begun.

Modern botanical research has shown that the tree-line in the early days of the Settlement reached as far up as 500 metres above sea-level (today it is no more than 300 metres) and that most of the country, with the exception of recent lava-fields, glacier sands and the soggiest marshland, was overgrown with birch wood and dwarf willow with occasional rowans and aspens. It has been estimated that 25 per cent of the land was tree-covered; today, the figure is only 1 per cent. Overall, it is believed that at the time of the Settlement as much as 60 per cent of the surface of Iceland had a covering of vegetation of some sort—all but the high plateaux of the interior, in fact. Today that figure is only 21 per cent, consisting of 20 per cent rough grazing and only 1 per cent arable land.

What caused this catastrophic decline that turned huge areas of fertile land into bleak deserts and semi-deserts?

Partly the blame lies in the steady deterioration of the climate for all but the last century—the Little Ice Age of the late Middle Ages. Partly the blame can be found in incessant volcanic activity—lava-flows that destroyed farms and pastures, ash-falls that obliterated fertile valleys, glacier-bursts and floods that turned the low-lying coastal farmlands of the south into desolate plains of black sand. But the real culprit, without a doubt, has been man himself. Before Iceland was settled, there were no herbivorous animals living in the country—no indigenous land animals at all, indeed, except for the Arctic fox. By introducing livestock, the settlers shattered the country's natural ecology with heavy and uncontrolled grazing. Meanwhile the settlers busied themselves with felling the woods around their farmsteads for pastoral and agricultural purposes and to make charcoal for heating. As the woods disappeared, soil erosion set in; deprived of shelter from the keen wind and the anchoring carpet of vegetation, the soil began to blow away in all directions. Winter rains scoured the undefended hillsides and laid them bare. Today, diligent efforts are being made to turn the ecological clock back, but it is a desperately slow business.

The pattern of settlement was dictated by the demands of the terrain, as it was to be for centuries thereafter. Individual farms required a lot of land to be economically viable, and so settlement was widely dispersed and farmsteads flourished in the remotest upland valleys as well as down by the coasts. Physical communications were daunting. Torrential rivers, formidable mountains, impassable reaches of lava and huge distances were forbidding obstacles to social intercourse. But the settlers from Norway had brought with them a creature that made light of difficulty and distance—the hardy, nimble-footed Icelandic pony, the pure-bred *equus scandinavicus*. It was as important a catalyst for settlement by land as the *knörr* was by sea. Sturdy and docile, the pony carried everyone and everything on its back—and continued to do so, indeed, for a thousand years; the first road for wheeled vehicles was not built in Iceland until 1874. The Icelandic pony has not changed in the slightest over the centuries; it has never interbred with foreign stock, and is still the original Viking horse. It has a unique range of five gaits: step (*fetgangur*), trot (*brokk*), gallop (*stökk*), pace (*skeið*), and running walk, or rack (*tölt*), which is the distinctive gait of the Icelandic pony, setting it apart from other European breeds—the rider sits perfectly still in the saddle, while the pony positively glides along. Pony-riding in Iceland is now a pleasure and a sport rather than a necessity; to own a herd of ponies is something of a status symbol. There are some 60,000 ponies in Iceland now, adding romance and glamour to the landscape as they range free in the upland pastures. In the long Iceland Saga, the bond between man and horse has always been close and affectionate.

The earliest settlers, with the whole island to choose from, carved out huge tracts of land for themselves: Ingólfur Arnarson, the First Settler, for instance, laid claim to the whole of the south-western corner of Iceland. Each main settler would then parcel out his land-claim to his kinsmen and followers and freemen, thus building up close-knit clan communities of which the family head became leader by dint of wealth, personal authority and power of patronage. One eminent lady settler, Auður the Deep-Minded (*djúpúðga*), came from Norway via Scotland with twenty well-born freemen, many of them with their own families, and became the matriarch of the Laxdalers in *Laxdæla Saga* (see Ch 15). As time passed, land would be sold or let in smaller parcels to new arrivals. New settlers could no longer have their pick of what they wanted, and rules for limiting the size of land-claims were agreed: no man could take more land than he could run round in one day carrying a lighted torch, and no woman could take more land than a two-year-old heifer could go round in one day.

Landnámabók (*Book of Settlements*), originally compiled by Ari the Learned and others in the first half of the twelfth century (see Ch 12), is the major historical source about the Settlement of Iceland. It records the names, genealogies and biographies of some of the principal settlers, and their land-claims—some 430 of them in all. No other nation in Europe is blessed with such a remarkable record of its remembered history from the very outset. But in addition to *Landnámabók*, Iceland has a wealth of other sources about the lives and loves and deaths of the early settlers in the literature of the Icelandic sagas.

One of the greatest of the sagas, *Egils Saga*, the *Saga of Egill Skallagrímsson* (see Ch 14), gives us a glimpse of the way in which Egill's father, a diligent and determined pioneer, exploited the natural resources of the place and built up a prosperous stake in the new country. His name was Skallagrímur, a Norwegian farmer-Viking who had fallen foul of King Harald Fine-Hair and started a new life in Iceland at Borg, in Borgarfjörður, on the west coast; his son was the great Icelandic warrior-poet Egill Skallagrímsson, the eponymous hero of the epic *Egils Saga*:

Skallagrímur was a great man for hard work. He always had a lot of men working for him, busy getting in all the available supplies that might be useful for the household; for at first they had few livestock, considering how many people there were. What livestock they had were left to fend for themselves in the woods during the winter.

Skallagrímur was also a great ship-builder. There was no shortage of driftwood to be had west of Mýrar, so he built another farm at Álftanes; from there his men went out fishing and seal-hunting and egg-gathering, for there was plenty of everything available there. They also brought in all his driftwood. Whales were frequent visitors, too, and one could harpoon as many as one wanted. None of the wildlife was wary, for it was unaccustomed to man.

Skallagrímur had a third farm down by the sea in the west part of Mýrar, where it was even easier to get at the driftwood. He started sowing there, and called the place Akrar (Cornfields). There were some islands lying offshore where a whale had been beached, so they called them Hvalseyjar (Whale Isles). Skallagrímur also had his men go up the rivers looking for salmon, and settled

Oddur *einbúi* (Live-Alone) on the river Gljúfrá to look after the salmon-fishing there . . .

As Skallagrímur's livestock multiplied, the animals started making for the mountains in the summer. He found a big difference in the livestock, which were much bigger and fatter for having grazed on the high moorland, and above all in the sheep that wintered in the mountain valleys instead of being brought down. As a result, Skallagrímur had a house built up in the fells and ran it as a sheep-farm. A man called Gríss was put in charge of it, and Grísartunga is named after him.

And now Skallagrímur's wealth stood on more legs than one.

The Age of Settlement, as it is called—the first period of Iceland's history—is traditionally reckoned to have lasted for sixty years, from 870 to 930. By the end of that period, the population of the country was fairly substantial, although no one can now estimate it with any certainty: somewhere between 25,000 and 40,000 seems to be the consensus opinion of scholars. It was a pioneering, frontier society; those who worked hard and had chosen their land well, like Skallagrímur of Borg, were able to live well, if not luxuriously. Their work-force of hired farmhands and other dependants was supplemented by slaves or 'thralls'—mainly captives who had been taken during earlier Viking raids. It is often assumed that slavery was widespread in Iceland at this time, but there is no evidence that slaves played a significant part in the economy. The word 'slavery' now has profoundly emotive associations, with echoes of clanking chains and oppressive cruelty; but 'slaves' in Iceland seem to have been accorded much more sympathetic treatment than was common elsewhere. They enjoyed certain legal privileges, and could earn their freedom, and even some land of their own, through exemplary service or loyalty to their masters. Iceland, it seems clear, was never a proper slave-owning society in the fullest sense of the term; and the pioneering conditions of the Age of Settlement would have made it difficult in any case to maintain the formal distinction between slavery and freedom.

In any formative society, some men rise to the top like cream by dint of their prowess and personality, bolstered by family ties and accrued possessions. Most of the leading settlers had been men of substance in Norway or the British Isles (it needed considerable resources to be able to afford the cost of emigration, for one thing), and they settled naturally into a loose aristocracy or oligarchy of land-owning magnates. It was essentially a chieftain society (the Icelandic word is *höfðingi*, 'head'); and the authority of the chieftain was reinforced by some sort of priestly office. Most of the settlers, with some notable exceptions, were pagans; they believed in a loose pantheon of Norse gods and natural spirits, but not in any systematic way. Paganism as a formal religion was on the wane throughout the Northlands at this time, and would soon be replaced by Christianity; but during the pagan period the leading chieftains of Iceland also had religious functions to perform. Such men had the title of *goði*, (plural *goðar*), usually translated as 'priest-chieftain', and their office was the *goðorð*. It is not clear to what extent, if any, specifically religious duties like temple-worship were involved—there is some doubt whether pagan temples as such ever existed in Iceland—and the office could be inherited, bought or sold, divided, or even temporarily borrowed. But whatever the function of the office, the real power of the *goði* lay in the personal allegiance and number of his followers, whose interest he took care to safeguard in return.

Soon after the Age of Settlement began, it must have become apparent that some sort of organization was necessary to regulate the exercise of power and deal with disputes. We are told that local assemblies or Things (the Icelandic word is *þing*) were established, where local disagreements were settled by the chieftains with the help of specially appointed courts. These Things were judicial rather than legislative, however; there was still a need for a common law, a common system of authority, that would cover the whole country. To this end, in the year 930, the Icelanders combined to establish a General Assembly, the Althing (*Alþingi*), at Thingvellir (see Ch 7). The law-code that was adopted was based on Norwegian law, but with one fundamental difference: no provision was made for a monarchy. Iceland was to be a parliamentary commonwealth without a king—a unique experiment in medieval republicanism that was to stand for the next 330 years.

This was the first major milestone in the history of the newly-fledged nation. The second was the adoption of Christianity as the formal religion of Iceland around the year 1000 (see Ch 10). Quite apart from its extraordinary importance for the future cultural and spiritual development of the country, the occasion itself provided one of the most spectacular scenes from the whole Iceland Saga: the passion and drama of debate in the magnificent open-air setting of Thingvellir—pure theatre for the mind and the senses. It was one of the innumerable times when the Saga landscape gave an added dimension to the saga itself.

The introduction of Christianity had little immediate effect on the political or social structure of Iceland. Pagan priest-chieftains simply became Christian chieftains, with the added power and influence of church patronage at their disposal. Overall, the times became a little less turbulent, perhaps; indeed, the period from 1030 to 1120 is familiarly known as the Age of Peace, to differentiate it from the more disputatious decades of the Settlement and the early commonwealth. That earlier period, indeed, is known as the Saga Age—for it was during those first 160 years that most of the events occurred that were to be chronicled in the Icelandic sagas.

The Icelandic sagas were the major and most enduring achievement of medieval Iceland. Indeed, they were the outstanding achievement of European medieval literature. And to understand the nature and quality of that achievement, it is essential to see the sagas in the perspective of the landscape in which they grew; for the sagas did not simply happen. They were the outcome of a long process of cultural development, the ultimate flowering of a unique literary experience.

It was the Church that first brought books to Iceland, and thereby introduced Iceland into the mainstream of European intellectual thought. The art of writing was brought to Iceland early in the eleventh century by missionary English priests, but by the middle of the century the first native Icelandic bishop was appointed, with his see at his ancestral chieftain's estate at Skálholt (see Ch 11). Fifty years later, a second diocese was established in the north, at Hólar (see Ch 13), and these two sees were the educational and cultural power-houses of Iceland until late in the eighteenth century, when the little town of Reykjavík became the capital of the country.

As in other countries, the Church was the patron of learning and learned works. But the difference in Iceland was that the Church was national, rather than international. Its leading figures were the scions of the country's noblest families, men who were steeped in the country's traditions and culture; the churches themselves were under the control of lay patrons, who would either take ordination for themselves or take clerics into their service. So Iceland did not develop an exclusive clerical caste with a monopoly of literacy and learning; education at church schools was widespread and open to all, both men and women. Most important of all, literacy was taught not just in the official language of the Church—Latin—but in the vernacular, in Icelandic.

A key factor that influenced the way in which literacy began to flourish in Iceland was the saga landscape itself. Iceland was a totally rural country. There were no towns, no villages even. There was no single central point, like a royal court, to act as a magnet for the nation's talents and create a social and cultural élite. Priest, farmer, aristocrat, scholar, poet—they were all the same person. People lived on farms, often in considerable isolation; going to church every Sunday was not a feasible proposition for much of the population, so the Church had to go to the people, through the medium of books. Widespread literacy was necessary to ensure that at least one member of each household should be able to read

aloud the homilies and edifying sermons that would otherwise
have been preached from the pulpit; and to be comprehen-
sible to the people, these sermons had to be in Icelandic, not
Latin.

Naturally enough, the very first books that came to Iceland
were in Latin. And the very first historical writing in Iceland,
by Sæmundur the Learned (see Ch 12), was also in Latin. But
from the earliest years of the twelfth century, men started to
write books in Icelandic. At first this vernacular prose-writing
of learned works was purely functional: the earliest known
work in Icelandic was a transcription of the complex code of
laws of the old Icelandic commonwealth. However, it was
quickly followed by historical works by scholars like Ari the
Learned, and religious works. Throughout the twelfth century, the written language was exercised extensively on all the
familiar subjects of medieval scholarly literature—saints'
lives, chronicles, translations, mathematics, geography, navi-
gation, travel, astronomy, philosophy, poetics, grammar,
and so on. Hand in hand with all this literary activity went the
need for book-production, the making of manuscript books.
At first these manuscripts were made in the scriptoria of the
cathedral schools and monasteries; but they were never the
exclusive possession of ecclesiastical libraries. Books were
available to all, and treasured by all, and soon were being
made in farmhouses all over the country, using calfskin
(vellum). The quills used were made from swans' feathers,
for the most part, and the ink was made by boiling the
bearberry plant (*sortulyng*: *Arctostaphylos uva-ursi*), which
provided a thick, glossy and happily durable substance. Many
manuscripts were also enhanced with elaborate decorations
involving the initial letters of each chapter, often cameo
illustrations of the subject-matter of the chapter—not as rich
and sophisticated as the illuminations in the best medieval
manuscripts of Europe, perhaps, but pleasing none the less.

While all this writing of learned works (*fræði*) was going
on, there was evolving a unique type of literary activity called
'saga'. The Icelandic word *saga* simply means 'something
said', and is cognate with the Old English word *saw*, meaning

'saying', but it has come to have the more specialized meaning of 'prose narrative'. In that sense it covers the same sort of ground as the Latin word *historia*, which means both 'history' and 'story'; but it also has the connotations of a word like 'legend', which comes from the Latin *legenda*, meaning 'things to be read'. And that is what 'saga' has come to mean: it is a comprehensive term that encompasses history, story, biography and legend.

In the same way, what are known collectively as the Icelandic sagas encompass several different kinds of writings. The earliest, in chronological terms, were Sagas of Saints (known in Icelandic as *heilagra manna sögur*), the biographies of various holy men and saints like the Apostles, or martyrs like Stephen and Sebastian, or Church Fathers like Ambrose, Gregory and Augustine. These religious writings were at first translations or adaptations of Latin originals; they were being written by the middle of the twelfth century, and judging by the number of early manuscripts that have survived, they were immensely popular. In style and diction they can be considered the forerunners of the 'classical' Icelandic sagas of the next century; one of their major characteristics is the vigour and vividness of their storytelling, their love of a good yarn, however far-fetched.

Another strand of saga-writing that was developing more or less simultaneously was that of Kings' Sagas—synoptic or individual biographies of kings of Norway (*konungasögur*). The first known work of this nature was a contemporary saga written by an Icelandic historian called Eiríkur Oddsson in the 1160s, covering the historical events in Norway from 1130–60. His book, which was called *Hryggjarstykki* (*Backbone Piece*), is now lost, but was much used by other historians, and from them we know that the author was scrupulous in citing the names of eye-witness informants. In the 1180s, a visiting Icelandic cleric, Abbot Karl Jónsson from the monastery of Thingeyrar (see Ch 13), wrote a biography of King Sverrir of Norway (*Sverris Saga*), the Faroese adventurer who usurped the Norwegian throne from around 1180 to 1202. This saga was composed under the king's personal supervision, and was later updated after the king's death in 1202. In fact the little monastery of Thingeyrar, in the north of Iceland, had become the centre of a school of early saga-writing by the end of the century, and produced sagas about two outstanding kings of Norway—King Olaf Tryggvason (995–1000) and King Olaf the Saint (1015–30)—and saga-biographies of native Icelandic bishops.

The thirteenth century is regarded as the golden age of saga-writing in Iceland. In that century, the composition of Kings' Sagas reached its height with the prodigious history of the kings of Norway known as *Heimskringla*. It was written around 1225–35 by the great historian and saga-writer, Snorri Sturluson (see Ch 14), the most celebrated figure in medieval Icelandic literature. It is an immense work, a complete history of Norway from the mythological mists of prehistoric times onwards, told in a series of saga-biographies of individual kings. The vastness of its scope and conception is implicit in the very first words, the words that gave it its name—'*Heims kringla* . . .' 'The orb of the world, on which mankind dwells . . .' Snorri also wrote the so-called *Prose Edda*, or *Snorri's Edda*, which is a prose account of the mythological poems of Germanic prehistory which are to be found today in the unique collection known as the *Poetic Edda*; and he is considered by most scholars to have been the author of one of the major 'classical' Icelandic sagas, *Egils Saga*, which was written around 1230.

And that brings us to the 'classical' sagas, the sagas 'proper' as most people think of them: the Sagas of Icelanders, or Family Sagas as they used to be called (*Íslendingasögur*). They tell about people and events in Iceland during the formative years of the nation, the first 160 years of settlement; and as a result, this period is familiarly known as the Saga Age—the age about which the Sagas of Icelanders were written.

Some forty of these Sagas of Icelanders are now extant. They vary greatly in length, from short episodes of only a few pages to massive epics like *Njáls Saga*. Nearly all of them were written in the thirteenth century. Within that golden century there was a fifty-year period, from about 1230–80, when most of the major sagas were written, from *Egils Saga* around 1230 to *Njáls Saga* around 1280, with *Eyrbyggja Saga* and *Laxdœla Saga* in between, and *Grettis Saga* a few years later: these are recognized as the Big Five of the saga canon. It was not the custom for the authors to sign their works and none of them is known by name, with the exception of the presumed authorship of *Egils Saga* by the great Snorri Sturluson himself.

These Sagas of Icelanders were family chronicles featuring the early immigrants and the adventures of their families and direct descendants down to the third or fourth generations. They were written in the vernacular, in prose, and can best be described as historical novels—the first novels to be written in Europe. They were not, strictly speaking, histories; they were imaginative works of art created around a historical framework and using many different sources: written records and genealogies, traditional oral stories, earlier sagas, fragments of remembered verses uttered on special occasions. Their purpose was to entertain and edify their audience, like the great novels of the nineteenth century. The major characters were undoubtedly historical figures, and the dramas in which they took part were for the most part well-attested historical events; but how these characters were portrayed, their dialogue, the significance of what they did and how they did it—all that was the business of the author.

The style of the sagas is laconic and dry, the plots are frequently complex and intricately woven, the dialogue terse and epigrammatic. They make no concessions to the reader, who is expected to draw his own conclusions from between the lines. Within the hard sweep and drive of the narrative there are profound insights into the mainsprings of human behaviour, great subtleties of touch, all the more effective because they are so understated. At their best, the Sagas of Icelanders are works of remarkable literary craftsmanship and compelling creative genius. They are essentially if not conventionally heroic, in that they portray individuals at the very limits of their capacities, stoically facing the imperatives of their destiny and the remorseless social code of honour and revenge by which they lived. Tragic dilemmas can only be resolved by uncompromising courage, fear can only be overcome by manliness. It can be a chilling ethos, without comfort or consolation, but it compels admiration none the less. Under the rough-hewn surface there are ripples of irony, of humour even, areas of surprising gentleness at times, of love and loyalty and devotion.

Above all, the sagas are marvellous stories in their own right. These muscled, powerful narratives carry the reader captive into a world where men and women live out their lives against a wild and untamed natural background. There is violence, yes, killings and counter-killings; there are merciless blood-feuds that overwhelm whole families; but there is nobility, too, a grandeur of spirit that elevates even the most mundane existence to immortality. But this is not a world of fable or legend; these were ordinary people who had greatness thrust upon them, people from a real past who spring vividly to life in the hands of master story-tellers. Realism is the key note, and that realism is heightened by the landscape in which the events are enacted: dramatic backdrops of mountain and valley, wild open spaces that positively invite action. The sagas, indeed, mirror the very landscape itself: rough-hewn and hard on the surface, formidable and forbidding, but with volcanic passions simmering just below the surface.

After the golden age of the classical Sagas of Icelanders in the thirteenth century, the artistic quality of saga-writing declined. The fourteenth century saw the growth of the so-called 'Legendary Sagas' (*fornaldarsögur*—Sagas of Ancient Times): fantastical tales of derring-do and magic, set in Scandinavia and on the Continent in prehistoric times, long before the Settlement of Iceland. Some of them are great fun, but they are not rated so highly as literary achievements. They were the popular pulp-fiction of their day, almost a pastiche of the saga style. There are some thirty-five of them extant now; the most celebrated is *Völsunga Saga*, the story of the Volsungs, of the curse of the Nibelung treasure, which so inspired Wagner and other nineteenth-century artists. Another popular genre of the fourteenth century consisted of translations of French chivalric romances, known as *riddarasögur* (Knights' Sagas); these were adapted and invented in enormous quantities from the middle of the thirteenth century onwards, and more than 250 of them are extant today.

There is another genre of medieval Icelandic literature, quite separate from the prose sagas, which should be mentioned in this introductory survey: the mythological and heroic poetry of the *Edda*, usually called the *Poetic Edda* to differentiate it from *Snorri's Edda*. The *Poetic Edda* is a collection of thirty-five poems and lays that reach back to the very roots of Germanic mythology and legend. They were not put together into a collection until around 1200, but they were composed very much earlier, in pagan times. The first fourteen poems recount stories about the old Norse gods and their exploits, and are our major source of information about Norse mythology; some are serious, some light-hearted, some are didactic, like *Hávamál* (*The Words of the High One*), which is a kind of handbook of Viking behaviour and morality; others are visionary, like the opening poem, *Völuspá* (*Sybil's Prophecy*), which is a profound and moving account in prophetic form of the creation of the world and the inevitable destruction of the old order at the Armageddon of paganism, the last great battle of Ragnarök, the Doom of the Gods.

The other twenty-one poems in the *Edda* tell the stories of legendary Germanic heroes. Some of these are known from the Migration Period in Europe (AD *c.* 300–500), historical kings like Attila the Hun (Atli), Ermanaric the Ostrogoth (Jörmunrekkr), and Gundicarius the Burgundian (Gunnar). Others are unidentifiable heroes of legend, like Sigurd (Sigurðr/Siegfried) who slew the dragon Fáfnir and rode through the flames to the bower of Brynhild, and his brother Helgi. In these poems, the heroic ethos of the Germanic warrior—and his lady-love—is raised to a majestic pitch of dramatic intensity that can hardly be found anywhere else in literature.

Snorri's Edda, on the other hand—the *Prose Edda* as it is also called—was written by Snorri Sturluson as a treatise on poetics, a handbook for poets who wanted to compose in the old style. For that purpose it was necessary to give an account of the old beliefs; Snorri uses the mythological poems from the *Poetic Edda* and makes of them a continuous narrative that tries to explain what Norse mythology was about. It is a mine of information about the ancient religion, for Snorri uses many old poems that are missing from the *Poetic Edda* as we have it today.

None of the original manuscripts of the early or classical saga literature has survived. Yet we know that the production of manuscript books was a tremendous industry in Iceland from the early twelfth century onwards. The first Bishop of Hólar, in the north of Iceland (see Ch 13), Jón Ögmundar-son, laid particular stress on educating the people, and established a brisk manuscript business at the cathedral, with a number of copyists fully engaged on the work of transcrib-ing. The oldest manuscripts were copied again as soon as they were worn out. The very oldest of the surviving manuscripts date from the late twelfth century, but most of them are mere fragments, and even they are only copies of earlier originals. There are not many survivors from the thirteenth century, either, even though that period was the heyday of saga composition.

The vast majority of surviving Icelandic vellums date from the fourteenth and fifteenth centuries; but the classical masterpieces of the thirteenth century never lost their popularity while the Legendary Sagas and Knights' Sagas were being churned out. No fewer than twenty-four vellum manuscripts of *Njáls Saga* are in existence today, although some of them are very fragmentary. In a nation where literacy was remarkably widespread, the sagas were regarded as serious entertainment; they were never relegated to library shelves, but were read aloud in farming households up and down the country. An Icelandic scribe who wrote out a copy of *Thiðreks Saga* around 1280 talked about the social value of the sagas in an Introduction:

With sagas one man can gladden many an hour, whereas most entertainments are difficult to arrange; some are very costly, some cannot be enjoyed without large numbers of people, some only entertain a very few people for a brief time, and some entail physical danger. But saga entertainment or poetry costs nothing and holds no dangers, and one man can entertain as many or as few as wish to listen; it is equally practicable night or day, by light or in darkness.

Physical circumstances conspired to provide the Icelanders with the means for this outpouring of literacy: the long winters gave them the time to indulge this national pastime, and the need for milk gave them a surplus of suckling calves whose skins, suitably treated, supplied the writing material required. For instance, in the 1390s, a wealthy farmer in the north of Iceland, Jón Hákonarson of Víðidalstunga, employed two priests as scribes for two years to copy and illuminate a great collection of sagas and royal histories; it took the lives of 113 calves to make the 225 leaves of the codex. This magnificent manuscript later passed into the possession of a farmer on the little island of Flatey in Breiða-fjörður on the west coast of Iceland, and became known as the *Flateyjarbók*—one of the most celebrated of all Icelandic manuscripts. But books never became the exclusive possession of any one class; they were available to all, and treasured by all. Anyone who could not afford the price of a new book would borrow one and copy it out himself.

The coming of printing after the Reformation in the middle of the sixteenth century did nothing to diminish the demand for manuscript books, for the printing press was a Church monopoly, and for a long time only religious works were allowed to be published. The introduction of paper made a huge difference, however; paper was very much cheaper to obtain, and much easier to write on. From now on, new manuscript copies were all made on paper, and with that the old vellums lost much of their usefulness. Many of the prized old books were kept as family heirlooms, but all too many were discarded or simply lost. Ari the Learned's *Íslendingabók* would have been lost to us entirely if an Icelandic bishop had not had two paper copies made of it in the middle of the seventeenth century, for the vellum from which the copies were made has vanished into oblivion.

Terentianus Maurus, the third-century Greek grammarian of Alexandria, in his *Tract on Letters*, wrote: *'Pro captu lectoris, habent sua fata libelli'*—'Books have their fate, depending on the capacity of the reader'. But there was more than the capacity of the reader involved here. Iceland had lost its independence in 1262 and become a colony, first of Norway and then of Denmark. Her economy suffered accordingly, and in addition the climate began to worsen dramatically. Devastating volcanic eruptions, severe winters, famines and pestilences ravaged the country, and the population fell alarmingly. Living conditions deteriorated; many of the great farm manors of the past degenerated into hovels, disease-ridden turf-covered cottages in which the peasants cowered against the weather and the constant threat of starvation. The Reformation brought no respite—quite the opposite: the Danish crown appropriated all the properties of the Church—about a fifth of all landed property in Iceland— and introduced forced unpaid labour on royal estates, and fearsome new penalties for heresy and sexual offences, with heavy fines, confiscations of property, and even death. In the seventeenth century, the Danish king clamped a royal trade monopoly on all commerce in Iceland, giving exclusive rights to selected Danish merchants who made up their own regulations, set their own prices at exorbitant levels, and reduced the population to total dependence on their often rotten and worm-eaten imports. It is almost impossible to exaggerate the misery and penury that Iceland suffered in the sixteenth and seventeenth centuries at the peak of Danish colonial oppression.

It is a miracle that Iceland survived at all; by 1708 the population, which had reached about 70,000 by the year 1100, had been more than halved, to 34,000. It is perhaps even more of a miracle that any kind of intellectual life survived;

but it did. Two tiny Latin schools, which had been established at the bishoprics of Skálholt and Hólar in 1552, managed to produce brilliant scholars and men of letters who kept the torch of learning alight—men like Arngrímur Jónsson (1568–1648), known as Arngrímur the Learned, who wrote notable treatises in Latin about the geography and political and cultural history of Iceland that aroused great interest abroad. He was also an enthusiastic collector of the old vellum manuscripts which were falling into disuse by then. Another distinguished scholar and collector of manuscripts was Brynjólfur Sveinsson (1605–75), Bishop of Skálholt (see Ch 11). It was he who rescued the priceless vellum copy of *Íslendingabók* and had it copied. He wanted to establish his own printing press at Skálholt to publish the Icelandic sagas, but was baulked by his colleague in Hólar who had the print monopoly and used it for religious works only; instead, in the hope of getting them published in Denmark, Bishop Brynjólfur sent some of his most precious manuscripts as a gift to the King of Denmark—including *Flateyjarbók*, and the only known manuscript of the *Poetic Edda*, which thereby became known as *Codex Regius*.

This flowering of Renaissance learning in Iceland coincided happily with the rise of antiquarianism abroad. Scandinavian scholars, fired by a desire to learn about their own past, were beginning to realize that the main sources were to be found in the ancient writings of the Icelanders in their vellum books. And now the efforts of Icelandic scholars to preserve and promote the old literature were reinforced by scholars in Denmark and elsewhere who were eager to get hold of more manuscripts and publish them, mainly in Latin translations.

The man who did more to rescue the surviving manuscripts than any other was a brilliant young Icelandic scholar called Árni Magnússon (1663–1730). He was brought up at the saga farmstead of Hvammur in the Dales, celebrated as the home of the pioneering matriarchal settler, Auður the Deep-Minded, in *Laxdæla Saga* (see Ch 15). Árni's family could claim descent from some of the most notable dynasties from the Settlement Age, and he grew up in an environment where learning and culture were revered. His grandfather was a clergyman who was also the local teacher and taught him Latin from the age of six; his uncle, another clergyman, started him on Greek and algebra from the age of twelve. Árni proved to be a precocious scholar, but could only pursue his studies during the winter, for he had to work on the home-farm all summer. At the age of seventeen he was admitted to the cathedral school at Skálholt, from which he graduated with great distinction three years later, in 1683. From there he was sent to the University of Copenhagen, which was then the only seat of higher learning open to young Icelanders. He soon graduated in theology, but his burning interest was in the literary antiquities of his homeland; he was lucky enough to obtain the patronage of great scholars like Thomas Bartholin, whom he assisted with his monumental edition of *Antiquitates* in 1689 ('Three Books of Danish Antiquities Concerning the Reason for Contempt of Death among the Danes While They Were Still Heathens, Collected from Old, Hitherto Unpublished Manuscripts and Monuments'). Árni became a secretary in the Royal Archives, and in 1701 he was appointed to a new chair at the University of Copenhagen as Professor of Danish Antiquities—the first Icelander ever to hold a university chair.

By this time there was stiff competition in Scandinavia to get hold of Icelandic vellums. Expeditions were sent out to find and fetch them as if they were rare new botanical specimens; one Royal Antiquary, despatched by the King of Denmark, was drowned in 1684 when his ship, laden with a cargo of uncatalogued vellums, was lost with all hands on the voyage back to Denmark. The Swedish College of Antiquities was also active in sending expeditions to Iceland to procure as much material as they could lay their hands on.

In 1702, Árni Magnússon was sent to Iceland by the king as one of two royal commissioners to carry out a land census of property throughout the country, and to carry out a general investigation of conditions in the country and the conduct of Danish officials and merchants. It gave Árni a unique opportunity of seeking out antiquities on his own account at the same time. For ten years, from 1702–12, he travelled the length and breadth of the land, looking for manuscripts wherever he went, cajoling, wheedling, haggling, begging, borrowing and buying up every single scrap of vellum he could find, whatever the price, and paying for them out of his own pocket. People said of him that he could sniff out old manuscripts like a bloodhound. He found one piece of vellum that had been cut to make an insole for a shoe; another page, from a copy of *Sturlunga Saga* dating to around 1400, had been trimmed by a tailor to make a pattern for the back of a waistcoat. Eventually he had amassed fifty-five cases of vellum manuscripts and paper copies and medieval documents. There were long delays before they could be shipped to him in Copenhagen; when they arrived at last in 1720, he installed them in his professorial residence in Store Kannikestraede, in the University Quarter, and immediately set two scribes to work to make copies of every item.

Then disaster struck. On 20 October 1728 the Great Fire of Copenhagen began. For several hours, Árni Magnússon thought himself safe; but on the second day the flames reached the University Quarter. Only then did Árni start to take precautions. All day long, until 5 o'clock in the evening, he and two helpers tried to empty the library as fast as they could. But by then it was too late to save all but the best. The oldest and most valuable manuscripts were rescued, but the bulk of the library, including all the printed books and paper copies and other documents, perished in the flames. Árni Magnússon never really recovered from this tragedy, and within fifteen months he was dead. On his deathbed he bequeathed the remnants of his great collection to the University of Copenhagen, to create an institute for their study.

These manuscripts, and others from the Royal Danish Library, are now being returned to Iceland through an act of unparalleled magnanimity by the Danish nation. A new Manuscript Institute, felicitously named Árnagarður, has been built in Reykjavík to receive them. On Wednesday, 21 April 1971—an unforgettable day for all Icelanders—a

Danish frigate came steaming into Reykjavík harbour bear-
ing priceless gifts: the first two manuscript treasures to be
handed over by Denmark to her former colony. One of them
was *Codex Regius*—the *Poetic Edda*; the other was *Flateyjarbók*. To date, more than a thousand manuscripts have been
returned.

The significance of these saga manuscripts to the people of
Iceland would be impossible to exaggerate. They have been
the root and stock of Icelandic culture, the life-blood of the
nation, the oldest living literature in Europe, enshrining the
origins of Icelandic society. The sagas not only preserved the
old language as a living tongue and a written language that is
closer to modern Icelandic than Shakespeare is to modern
English; they also helped to keep Icelanders alive throughout
the worst centuries of natural disasters and colonial
oppression.

Indeed, when the Icelanders took up the struggle for
freedom and independence from Denmark in the nineteenth
century, the saga literature was both their inspiration and
their justification. Their claims were based on ancient historical authority. The Icelanders had renounced their own
unique republicanism in 1262—at the height of the golden
age of saga-writing—by voting to give their allegiance to the
King of Norway. It had been a voluntary act of submission:
the Icelanders had grown weary of the ceaseless jockeying for
power between leading families in the land which had brought
the country to a virtual state of civil war. Through the Union
of Kalmar in 1397, which joined the three crowns of
Denmark, Norway and Sweden under Danish leadership,
Iceland was brought into the ambit of Denmark and eventually became a Danish colony, as Norway itself did. In the
nineteenth century, Norway was detached from Denmark
and given to Sweden after the Napoleonic wars; but Iceland
was not included in the cession, and remained a Danish
possession.

In the long struggle for independence that ensued, the
Icelanders maintained that the union with Norway in 1262
had been a purely personal relationship with the monarch,

whereas the Danes argued that Iceland had thereby actually been incorporated into the kingdom of Norway, and, subsequently, Denmark. The independence movement was fuelled by the rise of the Romantic movement in Europe, and by the July Revolution of 1830 in France. A generation of Romantic poets grew up in Iceland, ardent young men who drew their inspiration from the sagas and the poems of the *Poetic Edda*. Lyrical poets like Jónas Hallgrímsson (1807–45) passionately invoked the heroism of the sagas and wrote tenderly and proudly of Iceland's magnificent scenery; his clarion calls to his fellow-countrymen led to a remarkable literary revival and to a reawakened awareness of the nation's past and the country's natural beauty. Political pressure, steadily and thoughtfully applied, combined with this groundswell of patriotic pride, and proved ultimately irresistible; step by grudging step, Iceland was granted increasing autonomy in her own affairs, until full independence was achieved in 1944. The sagas had won; and the first claim that the Icelanders made on their former colonial masters was a request for the return of the saga manuscripts to their homeland.

In the past, the sagas used to be accepted as literal truth, pure gospel history; it is only in comparatively recent times that critical scholarship has indicated the extent to which the anonymous authors manipulated their material to suit the demands of their narrative art, remaining true to the spirit if not the letter of their sources. What helped to give the sagas their sense of absolute verisimilitude has always been their sense of place. The sagas and the landscape are inseparable. They were written in that landscape and about that landscape, which adds immeasurably to their immediacy. And that saga landscape has scarcely changed over the centuries. It has never become cluttered with industrial progress on a grand scale. Iceland's history is a story of evolution, not revolution: farm houses have been built and rebuilt, generation after generation, on precisely the same sites as the original settlers selected, for they had chosen well. Place-names have hardly varied for 1100 years, and unbroken popular traditions have kept alive a host of stories about individual features and individual exploits.

One can stand today at the sites where the saga events are said to have occurred, and recognize every detail of the landscape. The dramas of the past seem to roll before your very eyes, and you begin to understand more clearly than ever before not only how things happened but also why things happened. Farmers who live on sites hallowed by saga history seem to live the sagas, too; for them, the events of the past might have happened yesterday, and they will point out to you every stick and stone with historical associations, recount the saga tales as if they were topical stories, speak of the long-dead saga heroes as if they were intimate friends. However lonely the landscapes, they are peopled by the constant presence of the past.

A recent book on Iceland's early history, by a distinguished Icelandic scholar (*Íslendinga Saga*, by the late Jón Jóhannesson, 1956), contains hardly any references to the sagas or the events they purport to describe. In *Iceland Saga*, however, I have gone to the opposite extreme: I have tried to tell the early story of Iceland mainly in terms of the saga literature, but taking into account whatever further evidence modern scholarship has provided. The story is told, in roughly chronological order, in terms of places and people—the places and people that are so familiar to all Icelanders from the sagas. I have tried, wherever possible, to relate them to Iceland as it is today, for Iceland is a country where the past and the present still sit together in casual and comfortable harmony. Some years ago, I used to spend my summer holidays working as a tourist guide in Iceland, taking visitors round the saga sites, telling the saga stories at the places were they happened; and that sense of pilgrimage is what this handbook to the Iceland Saga is intended to celebrate.

CHAPTER 2

Reykjavík: the First Settler

Ingolfr hét maðr nórænn, es sannliga es sagt at færi
fyrst þaðan til Íslands . . .
Hann byggði suðr í Reykjarvík.

A Norwegian called Ingólfur is reliably reported to have
been the first man to leave Norway for Iceland . . .
He settled in the south, at Reykjavík.

(*Íslendingabók*)

There always has to be a 'first'. We are never fully satisfied
with our picture of the past until we can pinpoint and highlight
a moment of origin, a birth, a happening, a person, a place,
with which to give a story a beginning. And in Iceland, as if by
providence, we have a First Settler, a Pioneer, a prime
progenitor of the nation: a man called Ingólfur. We have this
on the authority of Iceland's first vernacular historian, Ari the
Learned, in his *Íslendingabók* (*Book of Icelanders*), written
in the 1120s, some 250 years after the event. And today there
is a high and handsome statue superintending Reykjavík
harbour to make the point: Ingólfur Arnarson—First Settler
of Iceland.

Íslendingabók is only a brief historical summary; *Landnámabók* (*Book of Settlements*), in whose original compila-
tion Ari the Learned is believed to have played a leading part,
is a much more comprehensive and detailed book, and this
tells us that although Ingólfur Arnarson was the first man to
settle permanently in Iceland, around AD 874, there were at
least three other Norsemen who had reached and explored
Iceland before him. One was a Viking called Naddoddur,
who was driven off course on a voyage between Norway and

the Faroes around the year 850 and made land on the east coast in a narrow steep-sided fjord called Reyðarfjörður (Rorqual Fjord); he climbed a mountain to get a good vantage point, but saw no sign of human habitation. As he was sailing away that autumn, bound for the Faroes, snow started falling, so he called the country Snæland (Snowland), and was full of praise for it. That was Iceland's first 'modern' name, after Thule.

A Swedish Viking adventurer called Garðar Svavarsson was more ambitious. He set off in search of this Snæland guided, we are told, by his mother, who had second sight. He sailed right round the country, thereby proving that it was an island. He spent the winter in the north of Iceland, on the broad bay of Skjálfandi (Shivering Fjord), where he built himself some houses; so the place was, naturally, called Húsavík (Houses Bay). Today it is a substantial township with a population of some 2,500. Garðar Svavarsson was delighted with his find and named it Garðarshólmur (Garðar's Isle) in an attempt to stake a claim on history, at least. When he was setting sail for home the following spring, a man called Náttfari and a pair of slaves somehow got left behind and made a home for themselves at Náttfaravík, on the opposite side of the bay. Later, this Náttfari moved to more congenial upland surroundings in Reykjadalur, but was brusquely evicted by the first 'real' immigrants who came on the scene, and was sent packing back to Náttfaravík. Theoretically, Náttfari should be accorded the status of First Settler, but history has disqualified him on a technicality: his settlement was accidental.

Soon after Naddoddur and Garðar Svavarsson, a third and more determined explorer went in search of the new and uninhabited land—a Norwegian Viking called Flóki Vilgerðarson. He took all his family and livestock with him, intent on founding a permanent settlement there. Like Noah, he also took three birds with him, not doves, but ravens, to help him find the way, 'for in those days ocean-going mariners had no lodestone'; and for that reason he was known as Hrafna-Flóki (Ravens-Flóki). When he released the first raven it flew straight back the way they had come. A little later the second bird was released; it flew high into the air, looked around, and returned to the ship. The third bird, however, flew straight ahead and disappeared over the horizon. Flóki set course in the same direction, and soon they caught sight of land:

> They made land at a place called Vatnsfjörður on Barðaströnd [on the west coast]. The fjord teemed with fish of all kinds, and they were so busy fishing that they paid no heed to gathering hay for the winter; and that winter, all their livestock starved to death.
>
> The spring was extremely cold. Flóki climbed a high mountain and looked north towards the coast, and saw a fjord full of drift-ice; so they called the country Ísland [Ice-Land], and that has been its name ever since.
>
> (*Landnámabók*)

And so, contrary to what one might expect, it was the ice-floes choking the coastline and not the spectacular glaciers that earned Iceland its inhospitable name.

Because of bad sailing weather, Flóki was forced to spend a second winter there. Thoroughly disgruntled, he returned to Norway and spoke unflatteringly of the country he had dubbed Ice Land. Two companions who had been with him on the expedition gave somewhat different accounts, however. One, a man called Herjólfur, said soberly enough that it had advantages as well as drawbacks. The other claimed that 'butter dripped from every blade of grass'; his name was Thórólfur, and his sunny optimism earned him the nickname of Thórólfur Butter (*smjör*). Ravens-Flóki himself later repented of his hasty decision, returned to Iceland and settled in Flókadalur on the north coast, just west of Skaga-fjörður. But by then it was too late: Flóki Vilgerðarson had missed his chance of immortality as the official First Settler of the land he had named so churlishly. That honour fell instead to Ingólfur Arnarson.

Flóki's abortive attempt at settlement is reckoned to have taken place around 860. According to the traditional chronology worked out by the early Icelandic historians, the real Settlement of Iceland began around 870.

Ingólfur Arnarson came of Viking stock in south-western Norway, in Hördaland; he was the son of a man called Örn (Eagle), the son of Björn-Ólfur (Bear-Wolf), the son of a semi-legendary hero called Hrómundur Gripsson (see Ch 13). The ancestry sounds impressive enough, but modern scholars find it too perfunctory, too trite, for their demanding tastes. In *Landnámabók* he is portrayed as a devout and god-fearing man; a pagan, to be sure, but a prudent one, and far-sighted.

Ingólfur grew up in what is now called the Viking Age. Historians mark the formal start of this period with the celebrated raid by Norwegian prowlers on the island monastery of Lindisfarne, off the north-east coast of England, in 793, but it is clear that 'Vikings'—a generic term for Scandinavian seafarers and pirates—had been on the move in the North Sea and the Baltic for several decades before then. They earned themselves an unsavoury reputation for violence and rapacity; their magnificent longships, lean and predatory, struck terror wherever they appeared. Today, the Vikings are enjoying a measure of rehabilitation; modern scholars tend to emphasize the more constructive aspects of their activities as traders, explorers, settlers, farmers, and craftsmen of the highest quality. But no one would call them angels, none the less.

Ingólfur had a kinsman and close friend called Hjörleifur. So close were they that they went through a ritual of blood-brotherhood, whereby they mingled blood from their veins and pledged their lives to one another. Like so many other energetic young Norwegians of their time, they joined in summer Viking expeditions across the North Sea, taking plunder wherever they could find it. After a particularly successful season, however, they fell out with their partners at a celebration feast—a matter of honour concerning Ingólfur's sister, Helga, who happened to be Hjörleifur's intended. It was more than enough to start a blood-feud. Ingólfur and Hjörleifur set upon their erstwhile comrades next spring and killed one of them, the son of a local chieftain; when the inevitable retaliatory raid came, they killed another of the chieftain's sons. Two killings in the same family could not possibly be condoned; mediators stepped in to put an end to the feud, and Ingólfur and Hjörleifur were forced to hand over their entire worldly wealth to the aggrieved chieftain as compensation for his loss.

There was obviously no future for the blood-brothers in Norway now, and they decided to emigrate. They had heard the rather mixed reports about the land Flóki had explored and named, so that summer they got themselves a good ship, a solid, ocean-going *knörr*, and sailed off to reconnoitre Iceland. They stayed there for the winter, and came to the conclusion that the southern part of the country offered better prospects than the north. Back in Norway next spring, they made their preparations to emigrate. Hjörleifur went off on a last Viking expedition to raise the necessary funds; he plundered in Ireland, which by then had become a favourite stamping-ground for seasonal raiding. One of his exploits there was to break into a prehistoric burial mound (a favourite Viking pastime, according to Irish annals); in the musty darkness he caught sight of a gleam of light from a sword being wielded by some creature who guarded the mound. Hjörleifur fought with this being and killed it, and took possession of the treasure in the mound. (This, it should be said, is a stock motif found in various other Viking yarns.) Hjörleifur also captured ten Irish slaves, who were to take bloody revenge for that indignity in due course.

Laden with booty, Hjörleifur returned triumphantly to Norway. The blood-brothers now had enough capital to fit out a proper expedition to Iceland, and bought two ships. That winter, Ingólfur held a great sacrifice to discover what the future held in store for him; but Hjörleifur, for whatever reason, would never sacrifice to the gods. The oracle told Ingólfur that his destiny lay in Iceland.

The following spring they got ready to sail. Hjörleifur, who was by now Ingólfur's brother-in-law, loaded up his ship with his Irish plunder and the ten slaves he had taken. Ingólfur took the rest of their common property; but he also put on board the sacred carved pillars of the ancestral high-seat in his home. These were hallowed to the gods of the pagan pantheon—Thór, presumably, the god of farmers and sea-farers, Freyr, the god of fertility, and perhaps Óðinn, the aristocratic god of war and poetry.

The year in which the two friends set sail for Iceland for good was 874, according to the compilers of *Landnámabók*: 'The summer that Ingólfur and Hjörleifur went to settle in Iceland, Harald Fine-Hair had been King of Norway for twelve years; that was 6073 years from the Creation of the World, and 874 years from the Incarnation of our Lord.'

At first they sailed in convoy, but lost contact with each other as they approached land from the south-east. As soon as Ingólfur caught his first glimpse of Iceland, he cast overboard his hallowed high-seat pillars, and vowed that he would make his home wherever they were washed ashore. In effect he was offering hostages to fortune, sending the pillars as ambassadors to parley with the guardian land-spirits of the place, lest his coming should offend or affright them. Then he himself landed at a promontory that has been known ever since as Ingólfshöfði (Ingólfur's Headland). It is a long, steep bluff of rock jutting far out to sea, 76 metres high and a paradise for sea birds nesting on its cliffs. In Ingólfur's day there was a sheltered, shallow haven for boats there, and the coastal plain was green with grass and scrub; since then, incessant glacier-bursts have reduced the hinterland to a barren waste of débris and black volcanic sand, and the wind has piled up a huge dune that gives access to the top of the promontory from the landward side. On the headland today there is a lighthouse, and a monument to Ingólfur that was erected there in 1974 on the occasion of the 1100th anniversary of his landing. It is one saga site that has been changed almost out of all recognition by the fierce play of natural forces down the centuries.

Hjörleifur, for his part, sailed for another hundred kilometres west along the coast to a promontory that has been known as Hjörleifshöfði ever since. Here, the topography has changed even more drastically than at Ingólfshöfði. In Hjörleifur's day it stood at the head of a shallow fjord; now the fjord is no more, and Hjörleifshöfði itself stands islanded three kilometres inland. The change has been wrought by several eruptions of the volcano Katla (Kettle), which lies deep under the ice-sheet of the glacier Mýrdalsjökull, immediately to the north; the subsequent glacier-bursts created a wide desert of black sand in all directions and pushed the shore-line far out to sea. It is an eerie sight, this sea-cliff rearing up out of an inland waste of sand; the sheer rock on the seaward side has been gouged into caves and overhangs by the action of the surf, but the surf is now far away. The top of the promontory is thickly grassed, starred with sea-pinks and moss campion; there was a little farm up there until earlier this century, but now there are only the gravestones of the last farmers. One of them was a noted amateur geologist, Markús Loftsson, who published in 1880 a masterly history of volcanism in Iceland—an appropriate scholarly pastime for a farmer of Hjörleifshöfði.

When Hjörleifur landed in that summer of 874, he set his ten Irish slaves to building two houses; their ruins were still visible in the thirteenth century, according to *Landnámabók*, and measured eighteen and nineteen fathoms in length (more than thirty metres). When spring came he wanted to sow; but he had only one ox with him, so he ordered his slaves to pull the plough. This was too much for their pride, and they hatched up a scheme to get rid of their Norwegian masters. They slaughtered the ox, and then reported that it had been killed by a brown bear. How was Hjörleifur to know that there were no brown bears in Iceland—only the occasional polar bear which floated across from Greenland accidentally on an ice-floe? Hjörleifur and his men fell for the ruse; they rushed into the woods in pursuit of the non-existent bear, and were picked off one by one and put to death by the mutinous slaves. It was the first and only slave revolt in the history of Iceland. As soon as the deed was done, the slaves took the rowing-boat from Hjörleifur's ship, piled the Norwegians' womenfolk into it, and fled for refuge to some islands they could see on the horizon to the south. That same spring, Ingólfur sent two of his own slaves, who were called Vífill and Karli, to scour the coastline to the west in search of his high-seat pillars. When they reached Hjörleifs-höfði they found Hjörleifur and his companions lying there, murdered, and turned back to tell Ingólfur the news. Ingólfur 'took their deaths badly', as *Landnámabók* puts it, and hurried to the scene. When he saw Hjörleifur's body, he said:

'It is a sad end for a warrior, to be slain by slaves; this is what happens to those who will not hold sacrifice.'

He noticed that the boat was missing, as well as the womenfolk of the murdered men, and guessed that the slaves had fled to the islands. He pursued them there and fell upon them, and killed them all; from then on the islands were known as Vestmannaeyjar—the 'Westmen' Isles, the islands of the Irishmen (usually transliterated now as 'Westmann').

Ingólfur brought the Norwegian womenfolk back to the mainland, and spent the winter at Hjörleifshöfði. Next spring he sent his two slaves off on their westward search again while he himself followed on behind, sailing a leisurely course along the coast. He spent the winter near a mountain that has been named in his honour Ingólfsfjall; it is a handsome hill, rearing more than 500 metres high, with steep screes that look as if they have been brushed upwards by a giant broom. Ingólfs-fjall is a relatively young mountain, born in a volcanic eruption during the Ice Ages when Iceland had been pressed down into the ocean by the crushing weight of the ice and the sea had reached in all the way over the southlands. Just to the west he could see the steaming hotsprings that now provide the natural heating for hundreds of acres of glasshouses for growing fruit, vegetables and flowers. Today, the spectacular little township of Hveragerði (Hotsprings Garden) houses the National Horticultural College, which is pioneering the use of undersoil heating to grow exotic tropical plants only 250 kilometres south of the Arctic Circle.

During that winter at Ingólfsfjall, news came that the high-seat pillars had been found at last. It is astonishing that they should have been found at all, considering the colossal amount of flotsam that had piled up on Iceland's shores down the millennia. Early next spring he set off, travelling west over the high moorlands of Hellisheiði (Cavern Heath) and Svínahraun (Swine Lava), and down towards the broad waters of Faxaflói (Faxa Bay). The pillars were lying on the shore under a little hillock which he named Arnarhóll— Eagle Mount. All around were rolling green grasslands that appeared to steam with the vapour of countless hotsprings. Here he settled, obedient to the will of the gods and the guardian spirits of the land, and called it Reykjavík: Smoky Bay.

After that, unaccountably, there is total silence about Ingólfur Arnarson in the sources. All we know is that he laid claim to a huge swathe of land covering the south-west corner of Iceland, which he then parcelled out to his kinsmen and supporters to create what must have been a major power bloc in this new island fiefdom. The mantle of his status as First Settler became a dynastic heirloom. His son, Thorsteinn Ingólfsson, is credited with founding the first district assembly (þing), at Kjalarnes, north across the bay of Kollafjörður from Reykjavík; and when Iceland's parliament, the Althing (alþingi), was founded in 930, it was Thorsteinn, scion of the First Family in the land, who was elected to the honorary post of Supreme Chieftain (allsherjargoði). Ingólfur's grandson, Thorkell *máni* (Moon), was Law-Speaker of the Althing for many years, and was remembered as the noblest pagan who ever lived in Iceland:

> In his final illness he had himself carried out to a shaft of sunshine, and commended himself to the god who had created the sun. He had lived a life as blameless as that of the best of Christians.
>
> (*Landnámabók*)

And Ingólfur's great-grandson, Thormóður Thorkelsson, was Supreme Chieftain of the Althing at the time of the Conversion of Iceland to Christianity by parliamentary decree around the year 1000.

With that, Ingólfur Arnarson and his posterity simply vanish from the stage. Their part was played. They had fulfilled the role required of them by destiny, by history and by story. They had been put on a pedestal of piety, they had been the 'good' pagans who had presided over the fortunes of the stripling nation in its formative years, and ushered it to the very threshold of Christianity when, in medieval eyes, real history began. No more was required of them.

To modern eyes, Ingólfur Arnarson seems almost a folklore hero rather than a historical person. No wonder scholars tend to be suspicious about the authenticity of his credentials. Despite his key position in Iceland's early history, no major saga was ever written about him, which is surprising, to say the least. He seems to come too pat upon the stage, of dubious antecedents, sprung fully-fledged as if from the forehead of a god. And with his founding-father role fulfilled, he strides off into the invincible realm of hallowed legend, there to live immortal in the afterglow of memory, impervious to doubt or question. Náttfari and his accidental settlement could never have filled the bill. If Ingólfur Arnarson had not existed, it would clearly have been necessary to invent him.

Some years ago I was with a Swiss tourist, paying due homage at the statue of Ingólfur Arnarson overlooking Reykjavík harbour. It was fashioned by the sculptor Einar Jónsson in the 1920s in the muscled, heroic style of the time. For a long time the Swiss lady gazed earnestly up at his stern and steadfast countenance; and then she murmured, '*Comme ils étaient beaux à l'époque!*'—'How handsome they were in those days!' It is what a First Settler *should* look like.

Today, eleven centuries after the arrival of Ingólfur Arnarson, Reykjavík is the capital of Iceland. Oddly enough, it has never been officially designated as the capital city. It has simply happened. And although there is no direct connection between Ingólfur's pioneering settlement and the creation of an urban capital, there is a certain geographical and historical inevitability about it: Reykjavík has become the capital because it was the best place for a capital to be. The natural or supernatural elements that impelled Ingólfur's high-seat pillars to this place made no mistake.

One can still easily visualize the scene that met Ingólfur's eyes as he came riding westwards over the high lava moorlands and looked down over the bumpy peninsula that jutted north-westwards into the immensity of Faxaflói Bay. At his feet, the braided waters of the Elliðaár (Elliði's Rivers) teemed with salmon, as they do to this day. Beyond, at the broadest part of the peninsula, he could see plumes of what looked like smoke rising from the ground of a wide valley— the natural hotsprings that inspired the name Reykjavík and also Laugardalur (Hotsprings Valley), now the site of a fine sports complex and exhibition centre. Farther on, between two swelling hills, lay another, smaller valley, with a little lake; that lake is now an enchanting feature of the city centre, almost a toy lake, in fact, known as the Tjörn (Pond). From the lake a stream ran northwards to the shore (it is now channelled under Lækjargata, or Rivulet Street, just like Fleet Street in London which means precisely the same); at the mouth of the river was a sheltered haven with sloping beaches, ideal for Viking boats, which has now been built up into Reykjavík's excellent harbour. All around, the hillsides were covered with trees and brushwood that would provide plentiful fuel. Small islets dotted the offshore waters; their names evoke their natural resources—Viðey (trees), Engey (pasture), Þerney (nesting terns). To the north lay Hvalfjörður (Whale Fjord), to the south Kopavogur (Seal-pup Creek)—resource-names again.

What Ingólfur saw, in effect, was a cornucopia of natural resources, a bountiful larder on land and sea that would provide well for his kinsmen and followers. On a fine summer's day it is an idyllic sight still, if anything enhanced by the patchwork of gaily painted roofs and green parklands of the modern city.

Curiously enough, not everyone in Ingólfur's party was impressed by Reykjavík as a place to settle. One of the two slaves who had found the high-seat pillars, a man called Karli, was disgusted with it: 'It was to no good purpose that we travelled across such good country, if we are to settle on this out-of-the-way headland.' And with that, he disappeared, taking a slave girl with him, to make a home much farther inland, by the shores of the great lake of Ölfusvatn which would later be renamed Thingvallavatn—Thingvellir Lake (see Ch 7).

Ingólfur and his descendants clearly prospered. Ingólfur staked out an enormous land-claim—the whole south-western corner of the country, from the head of Hvalfjörður down to the salmon-haunted estuary of the Ölfusá (Ölfus River) on the south coast, skirting the western shore of Thingvallavatn. In order to bolster his position as chieftain of this vast area, he parcelled out large districts to kinsmen or trusted friends who followed him to Iceland. Soon there were substantial farmsteads established at all key points, manor farms tenanted by people owing some sort of moral allegiance, at least, to Ingólfur. For instance, *Landnámabók* tells us of one early settler, a redoubtable lady called Steinunn the Old, who was a kinswoman of Ingólfur's; she followed him to Iceland and stayed with him at Reykjavík the first winter (she had probably been widowed during a Viking expedition to the British Isles). He offered to make her a gift of the whole of the northern 'toe' of the Reykjanes peninsula. Steinunn the Old insisted on paying for it, however, and gave him in exchange a valuable embroidered cloak with hood attached (*hekla*), 'because she thought this would make it more difficult to break the agreement'. Thus, in the first recorded real-estate deal in Iceland, for the price of a cloak Steinunn the Old acquired the lands that now house the international airport of Keflavík.

Meanwhile, the original manor farm at Reykjavík grew in extent and influence. Satellite farmsteads were established at the end of the peninsula to the west, at Seltjarnarnes, and just to the east of Reykjavík, at Laugarnes. But as time went by, the prosperity of Reykjavík began to dwindle as the lands were divided and sub-divided. In the year 1226 an Augustinian monastery was founded on the islet of Viðey, off Reykjavík, which quickly became rich and powerful by acquiring many of the lands of Reykjavík and their income. The imposing manor farm of Bessastaðir (now the official residence of the President of Iceland), handsomely sited on the little peninsula of Álftanes (Swans Ness) across the fjord to the south of Reykjavík, was taken over as crown property when Iceland surrendered its independence in 1262, and became the residence of foreign governors-general appointed by the king.

Reykjavík provided the best harbourage in south-western Iceland, so the Danish authorities had a vested interest in controlling it for trade purposes. Between the hammer and anvil of church and state, Reykjavík was being crushed to death. After the Reformation, when all church property was confiscated by the crown, the lands of the monastery of Viðey fell into royal hands; and in 1613 Reykjavík itself was purchased by the crown, under duress, and ceased to be a hereditary estate. A small shanty town of huts and hovels grew up there, to accommodate the casual labour required by the Danish traders to catch fish. Throughout the seventeenth century, the Danish trade monopoly, and the absolute monarchy of the Danish king, became more and more oppressive. Abuses and outrages abounded. The value of property plummeted. The general wretchedness and misery of the people was appalling: in the 1703 census, it was noted that one in ten Icelanders was a parish pauper.

The turning point, both for Reykjavík and the rest of Iceland, came in the middle of the eighteenth century, when the conditions in Iceland were beginning to cause concern even to the Danish crown. In an attempt to curb the flagrant rapacity of the Danish traders, the crown appointed a native Icelander to the important office of *landfógeti*—Royal Superintendent, with special responsibility for tax revenues and economic affairs in Iceland. His name was Skúli Magnússon, a tough, self-made Northerner who had made a reputation for himself as a hard-nosed sheriff, or district magistrate (*sýslumaður*). He had all the makings of a great entrepreneur, a man with a stubborn vision of Iceland's commercial potential and an endless capacity for hard work.

To set an example, he persuaded the crown to hand over the island of Viðey for his headquarters, and there he built an imposing manor, not of timber but of hewn stone; it was the first stone building in Iceland, and is now in the care of the National Museum.

Skúli realized that he had to break the stranglehold trade monopoly of the Danish traders, and establish native industries to exploit Iceland's resources and benefit from them. To that end, and with surprisingly generous royal support, he founded a joint-stock company in 1752 with permission to build premises at Reykjavík. He built a woollen mill and imported German weavers to teach Icelanders new skills. He built a fulling mill, a rope-works, and a tannery. He brought farmers from Denmark and Norway to teach new agricultural methods, he imported trees to start new plantations, and he bought fishing-smacks so that Iceland could start its own fishing fleet.

The Danish traders fought all these initiatives tooth and nail, of course. Skúli Magnússon fought equally hard to keep them going, spending much of his time in Denmark on complicated lawsuits; but the new industries never really got off the ground, although they employed between sixty and a hundred men. The technology did not work, and the foreigners imported to show the Icelanders better ways were feckless for the most part. After twenty strenuous and despairing years, the whole enterprise collapsed, leaving heavy debts. Skúli himself, a difficult, headstrong man at the best of times, eventually became bankrupt and lost his official post; he died in penury on Viðey in 1794.

Despite the crushing failure of Skúli's industrial enterprise, his efforts were to bear fruit in other directions. He had created the first street in Iceland: Reykjavík's Main Street (Aðalstræti), where The Premises, as they were called, were built. Happily, one of the buildings from the 1750s still survives, the oldest house in Reykjavík: it is not quite the original weaving shed, which burned down in 1764, but the successor building that replaced it immediately after the fire. This building has been carefully conserved, and is now a little

restaurant called, appropriately, Fógetinn, in Skúli Magnússon's honour. Across the street, in the little ornamental
garden on the site of the old town church, there stands a
somewhat idealized statue of Skúli himself. It was due to Skúli's efforts that the hated trade monopoly
was ended in 1787, and Icelanders were allowed to participate
in trade as Danish subjects. Foreign traders were still banned,
however. With his Premises, Skúli had also established an
embryonic focal centre, which now began to draw to itself the
various institutions and functions necessary for a 'capital',
however miniature. Ironically, the first public building to be
erected in Reykjavík, in 1765–70, built of hewn stone like
Skúli Magnússon's house on Viðey, was a prison. It is an
exceptionally handsome building, still beautifully preserved
at the base of Arnarhóll below the statue of Ingólfur Arnarson and overlooking Lækjartorg (Rivulet Square). As a
prison, the building proved a spectacular failure, and many
prisoners died of malnutrition and disease; it was later converted for use as the office and home of the Danish governor-
general. Today the Stjórnarráðshús (Cabinet Office), as it is
called, elegantly houses the offices of the President of Iceland
and the Prime Minister.

The most significant event in Reykjavík's development
occurred on 18 August 1786, when the tiny hamlet was
granted, by royal decree, a municipal charter as a market
town. Its total population at the time numbered all of 167
souls! At once, the major institutions of church and state
began to gravitate towards Reykjavík. The bishoprics of
Skálholt and Hólar were abolished and amalgamated into a
single diocese centred on Reykjavík with a brand-new stone
Lutheran cathedral that was completed in 1796. The school
that had been associated with Skálholt for centuries was also
moved to Reykjavík, but the new house built for it proved so
shoddy that it was quickly moved again, to Bessastaðir; but in
1845 it returned to a beautiful new timber building overlooking Lækjargata which still serves as the Menntaskóli (Grammar School) of Reykjavík. Finally the Althing was moved
from Thingvellir to Reykjavík. This was not as significant as it

sounds, however. Under Danish rule, the Althing had been steadily shorn of its legislative and judicial functions until it was a parliament in name only. When it assembled for the last time at Thingvellir in 1798 the brief session was attended by only twelve representatives, eight of whom were government officials. No sooner had it been moved to Reykjavík than it was abolished, in 1800, and replaced by a new Supreme Court that would exercise what was left of its judicial powers. It was not until 1845 that the Althing was re-established as a national assembly, in response to irresistible popular pressure; and in 1881 it was given proper housing in a fine new stone building at Austurvöllur beside the cathedral — Iceland's Parliament House (Alþingishús) to this day.

And so Reykjavík began, slowly but steadily, to burgeon in the nineteenth century. But it was still very much a Danish township, a Danish trading-post with the trappings of authority and a veneer of Danish-speaking bourgeoisie. European travellers, however sympathetic, could not avoid being rather disparaging about this stripling 'capital' — men like Sir George Steuart Mackenzie, for instance, in his *Travels in the Island of Iceland, during the Summer of the year 1810*:

> Viewed from the sea the capital of Iceland seems of a mean appearance . . . The houses . . . are formed of wood, coated on the outside with a mixture of tar and red clay . . . The church, a clumsy building covered with tiles . . . is in a sad state of dilapidation, the winds and rain having access to every part of it . . . It is not much frequented on ordinary Sundays . . . In the neighbourhood of the town there is a considerable number of cottages, all very mean, and inhabited for the most part by the people who work for the merchants . . .

None the less, Reykjavík gradually began to assume the mantle of cultural and political capital of the country. It was Reykjavík that saw all the major stages of the independence battle, even though it was led mainly from abroad by the great nationalist leader Jón Sigurðsson (1811–79), whose statue now stands facing the Althing building in the middle of

Austurvöllur Square. In 1874 the King of Denmark sailed to Iceland on the first royal visit by a reigning monarch, to grant the Icelanders a measure of autonomy in their domestic affairs. In 1904, the granting of full home rule was announced in a ceremony outside the Cabinet Office. In 1918, Iceland became a sovereign state in personal union with the King of Denmark; and finally, on 17 June 1944, this Act of Union came to an end, and Iceland became a fully independent republic once again.

By now there could be no doubt in anyone's mind that Reykjavík was the capital city of the nation. The population had grown substantially, from 2,000 in 1870; by the time of the declaration of independence in 1944 it had risen to 45,000. The population of Reykjavík proper is now 90,000, but the Reykjavík conurbation, including the satellite towns of Kopavogur and Hafnafjöröur, totals 132,000—more than half the population of the whole of Iceland (242,750 in December 1985).

Reykjavík is now a modern metropolis, a truly European city in the best sense of the term. Culturally and commercially and administratively, it is the power-house of the nation: a vigorous, self-confident, essentially civilized city. The University of Iceland is there now, founded in 1911. There is no atmospheric pollution, for every building is heated by natural hot water from under the ground. It is clean, colourful and cheery. When Reykjavík celebrated its bicentenary on 18 August 1986 it had every cause to congratulate itself.

The Old Town of Reykjavík, the nucleus round which the city began to grow, is still the city centre, even though the city itself has spread for miles inland over the peninsula. The hub is the grassy square of Austurvöllur, with the harbour to the north and the little Tjörn to the south. It is an area of immense charm and old-fashioned flavour; many of the older buildings have been mercifully preserved, and converted into boutiques and small restaurants.

But there are even older remains, too. Right under the Old Town, archaeologists have now unearthed unmistakable traces of a very early farmstead—presumably Ingólfur

Arnarson's original settlement at Reykjavík. He had built his home at the corner of Aðalstræti (Main Street) and Suðurgata (South Road), quite close to the shores of the Tjörn. His path down to the harbour where he had drawn up his immigrant ship took the same lines as Aðalstræti does today. Pollen analysis shows his homefield for hay was Austurvöllur (East Field), the grassy square where the statue of that other national hero, Jón Sigurðsson, now stands.

It is historical coincidence, of course. But what an extraordinarily happy coincidence it has turned out to be.

CHAPTER 3

Some Early Settlers

It is often said that writing about the Settlements is irrelevant learning; but we think we can the better meet the criticism of foreigners when they accuse us of being descended from slaves or scoundrels if we know for certain the truth about our ancestry. And for those who want to know ancient lore and how to trace genealogies, it is better to start at the beginning than to come in at the middle. Anyway, all civilized nations want to know about the origins of their own society and the beginnings of their own race.

(Landnámabók: Þórðarbók)

Landnámabók, the *Book of Settlements*, is a goldmine of stories about the early settlers of Iceland and how they chose their settlement sites and named the features of the landscape. Some of them sound rather far-fetched and are told tongue in cheek. Some are well-rounded little episodes, miniature sagas in their own right. All of them reveal an earnest desire to know the context in which Icelandic society was born, and to correct any misconceptions that foreigners might have about this remote country that had been colonized by the dreaded Vikings; that is made quite clear in the apologia for the study of genealogy and the Settlement which is found in *Þórðarbók* (*Thórður's Book*), a late version of *Landnámabók* which none the less uses discarded material from the lost original version by Ari the Learned and others in the twelfth century. In fact, there were relatively few 'professional' Vikings amongst the settlers, although their stories tend to be the most vivid. Most of the settlers were simply farmers intent on making a new life for themselves in virgin

territory. Some of them had good family connections in
Norway or the British Isles, and prided themselves on this,
although their ancestry was probably not quite as exalted as
they wanted their neighbours to believe; it is only human to
want to idealize one's antecedents, whether by upgrading
them or, through inverted snobbery, by self-consciously
downgrading them. No one wants to be accused of being
'descended from slaves and scoundrels', especially in a pioneering society like Iceland where kinship and ancestry
played an important part in the fabric of the new society.

Most of the early settlers were pagans who believed in Thór
and Freyr and, to a lesser extent, Óðinn (see Ch 5). A very
few of them were noted for being Christian, having come into
contact with Christianity in the British Isles (see Ch 4). But all
of them, pagan or Christian, had a profound respect for the
natural spirits which were thought to inhabit the land and
look after it. The *Hauksbók* version of *Landnámabók* says:

> It was the first tenet of the pagan laws of Iceland that men
> should not take ships with curved beaks to sea. But if
> they did, they were to remove the beaks before they
> came within sight of land, so as not to approach land with
> gaping prows and snarling snouts and thereby affright
> the land-spirits.

These land-spirits (*landvættir*) lived in rocks and woods and
other natural features of the landscape, and needed to be
propitiated; the landscape was a potent factor in the Settlement, alive with supernatural beings, dwarfs and trolls and
elves and 'hidden people' (*huldufolk*). Icelandic folklore is
full of tales about these creatures; belief in them was probably
deeper and more pervasive than formal paganism, or even
formal Christianity, and lingers still to this day, not only in the
farming districts but in more sophisticated urban surroundings as well. There are still innumerable fairy rings and
enchanted spots (*álagablettir*) all over Iceland where elves
and sprites are said to dwell, and which must not be disturbed
at any price.

Thorsteinn Rednose: the Sacred Waterfall
High above Rangárvellir (Rang River Plains), where so much of the action of *Njáls Saga* takes place, lies the now abandoned farmstead of Rauðnefsstaðir (Rednose-Stead), in the district of Hólmslönd (Holm-Lands).

According to *Landnámabók*, the first settler here was a man called Hrólfur *rauðskeggr* (Redbeard), who claimed all the land between Rangá and Fiská (Fish River) and made his home at a place called Foss (Waterfall). It was inherited by his son, Thorsteinn *rauðnefr* (Rednose), and the name of the farm was changed from Foss to Rauðnefsstaðir, presumably as a reflection of the stature of the new owner. But the waterfall after which the farm had been named remained sacrosanct, as *Landnámabók* makes clear:

> Thorsteinn Rednose was a great sacrificer. He used to make sacrifices to the waterfall, and all the leftovers had to be thrown into it.

The spirits of the waterfall repaid his devotion handsomely. His farm prospered. His flock of sheep multiplied mightily. One year at the autumn round-up, the number of sheep in his sheep-fold was 2,400; no one bothered to count the remainder, because there was no room for them in the sheep-fold and they ran off. Thorsteinn Rednose developed a sixth sense about his sheep; each autumn he could see which of them were doomed to die, and he had those slaughtered, which greatly improved the quality of his stock. In the last autumn of his life he went to the sheep-fold and told his shepherd to slaughter any of the sheep he wanted: 'Either I am doomed to die, or the sheep are doomed to die, or all of us are.' On the night he died, his presentiment came true: all the sheep were swept by a gale into the waterfall and drowned.

The waterfall was named Leifðafoss (Leftovers Falls) as a result of all this. It is a busy, bustling cascade in the waters of the river Fiská just beside the farm. The farm prospered for centuries until 1947, when the pastures were ruined by heavy falls of volcanic ash from the eruption of Mount Hekla that year and the farm had to be abandoned. To the east of the river one can still make out the traces of a large enclosure, which local tradition claims is the sheep-fold of Thorsteinn Rednose; it is now a protected historical site.

Thórir Flap: the Sacred Grove

There was a man called Thórir *snepill* (Flap) who came out from Norway in the early days of the Settlement. He landed in the north of Iceland, in the Skjálfandi estuary, and laid claim to the chilly-sounding valley of Kaldakinn (Cold Cheek) down which the Skjálfandi river runs into the estuary. It was, and still is, good farming land; but Thórir Flap found no happiness there, and soon he crossed to the next valley to the west, Fnjóskadalur (Touchwood Valley), and took possession of it. This was much more to his taste, because there he found a grove of trees which he held to be sacred, and built his farm there, and named it Lundur (Grove), and made sacrifices there. Thórir Flap's granddaughter married a man who was to play a crucial part in one of the key events of Iceland's history—the conversion to Christianity (see Ch 10); his name was Thorgeir Thorkelsson, the *goði* (priest-chieftain) of nearby Ljósavatn (Lightwater), who was Law-Speaker of the Althing during that fateful session—the pagan arbitrator who came down on the side of Christianity.

The farm of Lundur is still an important homestead in the valley; and the sacred grove that Thórir Flap once worshipped is today part of the largest forest in Iceland, *Vaglaskógur*, which is now protected and used for experiments in reafforestation. It is a lovely place, with birch trees more than twelve metres in height, and all the more delightful for being so unusual in this treeless land.

Hrollaugur of Síða: Sacred Pillars

There are several instances in *Landnámabók* of settlers following the example of Ingólfur Arnarson and casting their high-seat pillars overboard within sight of land. Some scholars doubt whether this pious exercise took place at all,

Reykjavík, the capital of Iceland. In the centre, the Tjörn (Pond): the farm of the first settler, Ingólfur Arnarson, was between the Tjörn and the sea.

Ponies at pasture. The pure-bred Icelandic pony (*equus scandinavicus*) was the catalyst of settlement.

because the odds against ever finding them again must have been astronomical. But those who are reported to have carried out this practice tended to be well-born and wealthy, people who felt themselves committed by destiny to a new life in Iceland.

One such was a man called Hrollaugur, son of one of the most eminent chieftains of ninth-century Norway, Earl Rögnvald of Möre. Two of Hrollaugur's brothers carved for themselves special places in the history of the Viking Age. One was called Einar, who became better known as Turf-Einar, one of the first Norse earls of Orkney; he is said to have earned his nickname because he introduced to Orkney the idea of using turves of peat as fuel. The other was a giant of a man called Hrólfur, who was so big that no horse could bear his weight, and so he had to go everywhere on foot; for that reason he was known as Göngu-Hrólfur—Hrolf the Walker, or Ganger-Rolf. History would know him better as Rollo, the Viking who founded the duchy of Normandy and the Norman (Northman) dynasty that conquered England in 1066.

Hrollaugur was a very different kind of man. For one thing he was illegitimate, whereby we may assume that he was not considered fit for blue-blooded rule. When he asked his father if he could go to Orkney to take over the earldom there, which was vacant at the time, his father replied:

'Your temper is not suited to warfare. Your paths will take you to Iceland, where you will be highly thought of and have many descendants, but your destiny does not lie here.'

So Hrollaugur sailed off to Iceland with his family, and with the blessing of no less a person than King Harald Fine-Hair of Norway himself. He threw his high-seat pillars overboard in the approved fashion, and they were washed ashore in the south-east corner of Iceland, at Hornafjörður. Hrollaugur settled in the Síða (Side) district and became a great chieftain. He never went back to Norway, but kept up his friendship with King Harald, who sent him a sword, a drinking-horn and a gold ring weighing five ounces, all of which became prized heirlooms for generations and greatly enhanced the family's standing. Among his distinguished descendants, as his father had prophesied, were Síðu-Hallur (Hallur of Síða), the wise Christian chieftain who would play an important conciliatory role in the dramas of *Njáls Saga*, and some of the early bishops of the Icelandic Church, including Jón Ögmundarson, the first bishop of Hólar (see Ch 13).

Kráku-Hreiðar: Self-Reliance

The settlement of Iceland was a comparatively peaceful affair. In the whole of *Landnámabók* there are only half a dozen references to men who were prepared to use violence to acquire land for themselves. Such men believed more in their own might and main than in any supernatural assistance.

There was a man called Kráku-Hreiðar (Crow-Hreiðar), a Norwegian Viking who emigrated to Iceland with his father. When they made landfall, Hreiðar went up to the mast and said he had no intention of throwing his high-seat pillars overboard, because he thought it a stupid way of making important decisions. Instead, he said he would ask the god Thór for guidance on where to settle, and if the place were settled already, he would fight for it. He put into Skagafjörður, in the north of Iceland, and sailed up to Borgarstrand, where his ship was wrecked. He spent the winter as the guest of an established settler. In the spring he was asked what he intended to do, and Kráku-Hreiðar replied that he intended to challenge a neighbour to a duel for his land. His host discouraged him, saying that that sort of thing always turned out badly, and advised him instead to go and seek advice from the most respected man in the district, Eiríkur of Hof, in Goðdalir (God Dales). Eiríkur deplored the idea of fighting, and said it was absurd for men to quarrel when the land was so thinly populated. Instead, he offered to give Kráku-Hreiðar a generous slice of his own land elsewhere, and said that Thór must have guided him after all, for the land lay in the direction that the prow of the wrecked ship had been pointing. Kráku-Hreiðar accepted the offer, and bloodshed was averted.

Kveld-Úlfur: Coffin Guidance
A bizarre variant of the pillars theme occurs in the story of the
emigration of Kveld-Úlfur, the father of Skallagrímur and
grandfather of Egill Skallagrímsson, the eponymous hero of
Egils Saga. Kveld-Úlfur was a friend of Ingólfur Arnarson;
and when he fell foul of King Harald Fine-Hair, he and his son
Skallagrímur set sail for Iceland in two ships, each with thirty
men aboard. Father and son kept in contact on their ships for
most of the way. But when they were almost at journey's end,
Kveld-Úlfur fell ill. He asked his men to make a coffin for him
should he die at sea, and to tell his son Skallagrímur to build
his home in Iceland near the spot where the coffin came
ashore, if that were possible. Then Kveld-Úlfur died, and his
coffin was consigned to the sea.

The two ships sailed round Reykjanes and past it, for they
knew that all the land had been taken by Ingólfur Arnarson.
As they nosed into Borgarfjörður, they lost touch with one
another and made land separately. As luck would have it, the
coffin was found almost at once. Skallagrímur liked the look
of the land, and laid claim to the huge area of Mýrar
(Marshes), and built his farm near the creek where the coffin
had come ashore, and called it Borg (Burg) and the fjord
Borgarfjörður.

Sel-Thórir: Horse Sense
The style and tone of *Landnámabók* are so matter-of-fact that
it is easy to slide past even the most extraordinary tale as if it
were an everyday event. Take the way in which Sel-Thórir
was guided to his settlement, for instance.

There was a Norwegian called Grímur who came to
Iceland looking for land. He arrived late in the summer
and settled temporarily on Grímsey in Steingrímsfjörður, in
the north. In the autumn he went fishing, with his young son
Thórir lying in the prow, safely tucked into a sealskin bag
that was fastened at the neck. Suddenly, Grímur hooked a
merman, and when he had hauled him to the surface,
Grímur asked: 'What can you tell us about our futures?

Where in Iceland should we settle?'

The merman replied that there was little point in making prophecies about Grímur (implying that he had not long to live): 'But as for the boy in the sealskin bag, he will settle and claim land at the spot where your mare, Skálm, lies down under her load.' Not another word could Grímur get out of the creature.

Later that winter Grímur and his farmhands went out fishing again, leaving the boy behind. And the merman's prophecy came true, for the boat foundered and all the menfolk were drowned.

Thórir, who was now nicknamed Sel-Thórir because of the sealskin bag, was left alone with his mother. In the spring they travelled across the moors to Breiðafjörður. The mare, Skálm, walked ahead of them, but never once did she lie down. They spent the winter on a headland in Breiðafjörður called Skálmarnes in the mare's honour. When mother and son set out on their travels again next spring they turned south across the moorlands towards Borgarfjörður. Skálm was in the lead as usual; and just as they were passing two red-coloured sand-dunes, Skálm lay down under her load. Sel-Thórir and his mother now reckoned that they had been guided to the place where they should settle; he took possession of the land between mountains and sea, and made his home at Rauðamelur ytri (Outer Red-Hill), just where the modern highway to Snæfellsnes swings westwards into the peninsula.

It is a spectacular location. The two 'red-coloured sand-dunes' are, in fact, two magnificent volcanic cone-craters rising a hundred metres above the surrounding lava-fields, burnt black and red. Sel-Thórir built his farm at the edge of this formidable stretch of lava; and there he became a great chieftain.

There is an intriguing postscript to this story in *Land-námabók* concerning another handsome crater not far away, called Eldborg:

When Sel-Thórir was old and blind, he went out one

evening and 'saw' a huge, evil-looking man come rowing into Kaldárós [Cold River Estuary] in an iron boat. This man walked up to a farm called Hrip and started digging there at the door of the sheep-shed. That very night there was a volcanic eruption there, from which the lava-field of Borgarhraun ran. Where the farm had stood there is now the crater.

Eldborg (Fire Burg) is a beautiful ring-wall crater shaped like a natural walled fortress. It is elliptical, some 200 metres long, rising sixty metres above the surrounding sea of lava. The walls are thin and very steep, a slender stockade of cliff-like ramparts made up of spatter-layers of frothy, molten lava spilling out of the crater. There have been two eruptions here; the first took place thousands of years ago, but the second was very much more recent. *Landnámabók* says that it was Eldborg itself that Sel-Thórir witnessed erupting; but recent scientific analysis of the lava has shown that it was a crater a little to the north, called Rauðhálsar, which erupted during the Settlement Age around the year 900. So, although the *Landnámabók* account has confused the two craters, it represents a fascinating folk-memory of a volcano in sudden action, larded with the folklore motif of the giant in his iron boat.

'Eldborg' has become a technical type-name for this kind of ring-wall crater, which is very unusual outside Iceland.

Ketilbjörn the Old: the Late-Comer

Even late-comers from Norway, if they were well-born and had well-placed family connections, could land on their feet in the new country, with a little help from their friends: men like Ketilbjörn the Old, for instance.

Ketilbjörn was a man of repute in Naumdalen, in Norway, the nephew of a notable Norwegian chieftain, Earl Hakon Grjotgardsson. He married extremely well; his wife was Helga, the daughter of Thórður *skeggi* (Beard) and an English princess—Vilborg, the daughter of King Oswald and granddaughter of the celebrated King Edmund of East

Anglia, who was martyred by the Danes in AD 870 and quickly canonized. The genealogy, it must be admitted, is somewhat suspect: 'King Oswald' is hard to identify, and there is no mention of his alleged wife, an illegitimate daughter of St Edmund, except in the Icelandic sources. But no matter: the Icelanders themselves believed in the royal connection.

Thórður Beard was a kinsman of Ingólfur Arnarson; he, too, emigrated to Iceland and was invited by Ingólfur to settle on part of his own huge land-claim, in the Mosfell district near Reykjavík, and built his farm at Skeggjastaðir.

Some years later, Ketilbjörn the Old decided to emigrate to Iceland; by this time most of the land near the sea had been taken. He made land in the estuary of the salmon-river on the threshold of Reykjavík; his ship was called *Ellidi* (a poetic synonym for ship), and that is how the braided rivers by Reykjavík got their name, Elliðaár. Ketilbjörn spent the winter with his father-in-law, Thórður Beard. In the spring he travelled east across the moors looking for a suitable place to settle. He came to the great lava arena that would soon become known as Thingvellir, the home of the Althing; the river that cascades over the lava cliffs there was still ice-bound, and when they hacked at the ice to get water, one of their axes fell into the river and was lost. So they called it Öxará (Axe River). Later, when the Althing was established, this river would be diverted to make better room for the Althing.

Ketilbjörn eventually took possession of the area known as Grímsnes, the district between the rivers Sog and Hvítá (White River), reaching up to Laugardalur and Biskups-tunga. Grímsnes is an idyllic part of the country; the southern section is a sea of lava, 6,000 years old now, that has been blurred by a thick blanket of grey and green moss and overgrown by brushwood and dwarf birch. The woodland is called Thrastaskógur (Thrush Wood), and in summer the air is heady with the scent of crowberry (*krækilyng*), ling (*beitilyng*) and bearberry (*sortulyng*). Today a gravel road undulates through it, a ribbon of bright red from the lava-slag and scoria quarried from the ash hills and craters all around.

Ketilbjörn built his home at the roots of a mountain called Mosfell, in a serene and fertile valley called Biskupstunga (Bishop's Tongue) that would play a central part in the subsequent history of Iceland; on a commanding height across the Brúará (Bridge River), his son Teitur Ketilbjarnarson built the manor farm of Skálholt (Sheiling Grove) which would become the power-house of the Church in Iceland and a major cultural centre down the centuries (see Ch 11). Teitur's grandson, Ísleifur Gissurarson, became the first native bishop of Iceland in 1056.

It is said of Ketilbjörn the Old in *Landnámabók* that he became immensely wealthy—so wealthy that he told his sons to forge a cross-beam of solid silver for the pagan temple at Mosfell. The sons refused—not out of any religious susceptibilities, perhaps, but because they did not want to see their inheritance squandered on such an extravagant gesture, temple or no temple. But Ketilbjörn had the last laugh. He hauled all the silver up to the top of Mosfell on a pair of oxen, and buried it there with the help of a slave and a bondmaid. He then killed the slaves so that no one would know the whereabouts of the silver, and Ketilbjörn the Old gleefully took the secret to his own grave.

Uni the Dane: the Earl Who Never Was
Not everyone made the grade as a settler. Uni *danski* (the Dane), son of Garðar Svavarsson who had discovered Iceland and modestly named it Garðarshólmur (see Ch 2), went to Iceland at the suggestion of King Harald Fine-Hair with the intention of taking over the new country in the king's name; King Harald had promised to make him Earl of Iceland in exchange. Uni made land with eleven companions in the north-east of Iceland, in Austfirðir (Eastfjords), and took the land around Lagarvatn. But Uni had a wretched time of it. As soon as people realized what his intentions were, they nicknamed him 'the Dane' and refused to sell him any livestock or help him in any way. Uni was forced to move over to south Álptafjörður, on the east coast, but found no place to stay there, either. Eventually he was taken in for the winter by a

man called Leiðólfur *kappi* (Champion). Uni fell in love with
Leiðólfur's daughter, Thórunn, and by spring she was expecting a child. Alarmed at what he had done, Uni decamped with
his followers; but Leiðólfur went after them—he wanted Uni
to marry his daughter and settle down and inherit the property in due course. But Uni had no wish to undertake such
responsibilities, and refused to go back. A battle ensued in
which many of Uni's men were killed, and Uni himself was
brought back against his will. At the first opportunity,
however, Uni ran away again. This time, when Leiðólfur
caught up with them, he was in such a rage that he slew Uni
and all the rest of his companions.

Better luck attended the child that Thórunn was carrying.
She gave birth to a boy called Hróar, who became a man of
distinction as the priest-chieftain of Tunga (*Tungugoði*) and
married the sister of Gunnar of Hlíðarendi, the peerless hero
of *Njáls Saga*.

Ingimundur the Old: the Patriarch of Vatnsdœla Saga

All the entries in *Landnámabók* are brief and episodic. They
are summaries of stories, rather than the stories themselves.
Many of the classical sagas used genealogical material from
Landnámabók in their own narratives; and the later recen-
sions of *Landnámabók* would sometimes summarize an existing saga and add it to the body of the book.

That is what happened to *Vatnsdœla Saga*, which was
written just after the middle of the thirteenth century; soon
afterwards, the account of the patriarchal settler, Ingimundur
the Old, was written into *Landnámabók* in short summary
form.

Vatnsdœla Saga is essentially a family chronicle, a conscien-
tious and sometimes self-conscious attempt to extol the
virtues of the pagan ancestors of an important dynasty in
northern Iceland, the Men of Vatnsdalur, the Vatnsdœlings:
heroes all, bathed in a benign glow of adumbrated
Christianity—'They believed in the One who made the sun
and rules all things'. It is not considered to be in the front rank
of major sagas; it lacks the grandeur and richness and literary

genius of the greatest classics like *Njáls Saga* and *Egils Saga* and *Laxdœla Saga*. But it has its charm, none the less, not least for the nostalgic attitude it reveals towards the past.

The area of settlement in *Vatnsdœla Saga* is the long green valley that runs serenely southwards from the broad waters of Húnaflói (Bears Bay) in the north of Iceland. The mouth of the valley is studded with an extraordinary stipple of large conical hillocks called Vatnsdalshólar, which were spawned when the mountainside collapsed in ruins as the glaciers retreated at the end of the last Ice Age, 10,000 years ago; they look like giant mole-hills breaking through the smooth valley floor. At the upper end of the valley lies the Settlement farmstead of Hof (Temple). It is idyllically sited in a grassy dell, and generations of diligent farmers have kept the land and its traditions green. It is an inviting place to visit, for it is still redolent of saga: all around are the places and place-names that hark back to the days of Ingimundur the Old, whose arrival in Iceland around the year 900 was ordained by destiny and brought about by magic and enchantment.

In the saga, Ingimundur is cast in the mould of the ideal Germanic hero, a lusty warrior in his youth who mellows into a mature and statesmanlike chieftain. He and his family, both before and after him, were considered men of luck, attended by a potent guardian force (*hamingja*) that bestowed on them an aura of good fortune. Ingimundur was the grandson of a powerful Norwegian chieftain, Ketill Raum, a name to con-jure with in the wild fastnesses of northern Norway. Ingimundur's father, Thorsteinn, was an adventurer who contrived to marry an earl's daughter despite slaying the earl's son (such was the power of the family luck), and Ingimundur himself was reared in the rough Viking school of freelance raiding and plundering:

> It was soon apparent that Ingimundur was resolute in attack and a man of valour, trusty of arm and weapon, steadfast and stout-hearted and a loyal friend, and most likely to become the best of pagan chieftains—as indeed he did.

When Harald Fine-Hair made his bid for the overlord-
ship of Norway, young Ingimundur picked the right side and
threw in his lot with Harald, and fought for him well and
bravely at the crucial battle of Hafrsfjord, off Stavanger, that
gave all Norway into his hands (see Ch 1). King Harald
rewarded all those who had supported him; and to
Ingimundur he gave a silver talisman, a figurine of the
fertility god Freyr. Basking in royal favour, Ingimundur now
seemed set to take over his father's ancestral estates and
become one of King Harald's right-hand men. But at this
point, fate took a hand. At a mid-winter feast a sorceress
from Lapland was hired to tell people's fortunes.
Ingimundur, with all the arrogant self-confidence of youth,
scoffed at the very idea of having his fortune told. But the
sorceress insisted:

> 'You shall make your home in the country of Iceland,
> which is still largely unsettled. There you will become a
> man of mark and live to a ripe old age, and your many
> progeny will be eminent in that land.'
> 'A likely tale!' said Ingimundur, 'considering that it is
> the one place I am determined never to go near. I would
> have a poor nose for a bargain if I sold all my rich and
> fertile patrimony to go to those wastelands.'
> 'Nevertheless,' said the Lapland woman, 'it shall
> come to pass as I say. And the proof of it is that the gift
> King Harald gave you at Hafrsfjord, the silver talisman
> of Freyr, has vanished from your purse, and has now
> reached the very copse where you will make your home;
> and when you build your house there, my words will be
> proved true.'

Despite his open disbelief the prophecy nagged at
Ingimundur's mind—especially when he discovered that the
Freyr amulet actually was missing. He told the king about this
strange event, and King Harald thought there might be
something in it after all. So Ingimundur hired a trio of
Lappish sorcerers and sent them on a magic mission to
Iceland to try to find the missing talisman. The shamans

spirited themselves to Iceland and searched around until they
found it; but whenever they tried to lay hands on it, it jumped
out of their grasp, and their advice to Ingimundur was that he
would have to go there and find it for himself.

So Ingimundur decided that there was nothing for it but to
emigrate to Iceland. Unlike most of the early settlers from
Norway, he went there with the king's blessing; not only that,
the king also approved marriage to an excellent lady called
Vigdís, who was the illegitimate daughter of the king's own
son-in-law. They landed in the north of Iceland, and began an
assiduous search of the valleys, looking for some especially
green place that the magicians had told him to expect.
Eventually they reached the mouth of Vatnsdalur with its
spectacular cluster of hillocks; and now Ingimundur felt he
was getting warm, for he recognized the lay of the land from
the Lapps' description.

It was then that his wife Vigdís, who was heavy with child,
called a halt:

> 'Here I must pause for a while,' she said, 'for I feel my
> pains upon me.'
> 'May all turn out for the best,' said Ingimundur.
> Then Vigdís gave birth to a baby girl. She was given
> the name of Thórdís, and Ingimundur said, 'This place
> shall be known as Thórdísarholt [Thórdís Copse].'

Today that historic birthplace is marked by a patch of
carefully-planted woodland, with a memorial stone to commemorate the unceremonious arrival of the first child to be
born in the Húnavatn district.

> They all then moved farther up the valley, and could
> see excellent land there, grassy and wooded. It was a
> beautiful scene, and everyone's spirits rose. Ingimundur
> laid claim to the whole of Vatnsdalur above Helgavatn
> and Urðarvatn . . .
> Ingimundur chose for himself a site in a lovely dell,
> and began to build. He put up a great temple there, 100
> feet long; and when they excavated the footings for his

high-seat pillars, he found his talisman, as had been foretold.

Then Ingimundur said, 'It is a true saying that no man may fight against his fate, so let us make the most of it. This homestead shall be called Hof.'

Looming over the present farm-site is a steep, saddle-backed hillock which is known locally as Goðhóll (God Hillock). On its top there are the grass-grown outlines of old walls, which tradition would have us believe are the remains of Ingimundur's temple, the *hof* after which he named his home and where the elusive talisman of Freyr was found; but the site has never been systematically excavated, and it could be anything.

From the top of Goðhóll one can look out over the broad acres of Vatnsdalur and identify all the places where the large events of the saga once happened. The story follows the fortunes of the family through four generations throughout the tenth century, to the coming of Christianity with the first missionaries in the 980s (see Ch 9). The saga is a chronicle of dramatic events, of killings and conciliations, of revenge and forgiveness, of heroism and villainy. It is a rich gallery of individuals; but none of his descendants dominates the scene as compellingly as Ingimundur the Old, the wise pater-familias, the considerate chieftain, the noble pagan whose virtues are those of a Christian before his time. His last act in life was a gesture designed to prevent his sons becoming embroiled in a blood-feud. To this day we can identify the very place in the river near Hof where Ingimundur, very old by then and well-nigh blind, tried to intervene in a quarrel between his sons and a rascally neighbour, Hrolleifur. He rode out into the river to separate them, and ordered his sons to withdraw. When the sons had gone, Hrolleifur spitefully threw a spear at Ingimundur which struck him in the waist. Ingimundur knew at once that the wound was mortal. He rode back home and dragged himself indoors, and seated himself on his cherished high-seat. Then he summoned one of his attendants:

'Go at once and tell Hrolleifur that before morning comes, my sons will be looking for him, to avenge their father. Let him see to it that he is away by daybreak. I am none the more avenged though Hrolleifur dies, and so long as I have any say, my duty is to safeguard anyone to whom I have ever given shelter, however it turns out afterwards.'

When his sons came home later that evening they found him sitting upright on his high-seat in the darkness, dead. Despite their father's wishes, his sons hunted Hrolleifur down and killed him; but the eldest, Thorsteinn, who took over the leadership of the Vatnsdœlings, recognized the significance of the gesture his father had made:

'We can comfort ourselves with the knowledge of the great difference there was between him and Hrolleifur. And my father will get his reward from the One who made the sun and all creation, whoever He may be; for it is certain that someone must have made it.'

CHAPTER 4

Early Christians

Svá segja vitrir menn, at nökkurir landnámsmenn hafi skírðir verit, þeir er byggt hafa Ísland, flestir þeir, er kómu vestan um haf . . .

Learned men say that some of the settlers of Iceland had been baptized, mostly those who came from the British Isles . . . *Some of them kept up their faith until they died. But in most families it did not last, for the sons of many of them built temples and made sacrifices.*

(Landnámabók)

According to *Landnámabók*, there was a sprinkling of practising Christians amongst the early settlers of Iceland. There were not very many of them—only about a dozen or so—and they seem to have had no lasting effect on the predominantly pagan bias of the community. Without exception, they had migrated to Iceland via the British Isles, especially Scotland and Ireland, where Celtic Christianity had been long established.

Nearly all of these early Christians in Iceland were connected with one powerful family that originated in Norway, from the western district of Sogn. Its progenitor was a leading chieftain called Björn *buna* (the meaning of the nickname is obscure). *Landnámabók* says of him that 'nearly all the most prominent Icelanders are descended from Björn *buna*', and indeed his name figures largely in the genealogies of the protagonists of many of the major Icelandic sagas. Björn *buna* had three sons—Ketill *flatnefr* (Flatnose), Hrappur and Helgi: 'they were all outstanding men, and a great deal will be said about them in this book'. In particular, it is the descendants of Ketill Flatnose who play the leading roles in the magnificent family chronicle of *Laxdæla Saga* (see Ch 15). Ketill Flatnose rose to prominence as a warrior chief in the Hebrides, in Scotland. Some sources suggest that he was sent there to pacify the islands on behalf of Harald Fine-Hair, King of Norway; once he had conquered the islands, however, he neglected to send tribute to Norway, thereby incurring the king's heavy displeasure and forfeiting his ancestral Norwegian estates. Other sources, however, indicate that he had gone to the Hebrides as a freelance Viking warrior long before King Harald's day. Whatever the truth of it, it is agreed that he took most of his family with him, apart from his elder son, Björn *austræni* (Easterner)—the nickname apparently refers to the fact that he remained in the east, in Norway, instead of going 'west-over-sea' to the British Isles. He was the only one of Ketill Flatnose's children who never accepted baptism: when he eventually left Norway, he visited his family in Scotland but did not like the look of things there, and emigrated to Iceland where he settled on the northern coast of Snæfellsnes, in Breiðafjörður, at a place called Bjarnarhöfn (Björn's Haven).

However, it is with the rest of Ketill Flatnose's offspring that we are concerned in this chapter: his other son, Helgi *bjólan* (another obscure nickname), and his three splendidly-named daughters—Auður *djúpúðga* (Deep-Minded), Thórunn *hyrna* (Horn) and Jórunn *manvitsbrekka* (Wisdom-Slope). And of these colourful characters, it is Auður the Deep-Minded who plays the most striking role in the Icelandic sagas, as the regal matriarch of *Laxdæla Saga*.

Auður the Deep-Minded

In *Laxdæla Saga*, Auður the Deep-Minded is known as Unnur; but there is no doubt that the earlier and more authentic form of the name, as used in *Landnámabók* and elsewhere, was Auður.

Auður went to the British Isles with her father, Ketill Flatnose. There she married a Viking warlord called Ólafur *hvíti* (White), who made himself King of Ireland and seems to have been known to Irish annalists as *Amblaibh mac Godfraidh*, or *Amblaibh conung*, King Olaf. This Olaf was killed in battle in 871, so Auður left Ireland for the Hebrides with her son, who was called Thorsteinn *rauði* (Red).

Thorsteinn the Red became a Viking warlord like his father, and laid about him to such good effect that he became king over much of Scotland, in name at least. He married Thuríður, the sister of Helgi *magri* (Lean), who would also emigrate to Iceland, and they had seven children: a son, Ólafur *feilan* (Wolf-Cub), and six daughters. Eventually his battle-luck ran out, and he was ambushed and killed in Caithness.

Now Auður showed her mettle. Stranded in a hostile country, and with a handful of grandchildren to look after, she somehow managed to have a ship built secretly in a forest, and set sail with all her surviving kinsfolk and a band of faithful followers. She was heading for Iceland; but on her way northwards, she stopped in Orkney, where she married off one of her granddaughters, and in the Faroes, where she married off another. Then she set sail for Iceland. It was around 895, as far as can be deduced.

Auður's brothers were already settled in Iceland by then, but she was too proud to accept hospitality from them for long. She wanted land of her own, and went off to explore the fertile valleys of the inner reaches of Breiðafjörður, leaving a trail of telling place-names in her wake. One headland was called Dögurðarnes, because that was where she took breakfast (*dögurðr*) one morning. Another was named Kambsnes, because that was where she lost a comb (*kambr*). Finally she made her home at Hvammur (Vale) in Skeggjadalur, at the far end of Hvammsfjörður. As the first settler in the area she took possession of the whole Dales district, which she proceeded to parcel out to her friends and followers with due regard to their lineage, social standing, and intrinsic qualities.

But now the traditions about this redoubtable lady diverge sharply. According to *Laxdæla Saga*, Auður the Deep-Minded was a pagan: she had thrown her high-seat pillars overboard as she approached land, and when she died, at a ripe old age, she was given a ship-burial down by the shore, with a load of treasure beside her. The sea has gnawed at the coastline over the centuries, and the presumed site of Auður's burial mound would have been consumed long ago. It would not have been as spectacular as the Sutton Hoo ship-burial from Anglo-Saxon times in Suffolk, or the rich Oseberg ship-burial in Norway, for these were great royal funerals; but five boat-burials, albeit very simple ones, have been excavated in Iceland, and the custom is well-attested there in pre-Christian times.

According to *Landnámabók*, however, Auður the Deep-Minded had been baptized in the British Isles, and was a devout Christian—so much so that she used to say her prayers at Krosshólar (Cross-Hills), and had crosses erected there.

Today the valley of Skeggjadalur is as green and welcoming as it must have been in Auður's day, facing south and soaking up the summer sun. The present farm of Hvammur stands a little farther up the valley than it did in Settlement days, apparently; on the eastern side of the valley there are still to be seen traces of the grass-grown foundations of some building from much earlier times. Just round the corner from the mouth of the valley there is a dramatic rocky outcrop near the coast. This is assumed to be the 'Krosshólar' of Auður's time, and a stone memorial cross has been erected at the top, inscribed with the words from *Landnámabók*: 'She used to say prayers at Krosshólar; she had crosses erected there, for she had been baptized and was devout in her faith.'

After Auður's death, however, her kinsmen reverted to paganism. They began to worship the hill itself, and built some sort of shrine there for sacrifices. They even believed that they would go into the hill when they died (see Ch 5).

The Church at Esjuberg

The first church in Iceland is said to have been built at Esjuberg, at the foot of the mountain Esja on Kjalarnes, across the bay of Kollafjörður to the north of Reykjavík. According to *Landnámabók*, it was two of Björn *buna*'s grandsons who were responsible for it.

The first settler on Kjalarnes was Helgi *bjólan*, the son of Ketill Flatnose. He went to Iceland from the Hebrides and went to see Ingólfur Arnarson, for Ingólfur was a kinsman of his. Ingólfur invited him to settle on Kjalarnes, which lay within his own huge land-take. According to *Landnámabók*, Helgi *bjólan* was a convert to Christianity.

Meanwhile his cousin Örlygur, the son of Hrappur (brother of Ketill Flatnose), was also making his way to Iceland. Hrappur had gone to the Hebrides with Ketill Flatnose, and there he had given his son Örlygur into fosterage with 'Bishop Patrick of the Hebrides' (no bishop of that name is known in the extant sources, however). Örlygur felt the same compulsion to go to Iceland as the rest of the family, and asked the bishop for guidance. The bishop provided him with timber for a church, an iron bell, a plenarium (*missale plenarium*: complete missal), and some consecrated earth that Örlygur was to place beneath the corner-posts of the church. The church was to be dedicated to Kolumkille (St Columba), the founder of Celtic Christianity on the Hebridean island of Iona in the sixth century.

They had a rough passage, and were storm-swept to the north-west of Iceland; when they eventually made landfall, Örlygur named the fjord they entered Patreksfjörður, in honour of his foster-father. In the following spring, Örlygur set sail again, and found his way to Kjalarnes, and stayed there with his cousin Helgi *bjólan*. Helgi gave him land on which to settle at Esjuberg, close to his own home at the foot of Mount Esja, and there Örlygur built St Columba's church, as he had promised. According to *Landnámabók*, 'Örlygur's kinsmen put their faith in Kolumkille, but did not take baptism.'

There has been a church at Esjuberg for many centuries now; but there are the remains of some very old buildings to be seen near the present farm, and they have been listed as a protected site — just in case!

Kirkjubæjarklaustur: the Cloister in the Lava

On the south coast of Iceland, at the edge of a ferocious lava-field between the glaciers of Mýrdalsjökull and Vatnajökull, there stands a tiny hamlet called Kirkjubæjarklaustur (Church Farm Cloister), a delightful oasis of green fertility. Originally, its name was simply Kirkjubær (Church Farm), but the name was lengthened when a Benedictine convent was founded there in 1186.

The first Icelandic settler at Kirkjubær was a man called Ketill *fíflski* (Foolish): 'He was a devout Christian, which is why the pagans called him foolish'. He was another of the Christian family of Ketill Flatnose; his mother was Ketill's daughter, Jórunn Wisdom-Slope, the sister of Auður the Deep-Minded. When Ketill the Foolish settled at Kirkjubær, it already had Christian associations, for this, according to *Landnámabók*, was one of the places where the pilgrim Irish monks, the *papar*, had made their home some years before the first Viking settlers arrived (see Ch 1). This tradition may have been inspired by a strange natural feature on the surface of a field on the outskirts of the hamlet: it is the flat top of a buried block of hexagonal basalt columns looking for all the world like a flagged stone floor and called—of course—*kirkjugólfið* (Church Floor).

Whatever the reason, there was a spell on the place: no pagan might live there. Indeed, after Ketill's death, a man called Hildir Eysteinsson wanted to move house to Kirkjubær, 'for he did not see why a pagan should not farm there; but as he was approaching the fence of the home-field, he dropped down dead.'

But the most spectacular event in the history of Kirkjubæjarklaustur occurred during the catastrophic eruption of the Laki Craters in 1783 that gave rise to the terrible 'Haze Famine' of 1783–4 (see Ch 1). As the craters vented their streams of lava in all directions, one wicked tongue of molten rock came grinding and growling straight towards the tiny settlement. This was not the kind of viscous lava that runs bright red in rivers, but an advancing wall of tumbling rock and scoria, as high as a tenement building, slow and remorseless as if pushed by a giant bulldozer. The eruption began on Whitsunday, 8 June; by Sunday 20 July, the lava-wall had almost reached the hamlet. The pastor, Jón Steingrímsson, summoned his terrified flock to the little church that stood in the path of the crushing lava. He ordered the doors to be closed, and then proceeded to preach with such fiery passion that all fears were stilled. And when the congregation stumbled out of the church at noon into the choking, smoking darkness they suddenly noticed that there was silence. The lava was no longer moving; the eruption from that particular crater had died down, only to belch out with renewed fury elsewhere. But Kirkjubæjarklaustur had been saved; and pastor Jón's passionate oratory from the pulpit that day has ever since been known as the *eldmessa*—the Fire Sermon.

Today, near the place where the old country church once stood, there is an elegant new memorial chapel of moulded concrete and wood, dedicated to the memory of the pastor whose courage and blazing faith are believed to have averted the wrath of God on that fateful day in 1783. There is no verbatim record of what he said in his Fire Sermon, alas; but his *Autobiography* has come to be considered a classic of its time.

Helgi the Lean: Hedging the Bets

The last of the family of Ketill Flatnose whose adherence to Christianity is mentioned in *Landnámabók* is Helgi *magri* (Lean). He was the son of another Viking adventurer, Eyvindur *austmaður* (Eastman), who married an Irish princess, and Helgi was brought up in Ireland, where he married the third of Ketill Flatnose's daughters, Thórunn *hyrna* (Horn); meanwhile, as we saw earlier, his sister Thuríður married Thórunn's nephew, Thorsteinn the Red, son of Auður the Deep-Minded.

But Helgi the Lean's commitment to Christianity, despite his Irish upbringing, was anything but whole-hearted:

> Helgi's faith was very mixed: he believed in Christ, but invoked Thór for sea-voyages and other hardships.

Thus, when he decided to emigrate to Iceland with his family, it was Thór whom he consulted as to where he should make land, and the oracle guided him to the north of Iceland, where he took possession of the whole of Eyjafjörður (Islands Fjord) and made his home a few kilometres up the valley at the head of the fjord. Having reached his destination safely with one brand of divine guidance, Helgi the Lean now switched his allegiance again and named his homestead Kristnes:

Helgi believed in Christ, and called his home after him.

Jörundur the Christian: Hermitage on Akranes

Landnámabók singles out one other Christian for special mention: his name was Jörundur, known to his neighbours as *kristni* (Christian).

Jörundur was of Celtic stock. He had emigrated from Ireland with his father and uncle, who had been the first settlers on the headland of Akranes, the headland on the north shore of Hvalfjörður, dominated by the striking mountain of Akrafjall which is clearly visible to the north of Reykjavík. The brothers had divided the lands round the headland between them; Jörundur's father, Ketill Bresason, settled at the site which has now grown into the bustling seaport of Akranes, while his uncle, Thormóður Bresason, took over the southern part and made his home at the historic manor farm of Innri-Hólmur (Inner Island).

Jörundur built a home for himself on his father's lands at Garðar (Gardens), which is now on the outskirts of modern Akranes. Landnámabók says of him that he kept his Christian faith steadfastly to his dying day, and became a hermit in his old age – the first recorded hermit in Iceland.

Jörundur's nephew, a man called Ásólfur, was even more committed: he seems to have become a monk in Ireland, and came to Iceland practically as a missionary, for he brought with him a party of eleven followers (it was apparently the custom of Celtic monks to travel in groups of twelve, like the Apostles). They made land on the south coast, on the lowlands under the Eyjafjöll mountains, and camped at a farm-site now known as Ásólfsskáli. *Landnámabók* says of him:

> He was a devout Christian and would have nothing to do with pagan people; he would not even accept food from them.

There was no need to accept food from them, however. No sooner had Ásólfur settled at Ásólfsskáli than the nearby stream started to teem with fish as never before — a clear case of God looking after His own. When the local farmers found out about this, they drove Ásólfur and his followers away, not wanting him to reap the benefit of this abundance. Ásólfur moved to another camp-site farther west, whereupon all the fish immediately left the stream at Ásólfsskáli and obligingly moved into the stream beside Ásólfur's new camp. Once more the pagan farmers drove him away, and he moved a little farther west to another stream, called the Írá (Irish River), whereupon the fish followed him to Írá as well. Even there the harassment continued, and Ásólfur now abandoned whatever mission he had set himself under the Eyjafjöll mountains and went to Akranes to seek shelter with his uncle Jörundur. Jörundur invited him to make his home with him at Garðar, but Ásólfur said he wanted to keep away from other people; so Jörundur built a little house for him on his own uncle's land at Innri-Hólmur, and arranged for him to get a regular supply of provisions.

At Innri-Hólmur, Ásólfur became a hermit and resident holy man. When he died, he was buried beside his hermitage. But he proved to be somewhat restless after death, and kept appearing to people in their dreams to complain about the condition of his bones. Eventually his bones were exhumed and placed in a wooden shrine, and a church was built on the spot, where his relics attracted a modicum of reverence.

There are no records of what happened to that first church; no doubt it fell into disuse as the initial Christian impetus brought by these few settlers petered out. But there was certainly a church there by the end of the eleventh century, when Innri-Hólmur had become a manor farm and estate of considerable consequence. There is a charming old church there now, built in 1891 but substantially renovated and refurbished over the years.

Landnámabók states explicitly that the early Christian families soon reverted to paganism. Iceland clearly lacked the church structure to keep the new religion nourished. But there must have been quite a number of Christian slaves from Ireland and the Hebrides in the households of those settlers who came from the west, and Christian concubines and wet-nurses. Furthermore, Icelanders who travelled abroad in the tenth century can hardly have avoided coming into contact with Christianity; there are several references in the sagas to Icelanders accepting a preliminary form of baptism called 'prime-signing' (*prima signatio*), which allowed them to mingle and trade with Christians even though they might not be fully committed to Christianity themselves. All in all, it seems likely that a quiet and unobtrusive awareness of Christianity existed in Iceland throughout the tenth century, which would have made the work of the first Christian missionaries in the 980s less arduous than in other pagan countries (see Ch 9).

However, to all intents and purposes, Iceland was a pagan country, and a pagan state. The vast majority of the settlers considered themselves pagans, and followed pagan practices, and no doubt believed, to a greater or lesser extent, in the gods of the Norse pantheon, as we shall see in the next chapter.

CHAPTER 5

The Worship of Thór

Land var alheiðit nær hundraði vetra.

Iceland was completely pagan for about 120 years.

(*Landnámabók*)

A couple of kilometres past the farm of Draghals in the spectacularly beautiful valley of Svínadalur, in Borgarfjörður, there stands a huge, glowering plaster effigy of the god Thór. It is a distinctly makeshift affair, created to celebrate the granting of official state recognition, in May 1973, to an eccentric new religious sect in Iceland, the so-called *Ásatrú*. The word means 'belief in the Æsir', which was the name the Norsemen gave to their gods (singular *Áss*). *Ásatrú* is a self-conscious attempt to revive aspects of the ancient paganism of early Iceland.

The moving spirit behind this contemporary cult is a poetry-writing sheep-farmer called Sveinbjörn Beinteinsson. He is a splendid figure of a man, in his sixties now, with the face of an Old Testament prophet and a huge grey beard that cascades like a waterfall over his chest. He lives alone on the farm of Draghals with about fifty sheep and two cats. He styles himself the High Priest of the tiny handful of enthusiasts and hangers-on who comprise the sect—some eighty members in all.

Sveinbjörn has become a legend in his own lifetime, a part of the country's folklore. He is a quiet, sincere, undogmatic man, a man of considerable charm and amiability. He keeps his innermost thoughts to himself; he never tries to proselytize. He simply wants to resurrect the belief in Nature and the forces of Nature symbolized by the pagan gods, the faith

in oneself and one's own strength and abilities, that were at
the root of Icelandic culture. His is a very private sort of
religion that has become public almost as a joke. He is held in
the esteem that all Icelanders feel for true eccentrics; no one
takes the cult very seriously. Yet the *Ásatrúarmenn*, as they
call themselves, are legally empowered to baptize children,
confirm adolescents, marry the living and bury the dead. Not
many weddings have taken place as yet—only about half a
dozen, in fact—but they are duly registered in the National
Records Office, and can only be dissolved through the normal
lawful procedure of divorce. The ceremony is held in the open
air at the base of the effigy of Thór at Draghály with a
minimum of ritual: an invocation to the gods, a reading from
one of the old mythological texts, a prayer for good health
and happiness and fertility, and a toast or two. The weddings
at Draghály tend to be treated as media events, but there is no
lack of sincerity or conviction.

The sect represents a deliberate move back to Nature and
its supernatural forces, in a mixture of romanticism, national-
ism and theosophy. It has no systematic theology, as such;
and this is because Norse paganism was itself unsystematic. It
had no Bible, no Koran, no central authorized version of
doctrinal orthodoxy, no coherent or consistent concept of life
after death.

In the mythological writings of the *Edda* the Norse gods
formed a loose pantheon of deities and demigods that catered
for the varying tastes, needs and traditions of the people who
worshipped them. Most of them were depicted as warrior-
gods, reflecting the old Viking ethos of tough self-reliance in
everything to which the Viking put his hand, whether it was
the adventurer's sword, the farmer's plough, the seaman's
rudder, the merchant's scales, or the pioneer's axe. But there
were also deities who were essentially fertility gods and
goddesses embodying concepts of growth and natural
increase, of life and death, that were much older and more
primitive than Viking society. All these gods represented the
natural and supernatural forces inherent in the land and sea
and sky.

The distinction between the warrior-gods and the fertility gods is reflected in the mythology itself and in the way in which the mythology was rationalized by men like Snorri Sturluson in the thirteenth century. Snorri, as befitted a Christian scholar, demoted the pagan gods into ancient war-chiefs in order to provide a harmless framework in which he could justifiably tell stories about them without giving affront to the Church. Originally, according to Snorri, the Æsir had been nothing more than a tribe of warriors from *Ásaland* (Asia), where their chief city had been *Ásgarður*. Their neighbours there had been another tribe, called the Vanir, who pursued more peaceful occupations like farming and husbandry. In primeval times there had been a war between the Æsir and the Vanir; it had been a long and inconclusive struggle, which only ended when the gods made peace and exchanged hostages, and thus it was that a fertility god like Freyr came to join the warrior-gods like Óðinn and Thór in the pantheon of the Æsir in Ásgarður.

In this pantheon, the foremost of the gods were Óðinn, Thór and Freyr—but not as a trinity, and not necessarily in that order. In the literary sources, and especially in Snorri Sturluson's work, Óðinn is depicted as the paramount god, the All-Father, the god of war and poetic inspiration, the god of princes and poets. Thór was the god of thunder, the ruler of storms and tempests, the wielder of thunderbolts—a huge, red-haired, red-bearded man with blazing eyes and fiery eyebrows; he rode the heavens in a chariot drawn by two sacred goats, and at his passage thunder rumbled and crashed, the earth quaked, and lightning cracked. He was a boisterous, bluff fellow, gargantuan in appetite and not overburdened with intelligence. He was the cosmic police-man who guarded the world against the assaults of monsters and giants. Compared with Óðinn, the aristocratic god, Thór was the god of the ordinary people, the farmers, the peasants, the seamen, the settlers, the pioneers. Freyr, along with his twin sister Freyja, represented the more animal aspects of fertility and sexuality. His sacred animals were the boar and the stallion, and he was believed to control sunshine and the seasons and the natural increase of the earth. He was the symbol of the divine marriage between the sky and the earth that produces spring. Freyr and Freyja were the children of an ancient earth-god, Njörður, whose name is loosely related to the Germanic mother-earth goddess Nerthus.

By the time of the Settlement of Iceland, belief in the old gods seems to have become diluted. Men might still believe in the idea of a god, but the gods themselves were not considered all-powerful; rather, they were supra-mortals who were subject, like mankind itself, to the vagaries of inexorable, impersonal Fate. They were not so much to be worshipped as propitiated, as were the land-spirits of the country.

Although the brooding, baleful presence of Óðinn looms large in the mythological literature, there is hardly any evidence of Óðinn-worship in Iceland. This is hardly surprising. Óðinn was above all the patron god of Viking warlords and their court-poets; it was Óðinn who allotted victory in battle, and warriors who fell gloriously on the battlefield were dedicated to him. Icelandic society was never a military society, and therefore Óðinn had little relevance there.

The staple god of the Icelandic settlers was undoubtedly Thór, the patron god of farmers and fishermen. His name appears as an element in countless place-names and personal names. The First Settler himself, Ingólfur Arnarson, was clearly a Thór-worshipper, for his son was called Thorsteinn, his grandson Thorkell.

One of the major Icelandic sagas, *Eyrbyggja Saga* (*Saga of the Eyr-Dwellers*), offers a great deal of information about the worship of Thór in Iceland in early Settlement days, the kind of pagan beliefs and rituals that the pioneers were thought to have held dear when they first arrived. *Eyrbyggja Saga* is a sprawling, episodic chronicle about the peninsula of Snæfellsnes, on the west coast of Iceland, and the families who founded settlements there. It was written in the middle of the thirteenth century; the author was obviously a keen antiquarian, and has provided us with a wealth of information about the religious beliefs and folklore of the early Icelanders. But it has to be remembered that he was writing some three centuries after the events he described, and long after all pagan practices had been abandoned in Iceland.

Thórólfur Mostrarskeggi: the Patriarch of Eyrbyggja Saga
There was a powerful and wealthy chieftain called Hrólfur, who lived on the island of Mostur at the entrance to the Hardanger Fjord in south-western Norway. He was a big, formidable-looking man with a luxuriant beard that was said to have earned him the name of Mostrarskeggi (Mostur-beard). Hrólfur was the son of Örnólfur *fiskreki* (Rorqual), and was renowned for his fishing-luck. He was a close friend of Thór's, and was in charge of Thór's temple there on the island. So ardent was his worship of Thór that his name was changed from Hrólfur to Thórólfur.

In the year 884, ten years after Ingólfur Arnarson had set sail for Iceland, Thórólfur Mostrarskeggi fell foul of King Harald Fine-Hair of Norway and was outlawed. He held a great sacrifice to his friend and patron, Thór, and the oracle advised him to make for Iceland, for good reports of conditions there were now reaching Norway. So Thórólfur bought a large ocean-going ship and made it ready for the voyage, and sailed off with his family and all his household goods, as well as many of his friends who wanted to go with him. He dismantled the temple of Thór and loaded its timbers on board, and he also brought away some of the soil from under the pedestal of the effigy of Thór.

Reaching Iceland he rounded the headland of Reykjanes in the south-west; and when the wind dropped, he threw overboard the carved high-seat pillars with their effigy of Thór, just as Ingólfur Arnarson had done, and vowed that he would settle at whichever spot in Iceland Thór chose to send the pillars ashore. Sure enough, the pillars were observed to drift away from the ship at considerable speed round the promontory of Snæfellsnes. Then the wind sprang up again, and Thórólfur followed, and found himself in an enormously wide and deep bay with high mountains on either side, and so he named it Breiðafjörður (Broad Fjord). Eventually, after diligent searching, he found his high-seat pillars on the south

coast of Breiðafjörður lying on the shore of a little headland
that Thórólfur gratefully named Thórsnes; and there, after
staking out a large land-claim and hallowing it with fire, he
built a great manor farm and called it Hofstaðir—Temple
Stead.

There, too, according to *Eyrbyggja Saga*, he built a large
temple (*hof*), dedicated to his patron god Thór. Its description is marvellously detailed and circumstantial:

> He had a large temple erected there, with its entrance in
> one of the side-walls near the gable. Inside the door
> stood the high-seat pillars, with the so-called 'holy nails'
> (*reginnaglar*) fixed in them; and beyond them the whole
> interior was sanctuary. Farther in there was an area built
> much like the chancel (*sönghús*) in churches today, with
> a pedestal in the middle like an altar; on it lay a solid arm-
> ring weighing twenty ounces, on which all temple oaths
> were to be sworn. This ring was to be worn by the temple-
> priest (*hofgoði*) on his arm on all public occasions. There
> was a sacrificial bowl (*hlautbolli*) on the pedestal, too,
> with a sacrificial twig shaped like an aspergill, with which
> the blood (*hlaut*) of animals sacrificed to the gods was to
> be sprinkled. The effigies of the gods were arrayed in a
> circle right round the pedestal.

This vivid and meticulous description has given scholars a
great deal of trouble: the description is simply too good to be
true. Most scholars tend to believe that the pagan settlers of
Iceland never built special temples or cult-centres for worship; they prefer to think that local chieftains simply used
their own substantial homes as the venues for ceremonial
feasts and rituals.

At Thórólfur Mostrarskeggi's Hofstaðir today there is no
sign of any ancient structure that could be interpreted as a
temple. But there is another Hofstaðir in the north of Iceland,
at the side of the River Laxá near Mývatn, where a large
archaeological site was excavated in 1908. It was the remains
of a substantial long-house measuring more than forty metres
in length, built of stone and turf; at one end, an interior wall

divided off a much smaller chamber. The long-hall proper
(*skáli*) had a long-fire down the middle of the floor, with
raised platforms down the sides which could have seated
more than a hundred people.

There has been much argument about this structure. There
is no mention of a Hofstaðir near Mývatn in *Landnámabók* as
the home of an early settler; nor does it appear in any of the
sagas. But local tradition insisted that the site was called
Hofstaðir and had been associated with a pagan temple, and it
was this that inspired the 1908 excavation. No artefacts of
religious or ritual significance were found at the site; but the
archaeologists were in no doubt that they had found an
authentic temple site. This interpretation has been dismissed
as wishful thinking in some quarters; but many modern
scholars and historians are coming round again to the view
that it could well have been a temple, after all. There are no
fewer than forty-four historic sites in Iceland that have the
element *hof-* in their place-names; there are also four places
in *Landnámabók* named Hofstaðir—and of these, three
were specifically remembered as sites of temples or places of
worship.

Although paganism in Iceland was never as formally
institutionalized as Christianity was to become, there are
indications in the sources that there was a network of public
temples in pagan times, whose upkeep was the responsibility
of the local *goði*, or priest-chieftain; but whether these were
special buildings, or small shrines in the open air, is a moot
point. These temple-places were to be used for specific public
and judicial functions, according to a tantalizingly brief
passage in *Landnámabók* about the earliest pagan law-code
in Iceland:

> An arm-ring weighing not less than two ounces of silver
> must be kept on an altar in every public temple, and the
> *goði* is to wear this ring on his arm at all lawful assemblies
> he shall hold; it is his duty to redden it beforehand in the
> blood of the animal he has sacrificed there. Anyone who
> has business to transact there must swear an oath on this

ring and name two or more witnesses. 'I call to witness,' he should say, 'that I swear an oath on the sacred ring, a lawful oath: so help me Freyr and Njörður and the All-Powerful God . . .'

There can be little doubt that the 'All-Powerful God' (*hinn almáttki áss*) in this instance referred to Thór, the most widely venerated god in pagan Iceland.

Helgafell: the Holy Mountain

The focal point of *Eyrbyggja Saga*, both in terms of the topography and the narrative, is a handsome hill called Helgafell (Holy Fell). It is a flat-topped knob of dark grey columnar basalt, seventy-three metres high, south of the little seaport of Stykkishólmur. For Thórólfur Mostrarskeggi and his family and descendants, Helgafell was a place of special sanctity:

> Thórólfur held this mountain in such reverence that no one was allowed to look upon it unwashed, and no living creature, neither man nor beast, could be taken from it and killed. Thórólfur called this mountain Helgafell, and believed that he and all his kinsmen on the ness would enter into it when they died.

Thórólfur Mostrarskeggi died in the year 918, and his mortal remains were laid to rest in a barrow (*haugur*) on Thórsnes, whose name was now changed to Haugsnes. The prosperous patrimony he had built up at Hofstaðir was inherited by his young son, Thorsteinn *þorskabítr* (Cod-biter), who moved the family farm farther inland, to the foot of Helgafell. He had clearly inherited the family fishing-luck, as his nickname suggests, and his given name, Thorsteinn, indicates that he had been dedicated to the god Thór as a baby. But in the year 938, when he was still only twenty-five years old, Thorsteinn Cod-biter's fishing-luck ran out:

> That same autumn, Thorsteinn went out fishing round Höskuldsey. And one evening, as Thorsteinn's shepherd was tending sheep north of Helgafell, he saw the north

side of the mountain open up, and inside he could see great fires burning and hear the noise of feasting and clamour over the ale-horns. And as he strained his ears to make out what was being said, he heard Thorsteinn Cod-biter and his crew being welcomed, and Thorsteinn being ushered to the place of honour opposite his father.

That evening the shepherd told Thorsteinn's wife, Thóra, of the vision he had seen. She was deeply disturbed by it, and said it was a foreboding of serious tidings. In the morning some men brought news from Höskuldsey that Thorsteinn Cod-biter had been drowned on the fishing-trip. His death was considered a great loss.

And so Thorsteinn Cod-biter was gathered to his father and his forefathers in the sanctuary depths of Helgafell.

To this day, Helgafell has a special quality about it. On the grassy summit there are the remains of a small stone structure that some people think was once a chapel, and from there the view over the farthest reaches of Breiðafjörður and its innumerable islands is breath-taking. Tradition has it that those who make the short, steep climb up the hill without either talking or looking back will have three wishes granted, if they face towards the east, tell no one what the wishes were, and wish them from a good and true heart.

Snorri the Priest: the Sage of Helgafell

The most celebrated owner of the manor farm of Helgafell was Thorsteinn Cod-biter's grandson, Snorri the Priest (*goði*), the central character in *Eyrbyggja Saga*. In his long and eventful life (963–1031), Snorri the Priest played a prominent part in the early history of Iceland; he appears in several other Icelandic sagas, notably *Laxdæla Saga*, and although he was a pagan priest of Thór he had no hesitation in abandoning paganism when Christianity came to Iceland (see Ch 9). He built the first church at Helgafell immediately after the conversion of Iceland, and one of his many sons became a monk and joined a monastery in England.

Snorri the Priest was not a saga hero in the conventional

The hillocks of Vatnsdalshólar: they stand like giant mole-hills at the entrance to the valley in which Ingimundur the Old made his Settlement farm.

The bleak and forbidding mountains in the north of Iceland —
between Eyjafjörður and Skagafjörður. Settlers like Helgi the Lean
founded their farms in the valleys between the mountains.

sense of the term. He achieved power and standing in the community not through physical prowess and courage but through cunning and commonsense. The story of how he acquired Helgafell as a young man illustrates vividly the kind of man he was.

When Thorsteinn Cod-biter was drowned at sea and received into the company of his forefathers in Helgafell, he had left two young sons: Börkur the Stout, and Thorgrímur, who was dedicated to the god Thór at birth and nominated as the next *goði* of Helgafell. He was only a baby when his father died, but as soon as he reached legal age (probably twelve in those days) he assumed the office of temple-priest and became known as Thorgrímur *goði*.

The fate of Thorgrímur *goði* is starkly told in one of the most profound and complex of the Icelandic sagas—*Gísla Saga*, the saga of Gísli the Outlaw, a tragic and moving story of family feuding that has now been turned into a sombre feature film by the young Icelandic film-maker Ágúst Guðmundsson (*Útlaginn—The Outlaw*). Thorgrímur *goði* married the sister of the eponymous hero of the saga, Gísli Súrsson of Sæból in Dýrafjörður, in the Westfjords. His bride's name was Thórdís; her dowry was the farmstead of Sæból, and Thorgrímur *goði* moved in to live there, leaving his brother Börkur the Stout to run Helgafell. Gísli obligingly moved out of Sæból and built a new homestead nearby.

At first, all went well. Gísli and Thorgrímur liked and respected one another, and the family's standing in the community was greatly enhanced by the arrival of the wealthy and well-connected *goði* from Helgafell. But Gísli had another close friend, his brother-in-law Vésteinn; and gradually the family friendships became soured by jealousy. The upshot was that Thorgrímur *goði*, to uphold what he perceived to be his family honour, secretly murdered Vésteinn in his bed one night. He never acknowledged the killing; but Gísli suspected Thorgrímur of the crime, and to avenge Vésteinn he committed murder himself—killing Thorgrímur in his bed at night, also without acknowledging the deed. There was now unbearable tension between the two neighbouring households. No one knew for certain who the murderer had been, but the prime suspect was obviously Gísli.

Gísli's sister, Thórdís—Thorgrímur's widow—was pregnant at the time of her husband's death. A few days later she gave birth to a son, who was given the same name as his dead father (as was the custom in those days) and called Thorgrímur. The baby was sent away for fosterage, but he proved such a difficult child that his name was changed to Snorri, which means 'the turbulent one'. And that was how Snorri the Priest earned the name by which he would become famous in *Eyrbyggja Saga*.

Meanwhile, at Sæból, an uneasy truce prevailed between the two family households. Then one day Gísli let slip a remark about Thorgrímur's death which his sister overheard and interpreted as an admission of guilt. She was now caught in a classic tragic dilemma: should she seek vengeance for her murdered husband, at the expense of her own brother's life? For Thórdís, the imperative of revenge overrode everything else. She married Thorgrímur's brother, Börkur the Stout of Helgafell, and laid upon him the duty of vengeance. Börkur had Gísli declared an outlaw at the local *Thing*, and descended on his house with a force of forty men to kill him; but Gísli gave them the slip and took to the hills.

Having failed to catch Gísli and put him to death, as he was entitled to do by law, Börkur the Stout went back to Helgafell with Thórdís, and hired a cousin of his as a bounty-hunter to track Gísli down. It was to take him fifteen years, the long, bitter years of Gísli's outlawry as described in *Gísla Saga*.

Throughout those years, young Snorri was growing up in his foster-home. He felt an overwhelming resentment against Börkur the Stout, his uncle and now stepfather; for Börkur had taken over Helgafell and its chieftaincy, which Snorri considered his own natural patrimony from his murdered father, and Snorri was determined to get his hands on it by hook or by crook. To that end he went to Norway at the age of fourteen to seek his fortune, and came back a year later with a carefully-hoarded nest-egg of 120 ounces of silver. But he told no one of its existence. On his return he went to Helgafell to visit his mother; and now the long shadow of the tragedy of *Gísla Saga* fell upon Helgafell, too.

One evening that autumn the bounty-hunter whom Börkur the Stout had hired to track down Gísli came marching into the house at Helgafell with a band of twelve men, fully armed. He announced that he had at long last managed to corner the outlaw and bring him to his death, fifteen years after the murder of Thorgrímur *goði*. Börkur was overjoyed at the news, and told Thórdís and Snorri to give a hearty welcome to the man who had wiped clean an ugly stain on the family honour. But human nature is strange; although Thórdís had originally incited Börkur to the vengeance, and perhaps only married him in order to achieve it, now that the deed was done and her brother Gísli had been killed she could not bear it. She was trapped in the profoundly irreconcilable motives and emotions of family feud. As she was serving food to the bounty-hunter, the man who had killed her brother to avenge her husband, she dropped a spoon on the floor; and as she stooped to pick it up, she seized the man's sword and lunged at him with it under the table. The pommel caught on the edge of the table, checking the blow, but she inflicted a nasty wound on the man's thigh, none the less. Börkur leapt to his feet in a rage and struck Thórdís with his fist, but Snorri hurled himself at Börkur and shielded his mother from further punishment.

The following spring, at the local Thing, Snorri formally demanded from his stepfather Börkur his inheritance—a half-share of the estate of Helgafell. Börkur had no wish to enter into partnership with his nephew, so he proposed to pay Snorri in cash for his share of the estate. And now Snorri displayed the foresight and craftiness that would characterize all his later dealings:

'I think the fairest thing', said Snorri, 'would be for you to set whatever price on the estate you think fit, and then I will decide which one of us buys the other out.'

Börkur thought this over, and came to the conclusion

that Snorri could not possibly have enough money to pay up on the spot. So he valued a half-share in the estate at sixty ounces of silver ... and he stipulated that the money should be paid out there and then, cash on the nail, without loans from anyone else. 'It is up to you, now, Snorri', he said. 'Make up your mind.'

'It is quite obvious, kinsman,' said Snorri, 'that you must think me very short of money, since you set such a low price on Helgafell. But my choice is to buy my father's estate at the price you have set; so give me your hand on the bargain, and make over the land.'

'That I will not do,' said Börkur, 'until every penny is paid.'

With a flourish, Snorri produced his secret purse of silver and counted out the sixty ounces, and bought Börkur out. His mother, Thórdís, rubbed salt into her husband's discomfiture by declaring herself divorced from him because of the blow he had dealt her the previous autumn. So Börkur was forced to leave home, worsted by his young and scheming nephew, and Snorri acquired Helgafell and the chieftaincy that went with it. The year was 979, and Snorri was only sixteen years old. Such was the mark he would make as a chieftain that he became famous in the Iceland Saga simply as Snorri *goði*— Snorri the Priest:

> Snorri was a man of medium height, and rather slightly built; he was a handsome man with regular features, a fair complexion and blond hair, and a reddish beard. He was even-tempered for the most part, and it was hard to tell whether he was pleased or not. He was a shrewd man, and far-sighted, and never forgot a grudge. To his friends he always gave good advice, but to his enemies his counsels brought no comfort.
>
> He was now in charge of the temple, and was therefore called Snorri *goði*. He became a great chieftain, and many greatly envied him his power, for there were those who thought themselves in no way inferior to him in

birth, and much superior to him in support and proven
mettle in a fight.

The Berserks' Lava

One of those who resented the growing power of the young
goði of Helgafell was a big, formidable man called Styrr,
known as Víga-Styrr (Killer-Styrr). He was a tall, powerful
man with ginger hair and a large bony face with a prominent
nose—the very image of a tough Viking warrior. He was
Snorri's main rival for supremacy in the district.

Víga-Styrr lived a few kilometres to the west of Helgafell,
at a farm called Hraun (Lava) on the edge of a large tract of
rough and impassable lava. His brother, Vermundur the
Slender, lived at the other side of the lava-field, at the farm of
Bjarnarhöfn (Björn's Haven). This lava-field is comparatively young, only about 3,000 years old; it consists of
basalt scoria-lava—*apalhraun*, or a-a lava to give it its technical name. It looks like a congealed sea of angry, tossing
waves, shrouded in grey and yellow moss. A thousand years
ago, no one could cross it on foot, and when Víga-Styrr and
Vermundur wanted to visit one another's houses, they had to
make a long detour right round the edge of the lava-field.

One summer, Vermundur the Slender went to Norway on a
trading trip. While he was there, he was given an unusual
gift—a pair of berserks. They were huge, powerful men,
brothers, and had originally come from Sweden:

> They were berserks, and once they had worked them-
> selves up, they were completely beside themselves and
> went about like mad dogs, fearing neither fire nor
> weapons. For most of the time they were quite easy to get
> on with, as long as they were left in peace; but if anyone
> gave them the slightest offence, they became extremely
> violent . . . They were fine men to have as allies, so long
> as their tempers remained under control.

Such were the two men whom Vermundur the Slender was
now given, to be his personal servants. Berserks were much

prized in Viking times for their ability to run amok in battle, when they seemed to be impervious to injury or pain; they would howl savagely and bite their shields, and in their frenzy (whether drugged or self-induced) they had the strength of ten men. The Old Icelandic word *berserkr* apparently means 'bear-shirted' (not 'bare-shirted', as is sometimes suggested), which has given rise to the idea that they actually wore bear-pelts in battle; but it may just have been a metaphor for bear-like strength. They were formidable thugs to have at your beck and call, and made admirable shock troops, but they could prove difficult to control.

Vermundur the Slender, in fact, found them distinctly alarming, and passed them over to his brother, Víga-Styrr, who seemed to have the right kind of toughness and tempera-ment to handle them.

All went well for a time at Hraun. The two berserks worked hard, and gave no trouble, until one of them, Halli by name, took a fancy to Styrr's handsome and imperious daughter, Ásdís, and demanded her hand in marriage—with menaces. Faced with this threat, Víga-Styrr swallowed his pride and went to consult his enemy and rival, Snorri *goði* of Helgafell. Snorri was only twenty years old at the time, but had already gained a reputation for wiliness and guile. Snorri was not slow to see an opportunity for personal advantage, and welcomed Víga-Styrr's overtures of friendship. He took Víga-Styrr to the top of Helgafell, 'for plans made there have seldom failed'. They sat there talking until evening, 'but no one knew what they talked about'.

As a result of their conversation, Víga-Styrr went back to his home at Hraun and offered the berserk a bargain: since Halli had no money to his name, he would have to earn the marriage by performing some great feat like the heroes of old, in lieu of a dowry. And the task that Víga-Styrr set Halli and his brother, Leiknir, was to make a road through the lava-field from Bjarnarhöfn to Hraun.

The berserks set to work with furious energy. Meanwhile, Víga-Styrr was just as busy, digging a huge hole in the ground at his farm to make a sunken sauna-bath. There was a skylight right above the oven so that water could be poured in from the outside, while the only entrance was through a trap-door.

On the last day of their labours, the young lady, Ásdís, paraded herself past them, wearing her finest clothes but pretending not to notice them. This spurred them on to even greater efforts. When they went home that night, with the task completed, they were completely worn out ('this is what happens to those who go berserk—once the rage leaves them, they seem to lose all their strength'). Víga-Styrr thanked them for their efforts and invited them to use the bath-house and then have a rest. Once the berserks were inside the bath-house, Víga-Styrr closed it and heaped a pile of rocks on the trap-door; and in front of it he spread a raw, wet ox-hide. Then he poured water through the skylight on to the oven below, and this made the bath-house so scaldingly hot that the berserks could not stand the heat and tried to force their way out through the trap-door. Halli managed to smash through and scramble outside, but he slipped on the ox-hide and Víga-Styrr dealt him a death-blow as he lay sprawled; and when Leiknir tried to get up through the trap-door, Víga-Styrr thrust a spear through him, and he fell back dead into the bath-house.

Víga-Styrr now had the bodies laid out for burial and took them over to the lava-field: 'There they were buried in a hollow so deep that nothing can be seen from it except the sky above; it is close to the pathway.'

As soon as Snorri the Priest heard the news of the berserks' deaths he went over to Hraun from Helgafell to collect his reward. He and Víga-Styrr spent the whole day talking together, and the outcome was that Víga-Styrr betrothed his daughter Ásdís to Snorri!

> Everyone agreed that both men had gained through this alliance. Snorri was the shrewder of the two, and a better counsellor, while Víga-Styrr was more of a man of action; and neither was short of kinsmen and supporters in the district.

From that day onwards, the lava-field has been known as

Berserkjahraun—the Berserks' Lava; and the Berserks' Road through it is still there, a clearly-marked pathway that must have cost immense labour to make, traversing the lava from Hraun to Bjarnarhöfn. In the heart of the lava-field, just beside the path, there is a large, deep hollow, a sunken amphitheatre, from which nothing can be seen except the sky above. This hollow contains a substantial stone cairn. It was excavated late last century, and was found to contain the bones of two men; they had not been particularly tall, apparently, but were said to have been exceptionally powerfully built.

CHAPTER 6

Priests of Freyr

Hrafnkell elskaði eigi annat goð meir en Frey, ok honum gaf hann alla ina beztu gripi sína hálfa við sik.

Hrafnkell loved Freyr above all other gods, and gave him a half-share in all his best treasures.

(*Hrafnkels Saga*)

Next to Thór, the sky-god, the second most widely venerated deity in pagan Iceland was the fertility god, Freyr; but the worship of Freyr was much more limited than that of Thór, and confined to particular families and places, especially in the east and south-east of Iceland.

A handful of men are specifically associated with Freyr-worship in the sources. One of the leading chieftains in the south-east of the country was known as Thórður Freysgoði (Freyr's Priest), and his descendants were known as the Freysgyðlingar, the 'priestlings of Freyr'. Thórður's sister was known as Thuríður *hofgyðja* (Temple-Priestess); and their home was near a headland called Freysnes. This bare reference in *Landnámabók* is all that is known about this family, and we are told nothing further about the nature of their religious functions; but there are one or two other references to 'temple-priestesses' in the sources, and it is assumed that they were engaged in cultic Freyr-worship because of the associations with Freyja, Freyr's twin sister and the goddess of sexual fertility.

Another man who is given the title of Freysgoði, surprisingly enough, is Thorgrímur *goði* of Helgafell, the father of Snorri the Priest (see Ch 5)—surprisingly, because in *Eyrbyggja Saga* it is made clear that Thorgrímur was dedicated at birth to the priesthood of Thór. However, in *Gísla Saga*, he is referred to as Freysgoði, and we are told a little about his relationship with his god. It was Thorgrímur's custom to hold a festival at the 'Winter Nights' early in October, at which he would welcome the coming of winter and offer sacrifice to Freyr. And Freyr duly repaid these devotions; for when Thorgrímur was buried in a barrow after his murder by Gísli, snow never lay on his cairn, and grass sprouted on the mound even in mid-winter: 'People believed that he must have been so beloved of Freyr for his sacrifices that the god would not allow frost to come between them.'

Víga-Glúms Saga: Freyr v. Óðinn

One Icelandic saga, from Eyjafjörður in the north of Iceland, seems to reflect a deep-rooted conflict between the worship of Óðinn and of Freyr. It is *Víga-Glúms Saga*, written around 1230, which tells the life-story of the hero Víga-Glúmur (Killer-Glúmur) from beginning to end, from truculent youth to blind and helpless old age: a full-scale biography, rather than a family chronicle like so many of the other Icelandic sagas.

Víga-Glúmur was born to high estate on the manor farm of Thverá that stands in the valley leading down to the head of Eyjafjörður (later, in 1155, it became the site of a Benedictine monastery and was renamed Munka-Thverá). He was born around the year 928. On his father's side, his great-grandfather was one of the most prominent of the early settlers of Iceland, Helgi the Lean (see Ch 4), who had laid claim to the whole of Eyjafjörður and made his home at Kristnes. On his mother's side, Glúmur's grandfather was a notable Norwegian Viking from the district of Voss, in south-western Norway, called Vigfúss.

As a young man, Víga-Glúmur was indolent and recalcitrant, reluctant to take on any farm work and a sore disappointment to his widowed mother. He was a tall, gangling youth, taciturn and reserved, and people thought him dull-witted. He did nothing to protect his mother when she became the target of ambitious in-laws who wanted the estate of Thverá for themselves and managed to edge mother and son out of their inheritance into a tumbledown farm nearby.

Glúmur's family on his father's side was particularly devoted to the god Freyr. His grandfather, the son of Helgi the Lean, had built a temple dedicated to Freyr across the river from his homestead at Thverá, and had the title of *goði*; and nearby there was a cornfield dedicated to Freyr that was called *Vitazgjafi*—'Certain Harvest'—because it was always fertile and never failed to produce a good crop. On his mother's side, however, his blood was pure Viking—and the chief Viking god was Óðinn, not Freyr or Thór.

When Glúmur was fifteen years old he went abroad to visit his grandfather in Norway, the old Viking Vigfúss of Voss. At first people laughed at him and his ungainliness; but he soon proved himself to be a chip off the old Viking block by felling an obstreperous berserk who had been terrorizing the neighbourhood. Vigfúss was delighted with his grandson's prowess; and when Glúmur returned to Iceland, he gave him three special family heirlooms that would bring him luck—a hooded cloak of dark-blue fur, a sword, and a gold-inlaid spear; and he told Glúmur that as long as he kept them in his possession, he would maintain the supremacy of his family position. The gift of these talismanic possessions points to the worship of Óðinn, for the spear was Óðinn's favourite weapon and the cloak his favourite garb. Furthermore, when old Vigfúss died, his guardian spirit (*hamingja*), visualized in a dream as a woman of gigantic stature, came to Iceland and made Glúmur her special ward. The implication in the saga is quite clear—that Víga-Glúmur was 'converted' to Óðinn-worship, the religion of his Viking forebears. Certainly, from then on his behaviour was that of a typical Viking warrior, ruthless, unscrupulous, guileful and uncompromising.

Back in Iceland, Glúmur's actions soon brought him into direct conflict with the god Freyr. The cause of the conflict was the cornfield, Vitazgjafi. It had been appropriated by the family in-laws, Thorkell the Tall and his son Sigmundur. Glúmur was no longer content to let them ride roughshod over his rights. One morning he put on the dark-blue cloak, and took down the gold-inlaid spear, and slew Sigmundur in the sacred cornfield—a desecration that was bound to anger the god. He followed up this manslaughter by driving Thorkell the Tall from Thverá and installing himself and his mother there instead. But before Thorkell left Thverá, he went to the sanctuary of Freyr, leading with him an old ox, and spoke as follows:

> 'Freyr,' he said, 'you have long been my trusted patron, and have received many gifts from me and rewarded them well. Now I give you this ox, in order that Glúmur may one day be forced to leave Thverá no less unwillingly than I go now. Let me now see some sign whether you accept my gift or not.'
>
> At that the ox shuddered and gave a bellow, and fell down dead; and Thorkell took it to mean that all was well, and felt easier in his heart now that he thought the sacrifice had been accepted.

But there was nothing that Freyr could do about Glúmur while he kept the symbols of Óðinn, the cloak and the spear, in his possession, and while he was under the protection of his family guardian spirit. For forty years, Víga-Glúmur lorded it over the district, subduing his enemies by force or guile. He compounded his sacrilege against Freyr by concealing his outlawed son, Vigfúss, within the precincts of the temple, thus violating its sanctuary. But still Freyr was powerless against him.

Eventually, however, Víga-Glúmur's own cleverness got the better of him. After a pitched battle against a confederacy of enemies, Glúmur tried to frustrate the consequent lawsuits for manslaughter by laying the blame for one of the killings on a minor who had been present at the battle. Everyone knew that this was just a legal manoeuvre to confuse the issue, for it was Glúmur himself who had struck the fatal blow. To settle the case, Glúmur was challenged to swear an oath in the temple of Freyr, denying responsibility for the killing. Glúmur accepted the challenge: before the altar of Freyr he placed on his arm the sacred ring, reddened with the blood of sacrifice, and swore his oath:

'I swear the temple oath by the ring, and I declare to the god, that I was not there, and I killed not there, and I reddened not spear-point nor sword-edge when the man was slain. Consider now my oath, all you wise men who are present.'

On the face of it, it was a straight denial; but buried in the Icelandic syntax was an archaic double negative that vitiated the oath by making it ambiguous. In defiance of destiny, Glúmur gave away his cloak and spear to the supporters who had stood by him on the battlefield; and now at last he was no longer impervious to the wrath of Freyr.

The double-edged oath that Glúmur had sworn was soon exposed, and Glúmur was now liable to be sentenced to outlawry for the manslaughter. Before Glúmur left for the court hearing, he had a strange dream:

He dreamed that people had come to Thverá to meet the god Freyr; they were crowded on the gravel banks by the river, where the god was sitting on a throne. He dreamed that he asked who the people were, and they replied, 'These are your departed kinsmen, and we are praying to Freyr that you will not be driven from the Thverá lands. But it is of no avail: Freyr answers shortly and angrily, and recalls the gift of an ox that Thorkell the Tall made to him.'

As the dream foretold, Glúmur's luck had run out. At the court hearing he managed to avoid a sentence of outlawry, but he forfeited the estates of Thverá and was banished from the district.

Víga-Glúmur left the district in disgrace, but with his head held high. He lived for another twenty years, growing blind in his old age. But the Viking spirit never died in him: even in his blindness, he planned to accost his enemies with a short sword concealed under his clothes, hoping to kill one or two of them, but nothing came of the plan.

That was the end of Víga-Glúmur's dealings with the men of Eyjafjörður. When Christianity came to Iceland, Glúmur had himself baptized, and lived for another three years after that. He was confirmed during his last illness, in 1003, and died in his white baptismal robe:

> It is said that Glúmur was for twenty years the greatest chieftain in Eyjafjörður, and that for another twenty years no one was more than his equal. It is also said that he was the doughtiest fighter in the land. And that is the end of the Saga of Glúmur.

Hrafnkels Saga: the Priest of Freyr

One of the most highly regarded of all the classical Icelandic sagas is *Hrafnkels Saga*, the Saga of Hrafnkell Freysgoði. It is nothing short of a masterpiece, a brilliantly wrought short novel that has been published and translated and written about more than any other saga. It was written around 1300, at the very end of the golden age of saga-writing.

It tells the story of a proud and domineering chieftain, Hrafnkell Hallfreðarson, the Priest of Freyr, who lived at the manor farm of Aðalból in Hrafnkelsdalur, in the east of Iceland, in the tenth century:

> He was an overbearing man, despite his many good qualities, and he forced everyone in the district to submit to his authority. He was kind and considerate to his own men, but harsh and ruthless towards his enemies, and to them he showed no justice. Hrafnkell fought many duels, but refused to pay compensation for any of the men he killed, and no one got any redress for whatever wrongs he committed.

He built a large temple at Aðalból and held great sacrifices to the gods. He loved Freyr above all other gods, and gave him a half-share in all his best treasures:

> Hrafnkell had one treasured possession which he held more dear than anything else he owned. It was a pale-

dun stallion, with a black mane and a black stripe down the back. He called the horse Freyfaxi (Freyr's Mane), and gave his patron Freyr a half-share in it. Hrafnkell loved this horse so fiercely that he swore a solemn oath that he would kill anyone who rode the stallion without his permission.

Hrafnkell's arrogant devotion to the god led inexorably to tragedy. One spring he took on as his shepherd a young man from a poor but honest family in the district, Einar Thorbjörnsson. He warned him specifically against riding Freyfaxi, on pain of death, and Einar agreed to this condition without demur, especially since there were plenty of other horses that he could use. But one day, thirty of Hrafnkell's sheep went missing. Einar scoured all the pastures without success, and after a week he decided he would have to ride up into the high moorlands to search for them. For some reason, all the mares in Freyfaxi's herd shied away from him, although normally they were quiet and docile. Only Freyfaxi stood his ground, as if offering himself to be ridden. With time pressing on, Einar decided to take a chance and ride the stallion, thinking that Hrafnkell would never find out.

Einar rode the horse hard all day. Eventually he found the missing sheep, lurking in a ravine which he had already searched first thing that morning. By now Freyfaxi was exhausted and covered with mud and sweat. No sooner had Einar dismounted than the horse bolted down the valley, all the way down to Aðalból, where Hrafnkell heard him neighing loudly at the door:

> Hrafnkell went outside, and when he saw Freyfaxi he said to him, 'It grieves me to see how you have been treated, my fosterling. You had your wits about you when you came to me, and this shall be avenged. Go back to your herd.'
> The stallion left immediately and went up the valley to his mares.

Hrafnkell slept soundly that night. Next morning he put on

blue clothing (the colour conventionally associated in the
sagas with deliberate missions to kill) and rode up the valley
to the summer shieling where Einar was tending the sheep.
Hrafnkell accused him of riding Freyfaxi, and Einar admitted
it. Without any hesitation, Hrafnkell dismounted and buried
his axe in Einar's defenceless skull.

Hrafnkell clearly regretted what he had felt bound by his
oath to do. He had never offered redress for any of his
killings, but when Einar's father, Thorbjörn, came seeking
compensation for his son's death, Hrafnkell offered generous
terms designed to raise the family out of their poverty:

> 'I shall supply your household with plenty of milk in the
> summer and meat in the autumn, and I shall keep on
> doing this every year for as long as you choose to live on
> your farm. I shall also provide for your sons and
> daughters, to give them a good start in life. From now on
> you need only tell me if there is anything in my posses-
> sion which you want, and you shall have it and never
> have to do without. You can keep on farming for as long
> as you like, and move over here and stay with me when
> you tire of it, and I shall look after you for the rest of your
> life.'

Under the circumstances, it was a remarkably good offer.
But in his pride and grief, Thorbjörn refused it: he wanted to
take the issue to court, where his dead son would be treated as
Hrafnkell's equal and atoned for accordingly, through
arbitration. It was a rash course, for the outcome of lawsuits
was often decided not by natural justice but by the relative
power and skill of the litigants. Hrafnkell's own pride was
affronted by the refusal of his terms, and he determined to
fight the court-case with all the strength and authority at his
command.

Thorbjörn appealed for help to his nephew, Sámur, a vain
and showy man who fancied himself as a lawyer. He was
taken aback at the suggestion that he should take on the
mighty Hrafnkell, but in the end, with great reluctance, he
agreed.

As Sámur had feared, the court proceedings went extremely badly. At the Althing next summer, when the case was being heard, Sámur and Thorbjörn tried unsuccessfully to solicit the aid of powerful chieftains, but no one was prepared to pick a quarrel with Hrafnkell. But suddenly, like some *deus ex machina*, two brothers from the Westfjords arrived who quixotically agreed to take on the case. With the help of their own supporters from the west, they managed to bar Hrafnkell's access to the court by sheer weight of numbers, and Hrafnkell was sentenced to full outlawry *in absentia*.

Winning a lawsuit in Iceland in those days was one thing; getting justice was another. There was no executive or police force to carry out the decisions of the court—that was up to the successful litigant. Hrafnkell rode home to Aðalból angry at the outcome of the case, but determined to ignore it; he did not believe that Sámur had the strength or the nerve to try to press the matter to its conclusion. Indeed, Sámur had no intention of doing such a thing. He was quite happy to have won a moral victory at least. But the brothers from the Westfjords warned him that Hrafnkell himself would take vengeance for his humiliation unless Sámur acted first, and insisted on helping him to see it through to the bitter end: Sámur would have to hold a court of confiscation at Hrafnkell's home and then expel him, or kill him, as it was now his right and duty to do.

At dawn one morning they fell upon Aðalból, catching Hrafnkell unawares. They seized Hrafnkell and all the able-bodied men in the household and bound them, and dragged them outside. Hrafnkell asked them to spare the lives of his men, but refused to beg for his own life; he only asked that he should be spared the humiliation of torture. But now, with Hrafnkell at his mercy, Sámur showed that he lacked the ultimate resolution and ruthlessness to be a chieftain himself: he could not bring himself to kill Hrafnkell, but instead he tortured him. He strung Hrafnkell and all his men up by a rope through their Achilles tendons, maiming them for life; then he drove Hrafnkell out of the district, and stripped him of his estates and authority as a *goði*. Sámur moved into Aðalból in Hrafnkell's place, and the temple of Freyr was desecrated and burnt to the ground. The stallion Freyfaxi, the cause of all the trouble, was then fetched. They led the beast to a cliff and pulled a bag over his head, then weighted him with boulders and pushed him over the cliff into a deep pool below: 'The cliff has been known as Freyfaxahamarr ever since.'

Meanwhile, Hrafnkell had moved farther east and bought himself a tumbledown farmstead. He renamed it Hrafnkels-staðir, and set to work trying to build it up. When he heard what had happened to Freyr's temple, and the stallion Frey-faxi, he said, 'I think it vain to believe in the gods.' He declared that he would worship them no longer, and kept his vow, and never offered sacrifice again.

By dint of hard work, Hrafnkell soon became rich and powerful again, and achieved such standing in his new community that 'everyone would stand or sit at his bidding'. His new chieftaincy was even more extensive than his old one had been:

> Hrafnkell was a changed man now, and much better liked than he used to be. He could still be as helpful and generous as before, but he had become gentler and quieter in every way.
>
> Sámur and Hrafnkell often met at assemblies, but they never spoke about their dealings. Sámur enjoyed his high position for six years. He was well liked by his supporters, for he did not forget the advice that the brothers had given him, and was quiet and gentle and ready to solve everyone's problems.

But the iron was still in Hrafnkell's soul. He was only biding his time before striking back at Sámur. Sámur had a brother called Eyvindur, a fine upstanding young man who was a successful trader, spending much of his time abroad. One summer, Eyvindur returned home with his ship. His journey from the coast to visit his brother at Aðalból took him past Hrafnkell's house in Fljótsdalur. As he rode by with five companions, he was spotted by an old washerwoman, who went rushing back to the house to tell Hrafnkell—and remind him in no uncertain terms of the old Viking duty of revenge:

'The old saying is true enough, that the older a man is, the feebler he is. The honour a man achieves early in life is worthless if he has to give it all up in disgrace, and hasn't the courage to fight for his rights ever again. It's a strange thing to happen to those who were once thought brave . . . Eyvindur Bjarnason was just crossing the river at Skálaford carrying a bright shield that shone in the sun. He would be a worthy target for revenge, an outstanding man like him.'

Hrafnkell needed no further incitement. Grimly, he put on his blue clothes again and gathered a group of eighteen able-bodied men, and together they set off in pursuit. Eyvindur knew himself to be innocent of any crime, and refused to run when he saw the pursuers on his trail. Hrafnkell and his men closed in, and without a word fell upon them, killing them all. That same night, before Sámur had had time to gather his supporters, he descended upon Aðalból and drove Sámur and his family off his former estates. There was no question of compensation this time for Hrafnkell's killing of an innocent man. Hrafnkell moved back into Aðalból and resumed his former chieftaincy and spent his remaining years in prosperity and peace. 'And so ends the Saga of Hrafnkell.'

CHAPTER 7

Thingvellir: Birth of a Nation

Með lögum skal land várt byggja, en með ólögum eyða.

With laws shall our land be built up, but with lawlessness laid waste.

(*Njáls Saga*)

Much the most important historic site in the whole of Iceland is Thingvellir: 'Parliament Plains'. It is the cradle of Iceland's history, the centre of stillness in the land. Today it is a national park, blessedly empty of man-made monuments; Thingvellir is a monument in itself, Iceland's Westminster and Runnymede combined, a place of private pilgrimage where people can imagine for themselves what it was like there in the days when the Althing was established and the nation was born.

It was there, on a day in late June around the year 930, that the people of the newly settled country came together for the first time to found a state. And what a birthplace they had chosen! Thingvellir is a huge natural arena, formed when the land rifted and lurched in convulsive geological subsidence thousands of years ago, leaving a great depression forty kilometres long and ten kilometres broad, bounded on both sides by cliffs of riven lava. The whole plain is seamed with cracks and crevices, all lying in the same direction from south-east to north-west; for Thingvellir lies athwart the Mid-Atlantic Ridge, where the Afro-European and North American tectonic plates are drifting apart (see Ch 1) at an average rate of about eight millimetres a year. Every now and again the earth splits and sinks again—the last time was during an earthquake in 1789, when the floor of Thingvellir subsided by about a metre. At each side of the great depression there is a major crevice—Hrafnagjá (Ravens Chasm) at the east side, and at the west side the much more prodigious Almannagjá (Everyman Chasm), where the cliff was split apart into a wide, plunging gorge.

The natural entrance to Thingvellir dips down through Almannagjá. At the top of the cliff, on a plateau of layered grey basalt lava, a panoramic view-dial identifies the ring of handsome mountains that circle that horizon: the low, classic shield-volcano of Skjaldbreiður (Broad-Shield) to the north, from which the lavas of Thingvellir flowed; the basalt peaks of Botnssúlur to the north-west and the table-mountain of Hrafnabjörg to the north-east; away in the distance, to the south-east, the shapely promontory of Ingólfsfjall, where the First Settler tarried on his way to Reykjavík; to the south the slopes of Hengill, wreathed in great plumes of geothermal steam. In the foreground to the north stands the bulk of Ármannsfell, which folklore insists is the home of a friendly neighbourhood giant, Ármann Dalmansson, the guardian spirit of the place. To the south, almost at the foot of the lava cliff, the arena dips into the expansive waters of the largest freshwater lake in Iceland, Thingvallavatn. A busy little river, the Öxará (Axe River), so named by the settler Ketil-björn the Old (see Ch 3), cascades over the western escarpment to the floor of the ravine and meanders towards the lake, enriching the grassy plain of the Althing area.

It is a spectacular site, and has a magical, almost mystical, effect on everyone who goes there; and it was a spectacular enterprise that the early Icelanders were embarking upon. After sixty years of pioneering settlement, the Icelanders were meeting to create a state the like of which had not been seen before in Europe—a republic: an oligarchic commonwealth, almost a democracy; a state without a king at a time in history when the idea of kingship, of royal authority, was becoming politically paramount.

In any frontier society, such as Iceland was at the time, the problem of law and order inevitably looms large. Within their own kinship groups the local chieftains, the *goðar*, had always exercised the authority of their position and administered

rough and ready justice amongst the men in their con-
stituencies. But what about disputes that spilled across these
boundaries? Obviously some sort of district assembly where a
group of local chieftains agreed to share authority was needed
to adjudicate killings and quarrels between men of different
local areas, to ward off potential blood-feuds by arbitration
and the award of proper money compensation to aggrieved
families, to settle brawls over shared fishing-rights, or dis-
puted driftwood, or stranded whales, or runaway slaves, or
straying sheep, or stolen horses.

According to *Íslendingabók*, the first such local assembly,
or district Thing (*þing*), was founded soon after the year 900
at Kjalarnes, north across the bay from Reykjavík, at the
instigation of the First Settler's son, Thorsteinn Ingólfsson,
and other chieftains in the area of Ingólfur's huge land-take.
Landnámabók adds that two of the leading chieftains
involved in this enterprise were Helgi *bjólan* and Örlygur of
Esjuberg, the main Christian settlers on Kjalarnes (see Ch 4).
We cannot be sure now where this first local Thing was held—
there are no indications on the promontory of Kjalarnes
itself, round the foot of Mount Esja; but further south, on the
outskirts of Reykjavík itself, a possible site is at present being
archaeologically investigated. It is called Thingsnes, a spit of
land running into the lake of Elliðavatn, from which the
Elliðaár rivers run down to the sea. The excavation has
revealed traces of a substantial man-made enclosure and
other very old structures, which may date back to the year
900.

Eyrbyggja Saga, that mine of antiquarian information (see
Ch 5), says that the first settler at Helgafell, Thórólfur
Mostrarskeggi, also founded a district assembly on Thórsnes,
the spit of land on which his high-seat pillars had been washed
ashore:

> Thórólfur used to hold all his courts on the point of the
> headland where Thór had come ashore, and that is where
> he established a district Thing. This place was so holy
> that he would not let anyone desecrate it, either with

bloodshed or with excrement; and for privy purposes they used a special rock in the sea which they called Dritsker (Dirt Skerry).

A few years later a brawl broke out there and blood was spilt, so the site was moved further inland, closer to Helgafell itself, to a place also called 'Thingvellir'. According to *Eyrbyggja Saga*, the site was still clearly visible in the thirteenth century:

> The circle where the court used to sentence people to be sacrificed can still be seen; inside the circle stands the Stone of Thór, on which the men chosen for sacrifice were broken, and the colour of blood can still be seen on the stone.
> Although this assembly place was held to be very sacred indeed, men were not forbidden to ease themselves there.

To this day, a large number of grass-grown humps are visible in the area, suggesting that there were once structures there to accommodate a large number of people. There is also a marshy expanse on which there stands a large and irregularly-shaped block of blue basaltic stone, with encrustations of red scoria that suggest the colour of blood. Like so much of the material in *Eyrbyggja Saga* purporting to describe pagan times and customs, this reference sounds particularly dubious; there is no direct evidence that human sacrifice was ever practised in Iceland.

Be that as it may, as the country became more populated during the Settlement Age (870–930) it must have become obvious that some sort of national organization, some sort of common law and administration of justice, was necessary; and once again, the political initiative came from the Reykjavík family and that first Thing on Kjalarnes. During the 920s a man named Úlfljótur, who was skilled in law, was sent to Norway to prepare a code of law derived from the laws current in south-west Norway, where the bulk of the settlers had come from, but one without provision for a monarchy.

He worked there for three years. Meanwhile his foster-brother, a man called Grímur *geitskör* (Goat Beard), was commissioned to conduct a survey in Iceland to acquaint people with the proposal for a national assembly, or Althing (*Alþingi*), and to find a suitable site for it—a sort of opinion poll, in effect. It so happened that an ideal site was available, right on the edge of Ingólfur Arnarson's land-take, some fifty kilometres from Reykjavík; the owner of the land had been found guilty of murder and his property had been confiscated. It was called Bláskógar (Blue Woods), but the name was changed to Thingvöllur (Assembly Plain), which common usage has pluralized to its present name of Thingvellir.

Thingvellir was the perfect site for the purpose. It had broad, flat reaches for encampments and tents, and for temporary booths (*búðir*), which were stone and turf structures that could be roofed with sailcloth. It had fresh water in abundance, a lake teeming with brown trout and arctic char (*murta*), and ample pasture for grazing. Above all, it was easy of access for the most densely populated areas of the country, the south and the west; but even the men of the Eastfjords thought nothing of a seventeen-day journey on horseback to attend.

And so, around the year 930, the first Althing was held at Thingvellir. In recognition of his legal experience, Úlfljótur, the law-maker, was appointed Law-Speaker (*lögsögumaður*) to get matters off on the proper footing; and the proceedings were duly hallowed by the First Settler's son, whose family would henceforth bear the honorary title of *allsherjargoði* (Supreme Chieftain).

The Althing has been called the oldest parliament in the world, even though it was more of an oligarchy than a representative democracy. Nevertheless it was a unique social and political experiment long before its time, long before Simon de Montfort's parliament in England in the thirteenth century. If Westminster is the Mother of Parliaments, then Thingvellir is the Grandmother of Parliaments.

Power rested entirely with the *goðar*, the priest-chieftains. It was decreed that there should be thirty-six of them—three from each of the twelve districts into which Iceland was administratively divided; later, this figure was increased to thirty-nine. There was only one salaried official, the Law-Speaker, who was elected by the *goðar* from amongst their own number for a term of three years (although he could be, and frequently was, re-elected). His functions were procedural, not executive; it was his task to conduct the meetings of the Althing, and to recite from memory the entire body of the law, one third for each year of his office. This was a vital function: until the whole law-code was committed to writing for the first time in 1117–18, the Law-Speaker was the living repository of the nation's laws—'With laws shall our land be built up, but with lawlessness laid waste.'

This public recitation of the law took place at the so-called Law Rock (*Lögberg*) which was the focal point of the Althing. This solid slope of basaltic ropey lava is on the eastern rim of the ravine that gives entry to Thingvellir, Almannagjá (Everyman Chasm), and is marked today by a flagpole. The proceedings of the Althing took place on the flat ground below, but the Law Rock provided a podium for oratory.

The Althing had two main functions, legislative and judicial, both of which were carried out by the *goðar*. Legislative work was carried out in the *Lögrétta* (Legislature), which consisted of all the *goðar* with the Law-Speaker as president. It convened within hallowed boundaries, sitting in a circle on three tiered rows of benches on a wooden floor and probably under an awning. The chieftains sat on the middle bench, each with two counsellors occupying the front and rear benches. The debates were held in public, but only the chieftains had the right to vote, and motions were carried on a simple majority. It was the task of the *Lögrétta* to pass new laws or amend old ones, to review court sentences if required, rescind outlawries and respond on the nation's behalf to overtures from foreign powers.

For its judicial function the Althing had four Quarter courts (one for each of the four Quarters of the country), which dealt with cases that had been remitted upwards by the three district Things in each Quarter. Each Quarter court consisted of thirty-six judges, chosen by the nine *goðar* of the Quarter; these judges, or jurymen as we would call them nowadays, had to be males of twelve years or more and free men with a permanent domicile. The prosecution and defence of each case was presented by one or other of the judge-jurymen, and the judges had to decide whether the accused was guilty or innocent as charged; the litigants could challenge the choice of a judge on the grounds of kinship with the parties concerned, or known bias. Verdicts were considered unanimous and binding if the number of dissenting votes did not exceed six. If there were a 'hung jury' the case was left unresolved; all too often, men took the law into their own hands, or challenged one another to single combat. These duels usually took place on an islet in the River Öxará; in Iceland, duelling was called *hólmganga*—'island-going'.

A duel attracted huge crowds of onlookers, as can be imagined. It was a highly formal, ritualistic occasion. It was not usually fought to the death—the drawing of first blood was frequently considered sufficient to decide the winner. It is clear that the duel was considered a form of ordeal, a way of letting the gods decide what the courts had been unable to unravel.

The most detailed account of the rules of duelling is found in *Kormáks Saga*, the saga of the warrior-poet Kormákur Ögmundarson and his lifelong frustrated love for a beautiful woman who married another. Kormákur poured out a stream of passionate love poetry to the lady, which forms the basis for the saga. He challenged the lady's husband to a duel (which, incidentally, he lost on a technicality):

> These were the rules for a duel: a cloak five ells square was to be laid down, with loops in the corners, and fastened with pegs rammed through the loops . . . Three borders or furrows, each a foot in breadth, were to be around the cloak, and at the edge of these borders there were to be four poles of hazelwood; when this had been done, the place was considered 'hazelled'. Each con-

testant was to have three shields, and when they had been destroyed the contestant was to return to the cloak, if he had stepped outside it, and defend himself with his weapons thereafter. He who had been challenged was to have the first blow. If one of the two was wounded so that blood flowed on to the cloak, the fight was stopped. If a contestant put one foot outside the hazelled area, he was said to have 'yielded ground'; if he put both feet outside it, he was said to have 'fled'. Each contestant was to have a second who held the shield before him. Whichever contestant came off the worse had to pay 'holm-ransom'—three marks of silver.

The last recorded duel on the islet in the Öxará involved another warrior-poet, Gunnlaugur *ormstunga* (Serpent-Tongue). *Gunnlaugs Saga* tells how he, too, challenged to a duel the husband of the lady he loved. The duel took place in the year 1007, and was inconclusive, in that the fight was stopped when Gunnlaugur's cheek was gashed by a piece of metal that flew off his opponent's broken sword. In the following year, duelling was formally banned, and a Fifth Court was instituted as a court of appeal and supreme court to deal with unresolved disputes from the Quarter courts.

Litigation was never an easy business in Iceland, as Sámur found to his cost in *Hrafnkels Saga* (see Ch 6). Despite the painfully correct procedures, too much depended on the power and connections of individual chieftains and the size of their following. Many of them were ruthless individuals who thought nothing of packing the jury and subverting the course of justice if it suited them to do so. The legal procedure was at best an uneasy check on the pride and violence of men who were used to getting their own way by force, men who felt it unmanly to submit a grievance to the arbitration of the law rather than avenging an insult with blood spilt. To such men, the concept of honour and injury overrode all other considerations; any slight, whether real or imagined, was seen as *skapraun*, a test of one's temper and manhood, and failure to respond to it meant losing face in the community and in one's family. Money compensation was at best a barely acceptable substitute for blood-revenge; if the demands of justice were thwarted by the intricacy of court procedure or the cunning of legalistic minds, the automatic resort was once again to violence. Furthermore, without an executive to carry out court decisions, sentences had to be enforced by the success-ful litigant—if he had the strength to do so. This was the fundamental flaw in the organization of the Icelandic com-monwealth. There were insufficient checks on the power of headstrong chieftains who set themselves above the law; and the political rights of individuals gradually became eroded as landed wealth and the chieftaincies that went with it became concentrated into fewer and fewer hands.

The death-throes of the old commonwealth began in the thirteenth century, during the so-called 'Sturlung Age', when greedy families and dynasties strove to achieve supreme power in the land (see Ch 14). Ambitious men sought backing from the King of Norway; private armies were raised, the homes of chieftains and their kin were attacked and burned, men were mutilated, women raped. The law stood helpless. Eventually the Icelanders, exhausted by the internecine rivalries and shocked by the outrages and betrayals commit-ted by their leaders, looked elsewhere for justice and swore allegiance to the King of Norway in 1262–4 under the Old Covenant (*gamli sáttmáli*). It spelt the end of the com-monwealth, the end of the great republican experiment. It coincided with the golden age of saga-writing, and helps to explain, perhaps, the popularity of a literature that harked back to the events of the Settlement Age, a time when men were men and honour mattered more than life itself.

And yet, despite all its imperfections, despite its vulner-ability and inherent failings, the Althing at Thingvellir was the heart and soul of the Icelandic nation for more than 300 years. It was held in midsummer for a fortnight each year in the open air, starting on the Thursday between the 18th and 24th of June (in honour of the god Thór), and could be attended by all free men and women. It was the great annual assembly for Icelanders from all walks of life and all parts of

the land. To Thingvellir every summer came the chieftains
with their formidable retinues. Here came farmers and farmhands, travellers and traders, friends and foes. For the two
weeks of the Althing, Thingvellir became a township of tents
and temporary booths. It was both parliament and fair-
ground, senate and circus. There were beer-tents and soup-
kitchens, trade marts and sporting events. It was the largest
social gathering of the year, a place where elders debated
while youngsters courted, where sword-grinders plied their
trade and hucksters shouted their wares, where gossip flew
while news was made, where old poems were remembered
and new stories embroidered, where plots were hatched and
marriages arranged, and occasional heads as well as hearts
were broken.

The importance of the Althing is constantly reflected in the
events of the Icelandic sagas. In *Njáls Saga*, for instance,
there are some great and memorable scenes at the Althing
that punctuate the action like exclamation marks. After the
burning of Njáll and his family in their home at Bergthórshvoll (see Ch 16) there is a magnificent court scene at the
Althing when all the cases of manslaughter are brought; and
when the cases are frustrated, the Althing erupts into battle.
But long before that, when the great sweep of the narrative is
getting into its stride, there is a vividly observed moment at
the Althing when the peerless hero of the saga, Gunnar of
Hlíðarendi, meets the beautiful and imperious woman who
will bring about his downfall, Hallgerður. Gunnar had just
returned from a triumphantly successful visit to Norway, and
his friends persuaded him to go to the Althing, dressed in all
his finery from the royal courts of Scandinavia, to see and be
seen:

> One day, as Gunnar was walking from the Law Rock,
> he went down past the booth of the men from Mosfell.
> There he saw some well-dressed women coming towards
> him; the one in the lead was the best dressed of all. As
> their paths crossed, this woman greeted him at once. He
> made a friendly reply, and asked her who she was. She

said that her name was Hallgerður, and that she was the daughter of Höskuldur Dala-Kollsson. She spoke to him boldly, and asked him to tell her about his travels. Gunnar replied that he would not deny her that. So they sat down and talked.

Hallgerður was wearing a red, richly-decorated tunic under a scarlet cloak trimmed all the way down with lace. Her beautiful thick hair flowed down over her bosom. Gunnar was wearing the robes that King Harald Gormsson had given him, with the gold arm-ring from Earl Hakon on his arm.

They talked aloud for a long time, until finally he asked if she were unmarried . . .

There are few material relics left of all that vivid, boisterous, teeming life that was lived at Thingvellir every summer. A scatter of grass-grown mounds on the plain at the foot of the Law Rock hints at the booths that once housed great chieftains, but none can be dated or identified with any certainty. But no matter. Thingvellir is a place for the imagination to soar, for romantic aspiration and inspiration alike. When the movement for political independence began to stir anew in the nineteenth century, it was to Thingvellir that the people flocked again to express their sense of historical identity and to recover a lost greatness. And when independence was finally regained, it was at Thingvellir that the Althing met in formal session in the open air again, to proclaim the sovereign republic on 17 June 1944.

CHAPTER 8

Stöng: How They Lived Then

Þá var öldin önnur,
Er Gaukur bjó á Stöng . . .

Those were the days,
When Gaukur lived at Stöng . . .

(Medieval ballad)

They lived in fine style, the people of the Saga Age. The huddled, multi-gabled farmhouses from the nineteenth century that have been preserved as examples of 'old Iceland'—at Keldur, for instance, or in the open-air museum at Árbær in Reykjavík—give a very misleading impression of the size and quality of houses in the commonwealth era. We get a much better idea from hints in the sagas themselves, and from archaeology.

Landnámabók gives an indication of the grandeur of some of the homes built by the early settlers. The first settler of Hjaltadalur, a man called Hjalti Thórðarson, built his home at Hólar, which later became the site of the bishopric for the north of Iceland (see Ch 13). When Hjalti died, his two sons, the Hjaltasons, hosted a memorial feast at Hólar which was long remembered:

> The most magnificent funeral feast ever held in Iceland was the one the Hjaltasons celebrated in honour of their father; there were no fewer than 1,440 guests, and all the important visitors were presented with gifts.

Another sumptuous residence was the house that Ólafur *pái* (the Peacock), one of the main characters in *Laxdæla Saga* (see Ch 15), built at Hjarðarholt in Laxárdalur around the year 960:

That summer Ólafur had a hall built at Hjarðarholt, larger and finer than anyone had ever seen before. The wainscoting and ceiling were adorned with fine carvings depicting the old legends; the craftsmanship was so superb that people thought the hall even more magnificent when the wall-hangings were not up.

At a wedding feast at Hjarðarholt, a poet called Úlfur Uggason presented a special poem he had written, a 'house lay' (*húsdrápa*), of which several verses are preserved in Snorri Sturluson's *Prose Edda*. These verses describe three of the scenes that were carved on the panels at Hjarðarholt: the funeral of the god Baldur, the swimming contest between Heimdallur and Loki, and Thór's attempt to catch the World Serpent on a fishing expedition – all of which were familiar stories from Norse mythology. The funeral feast held by Ólafur the Peacock at Hjarðarholt in memory of his father was reckoned to be the second largest feast ever held in Iceland, with no fewer than 1,080 guests.

The houses built by the first settlers were of the classic Norse long-house type: a single long-hall, which could be partitioned into separate chambers. Later, other rooms were added for specialized purposes—a weaving-room for the women, a larder, a privy and so on; the substantial farmsteadings to house the livestock and store fodder were built nearby. The overwhelming impression one gets from the large number of houses that have been excavated is one of sheer size; long-houses of forty metres or more, like Hofstaðir near Mývatn (see Ch 5), were by no means uncommon, and Hjarðarholt must have been considerably larger. The houses were built with stout timber frames and elaborate rafters; the outside walls were made of specially cut turves carefully stacked on foundations of unhewn stones, a metre thick or more, and the roofs were covered with turf as well. They looked a part of the landscape, like grass-grown ridges.

The best-preserved Saga Age house yet uncovered by archaeology is a farm called Stöng, near the head of the valley of Thjórsárdalur in the south of Iceland. It is often referred

Helgafell on Snæfellsnes: a holy mountain to the first settlers, and later the manor farm of Snorri the Priest. Guðrún of *Laxdæla Saga* lies buried near the church.

The great lava arena of Thingvellir, where the Althing met in the open air every summer. On the extreme left, the track through Almannagjá (Everyman Chasm); the flagpole in the distance marks the Law Rock. The river, Oxará, ran in a wider curve in those days, creating more flat space for meetings of the Assembly.

to, somewhat fancifully, as 'Iceland's Pompeii', because its preservation was due to a catastrophic volcanic eruption: in the year 1104 it was smothered under a tremendous outpouring of tephra from Iceland's most famous volcano, Mount Hekla. It was excavated in 1939 by a team of Scandinavian archaeologists.

Thjórsárdalur (Bull River Dale) is a remarkable valley. Its bedrock was formed some 8,000 years ago by the most prodigious lava-flow the world has known since the last Ice Age, a huge river of lava covering some 800 square kilometres that swept for 130 kilometres south to the sea. Time and moss and erosion gradually mellowed the unyielding lava; the minerals helped to create fertile new grassland, and a new river, the Thjórsá—now the mightiest river in Iceland— gnawed its way down to the coast. But it has remained an intensely volcanic area; to the east broods the majestic hog-backed ridge of Mount Hekla, queening it over the south-lands in a perpetual ermine mantle of snow, always threatening to erupt yet again.

The first recorded eruption of Hekla was in the year 1104. At that time there were at least twenty farmsteads in the upper reaches of Thjórsárdalur. Millions of tons of black sandy tephra, or volcanic ash, shrouded the green pastures. All the farms died. To this day it is a dark and barren wasteland, littered with lumps of lava and starred with unexpected clumps of flowers fighting to regain a foothold in the desert of sand. But now, through archaeology, one of those long-abandoned farms has come to life again: the farm of Stöng.

Stöng had its own saga. In the tenth century it was the home of a warrior-farmer called Gaukur Trandilsson. He was a redoubtable champion, but he was killed in single combat by his own foster-brother, Ásgrímur Elliða-Grímsson, who figures largely in *Njáls Saga*. There, Gaukur only gets a passing mention, when Ásgrímur justifies the killing as having been a matter of honour: 'Many people would say that I did not kill Gaukur until my hand was forced.' The author of *Njáls Saga*, and the audience for which *Njáls Saga* was written, clearly knew all about Gaukur Trandilsson and his fate; obviously, there was a separate saga about him already in existence. For a long time, this was only a scholarly assumption; but just before the last war, proof was found in one of the great vellum manuscript codices that Árni Magnússon had collected and taken to Copenhagen (see Ch 1). The codex is called *Möðruvallabók* (*Book of Möðruvellir*); it is a huge collection of sagas, no fewer than eleven of them, starting with *Njáls Saga*. It was compiled in the middle of the fourteenth century.

In *Möðruvallabók* there is a long space between *Njáls Saga* and the saga which follows it, *Egils Saga*. In this space there was some writing which was so worn that it was indecipherable. With the invention of ultra-violet lamps, however, it became possible to make out what the words were: 'Insert here *Gauks Saga Trandilssonar*; I am told that Grímur [Thorsteinsson], Esq., has a copy.'

Alas for posterity, the scribe never got hold of the copy of *Gauks Saga*, to add it to the great codex; and *Gauks Saga* has since then disappeared without trace—just one of the many gems of Icelandic saga literature that have been lost for all time.

Undoubtedly, it would have told us about the circumstances which forced Ásgrímur Elliða-Grímsson to fight and kill his own foster-brother. In its absence, we have to be satisfied with a hint that occurs in a snatch of a surviving medieval ballad:

> Those were the days,
> When Gaukur lived at Stöng;
> Then the way to Steinastaðir
> Wasn't long.

Steinastaðir was the name of a farm in the neighbourhood; and the clear implication is that Gaukur was having an affair with the housewife of Steinastaðir, who must have been a kinswoman of Ágrímur's, so that family honour was at stake.

But the most remarkable thing about Gaukur Trandilsson is that his name cropped up again in the most unlikely place imaginable, 200 years later and 600 kilometres away in Scotland: the magnificent Neolithic burial mound of Maeshowe, in the Orkneys, which is dated to around 2,700 BC. Maeshowe was known to the Vikings as Orkahaugur; and when the great mound was first excavated in 1861, it was apparent that the Vikings had broken into the tomb seven centuries earlier, and had left a mass of Viking runic graffiti on the walls.

The longest of these inscriptions is in the form of a four-line stanza:

> These runes were carved
> By the greatest rune-master west-over-sea,
> With the axe once owned by Gaukur
> Trandilsson in the south of Iceland.

What was Gaukur Trandilsson's axe from Stöng doing in that extraordinary place? The riddle was brilliantly solved by Professor Hermann Pálsson of Edinburgh University as an exercise in literary detective work. *Orkneyinga Saga* (*Saga of the Orkneymen*), which was written in Iceland early in the thirteenth century, tells us that in the 1150s, an Orkney earl called Rögnvaldur Kali led a detachment of Vikings on one of the Crusades; on his way home, he went by ship from Norway to the Orkneys. This ship had an Icelandic skipper, a man called Thórhallur Ásgrímsson, who was a direct descendant of Ásgrímur Elliða-Grímsson, the man who had killed Gaukur Trandilsson in single combat. After the duel, Ásgrímur would have taken the dead man's weapons, as was his right as the victor, and the axe would have become a family heirloom, handed down from father to son until it reached Thórhallur Ásgrímsson. We can now visualize what must have happened: when the Crusaders reached the Orkneys, they boisterously suggested a night out on the tiles, and ended up by breaking into Maeshowe—a popular Viking pastime by then, it appears. While they were inside, a boastful rune-master wanted to show off his prowess, and asked if anyone had a suitable implement. At that point, Thórhallur volunteered the use of his axe, and told the story of how it had come into his family's possession—and the runester promptly incorporated it into his graffito. Thus an immortal runic inscription was born.

At Stöng in Iceland, Gaukur Trandilsson had made a good life for himself. He had plenty of grazing for his sheep, he kept a herd of twenty cows in his byre, he had a smithy for making his own implements and weapons from home-smelted bog-iron ore. His household would have consisted of about twenty people. Yet it was only a medium-sized farm; Stöng was too far up the valley, too close to the line between vegetation and the desert of the high hinterland, to be really prosperous.

Stöng has now been recreated as a full-scale reconstruction a little further down the valley, at Skeljastaðir—the 'Commonwealth Farm' (*þjóðveldisbær*), as it is called. Only the tools that were available during the commonwealth era were used; the timber (a gift from Norway) was shaped by means of axes without the aid of saws or planes, and the axe-marks can be plainly seen on all the woodwork. The farm was a basic long-hall, seventeen metres long and six metres in breadth. It had a single door at one end of the long side facing down the valley. This door led into a vestibule which was also a storage room, which led in turn to the main room, the long-hall (*skáli*), which was the all-purpose room for the whole household. The walls were wainscoted, and there was a clear space between the panelling and the thick turf walls to prevent rotting. Down either side of the hall there were raised platforms on which people sat to work and eat, and where they stretched out to sleep. In the centre of one side there was a lockable bed-closet (*lokrekkja*) for the head of the family and his wife. The pillars holding up the rafters allowed the hall to be partitioned into three, to make separate quarters for men and women. There was a long-fire built into the earthen floor in the middle of the hall, and another fire-pit in the vestibule for cooking.

At the inner end of the hall a doorway led into another room which had been added on. This was a living-room (*stofa*), which was primarily a work-room for the women and perhaps also their bower. It had a sunken stone box for a fireplace in the middle of the floor, and benches down the side. There was an upright weaving-loom at the far end, and a special dais called the *kvennapallur* (women's platform) under which the textiles were stored as they were finished. This was where the womenfolk of the farm worked at the wool all the year round. Two sets of warp-threads hung from the beams at the top of the loom, kept taut by the weight of heavy stones; the weft was slipped through these threads and beaten upwards into place with a weaving-sword. To make a single length of cloth, the women had to walk several miles to and fro across the face of the loom. It was exhausting work, but it was essential to the economy of the farm; homespun cloth (*vaðmál*) was Iceland's staple export commodity in the early days, and was also used as a main unit of currency.

Two additional rooms, or back-houses, led off the main hall at right angles, rather like afterthoughts. One was a substantial larder (*búr*); on the earthen floor the imprints of three huge tubs for dairy products and pickled foods were still clearly visible when the farmhouse was excavated. The other room, whose entrance faced the front door across the vestibule, seems to have been a privy and possibly a bath-house for saunas; it had deep stone-set runnels along the walls.

The archaeological record in Iceland is relatively meagre. Very little perishable material has survived. But in the National Museum there is a magnificent carved door, dating from around 1200, that came from the church at Valthjófs-staður in the east of Iceland, but which had originally been made for the home of some secular chieftain. It was made of fir, and decorated with two Romanesque roundels carved in relief. The upper roundel depicts the classic medieval motif of the Knight and the Lion: the mounted knight rescues a lion from the clutches of a dragon, whereupon the lion becomes the knight's companion, and finally lies grieving on his tomb, which bears the inscription '[Behold] the mighty king is buried here, who slew this dragon'. The lower roundel is an intricate knot of four dragons, their wings and bodies intertwined round a centre formed by their intersecting feet. It would be fascinating to know what kind of heroic motifs a champion like Gaukur Trandilsson would have chosen to decorate his home at Stöng.

By the start of the nineteenth century, the long-hall style of architecture had undergone a complete re-orientation. The hall itself had shrunk to a narrow passagę with small rooms leading off it, each with its separate gable. The original bath-room (*baðstofa*) gradually became the living-room and communal bedroom, no doubt because it was the warmest place in the house. The cow-sheds and stables were built to adjoin the farmhouse, and in some cases the living-room was built directly above the animal-shed, to utilize the body-heat of the livestock below. Architecture in Iceland has always reflected external conditions; as the cold intensified, the houses huddled in upon themselves, cowering deeper and deeper into the ground against the elements until they looked like burial mounds. Constantly damp, airless and disease-ridden, they were a far cry indeed from the great manor houses like Hjarðarholt, in the days when the way from Stöng to Steinastaðir wasn't long.

CHAPTER 9

The Hammer and the Cross

Ólafr rex Tryggvasonr . . . kom kristni í Norveg ok á Ísland. Hann sendi hingat til lands prest þann, es hét Þangbrandr ok hér kenndi mönnum kristni ok skírði þá alla, es við trú tóku.

King Olaf Tryggvason brought Christianity to Norway and into Iceland. He sent to this country a priest called Thang-brand, who taught people Christianity and baptized all those who accepted the faith.

(Íslendingabók)

Throughout the tenth century, while Iceland remained 'completely pagan' in Ari the Learned's words, the Church on the Continent was busy trying to infiltrate the Scandinavian kingdoms. Missions were sent to Sweden, to Norway and to Denmark, and were for the most part tolerated, even encouraged in some cases. In the 960s, King Harald Gormsson of Denmark—Harald Blue-Tooth—was converted to Christianity and raised the massive Jelling Stone to boast that he 'made the Danes Christian'. As the influence of the Church in Scandinavia increased, it was inevitable that Icelanders travelling abroad would come into contact with it. Some were so impressed that they submitted to baptism; a few even felt impelled to become missionaries, to spread the good news in their homeland. One such enthusiast was a young Icelander called Thorvaldur who, because of his wide travels, earned himself the nickname of *víðförli*—'Far-Farer'.

In the summer of 1981 the Bishop of Iceland unveiled an impressive memorial stone in a field near the farmstead of Stóra-Giljá, in the north of Iceland. It was erected to commemorate the first recorded Christian mission to Iceland, precisely a thousand years earlier and at that very place; for in the same field there lies a gigantic boulder called Gullsteinn (Goldstone), which was said to have been the home and haunt of a land-spirit—the first land-spirit in Iceland to be exorcized by the Cross.

The story is told in a short saga episode called *Þorvalds þáttur víðförla* (*Tale of Thorvaldur Far-Farer*), which relates the adventures of a country boy called Thorvaldur, the younger son of the wealthy farmer of Stóra-Giljá. Like many another youngster in the Saga Age, Thorvaldur went abroad to seek fame and fortune as a Viking mercenary. In newly-converted Denmark he found both, in the service of the formidable Svein Fork-Beard, prince of Denmark, scourge of England and father of a future king of England, Canute (Knútur) the Great. Thorvaldur accompanied Svein on several raiding expeditions west-over-sea, and won high praise for his loyalty and fighting prowess. But Thorvaldur was no blood-and-thunder Viking; he was merciful and charitable of heart, so much so that he spent all his booty on giving alms to the poor and ransoming captives, until 'even those who were robbed and pillaged by Svein's men loved Thorvaldur, and were loud in praise of his goodness'.

It comes as no surprise to read that when his travels took him to Germany he should take up with a Saxon missionary bishop called Frederick, by whom he was baptized into the Christian faith; nor that he should thereupon persuade this bishop to accompany him to Iceland to spread the gospel amongst his fellow-countrymen there.

In the *Tale* this first mission to Iceland in the year 981 is portrayed as a freelance enterprise; but it took place in the days of the powerful Archbishop Adaldag of Bremen (937–88), close friend and supporter of the German Holy Roman Emperors of the tenth century, and it is not unlikely that the Icelandic mission had some sort of formal backing from the Bremen bishopric.

Thorvaldur's aims were modest enough: he wanted to 'try to convert his father and mother and other close kinsfolk'. The visitors were given a good welcome at Stóra-Giljá, which

became their base, and Thorvaldur was soon busy proselytiz-
ing on Bishop Frederick's behalf, for the bishop spoke only
German. Many of Thorvaldur's kinsmen responded well and
accepted baptism; but his father, Koðrán, proved a harder
nut to crack. One day Bishop Frederick held a special mass
which Koðrán attended, more from courtesy than curiosity.
Koðrán was suitably impressed by the singing, the opulence
of the vestments, the fragrance of the incense and the bril-
liance of the candles, and was quite prepared to accept the
fact that his son had found himself a useful guardian spirit in
this foreign bishop:

> 'But I have a guardian spirit of my own who is very
> useful to me. He foretells the future for me, takes care of
> my livestock and tells me what I should be doing and
> what I should avoid; and because of this I put great trust
> in him, and have worshipped him for many years.'

> 'Where does your guardian spirit live?' asked
> Thorvaldur.

> 'He lives a short way from the farm in a large and
> handsome boulder,' said Koðrán.

> 'Then I shall make a bargain with you, father,' said
> Thorvaldur. 'You think your guardian spirit very strong,
> and say you put great trust in him, while the bishop
> whom you call my guardian spirit is but an ordinary man
> with no especial strength; but if by the power of God in
> heaven, in Whom we believe, he can drive out your
> guardian spirit from his stronghold, then it will be right
> for you to turn to this most powerful God, your Creator,
> who is the true God whom no strength may overcome.'

Koðrán readily agreed to this proposal. Next day the
bishop blessed a tub of boiling water and poured it over the
huge rock, chanting psalms and reciting prayers the while.
That very night the guardian spirit appeared to Koðrán in his
sleep, bedraggled and woebegone, complaining bitterly
about all the boiling water that was pouring through his roof,
scalding his children and spoiling his furniture. The next day
the bishop redoubled his efforts, and again the following day,

until the great boulder cracked. That night Koðrán's guardian spirit appeared to him for the last time, and spoke to him more in sorrow than in anger:

'This wicked man, the bishop of the Christians, has driven me from my own property. He has wrecked my house and drenched me in boiling water, ruined my clothes and utterly destroyed them, burned me and my people and driven me into exile to the farthest wilderness. This is the end of our association and friendship, and all because of your weakness. Who will now guard your goods and care for them as I have done in the past? You are said to be a good and righteous man, but you have evilly repaid my kindness to you.'

And so Koðrán was baptized, together with his wife and the rest of the household. To this day the great boulder is seamed with cracks that are said to bear witness to the struggle for Koðrán's soul between the bishop and the demon; and to symbolize this victory, it has been known as the Goldstone ever since.

In the following year, 982, Thorvaldur and the bishop set up home at Lækjamót in Víðidalur, and the *Tale* relates with much relish some picturesque stories of the bishop's battles with pagan fiends and demons. Few notables were converted; but the *Tale* claims success with a prominent settler's son, Thorvarður Spak-Böðvarsson, who built a church on his lands at Neðri-Áss in Hjaltadalur in the year 984 (although other sources suggest that he was baptized in England). Another convert is said to have been a man called Máni (Moon), known as Máni the Christian, who lived at Holt in Ásar and built a church there; there is an enclosure there called Mánagerði, in which Máni was said to have grown hay for his one cow, 'for he would rather toil with his own hands than have to mix with pagans, who hated him.'

The missionaries had no success at all when they travelled through the Westfjords; and when they tried to preach the new faith at the Althing they aroused positive hostility. The Icelanders found the bishop not only alien but effeminate; he

was beardless, as church regulations required, and the vestments he wore reminded them of skirts:

> Babies nine
> Has the bishop borne;
> And all of them
> Has Thorvaldur sired.

This insulting lampoon on the baptismal ceremony, with its
crude imputation of homosexuality, was a deliberate slander
of the grossest kind: in the early laws, insinuation of perversion was regarded as actionable. Thorvaldur lost his temper
and promptly slew two of his detractors, much to the bishop's
dismay, and the two missionaries were prosecuted for
manslaughter and sentenced to outlawry.

They left the country the following spring. Thorvaldur
never returned to his homeland, and went on to earn his
nickname of 'Far-Farer' by faring far to Jerusalem and then
to Constantinople, where he was allegedly raised to high
estate by the Emperor of Byzantium and appointed overlord
of all the kings in Russia, no less. He ended his days there as a
recluse in a monastery he is said to have founded at a place
called Dröfn, which is thought to have been near Polotsk on
the River Dvina.

That first mission to Iceland (981–6) cannot be called a
spectacular success; indeed, *Kristni Saga* (*Chronicle of
Christianity*), which was compiled in the second half of the
thirteenth century, is dismissive of the whole enterprise: 'But
most people were little swayed by their words.' But for local
people, the story of Thorvaldur's adventures assumed heroic
saga proportions as time went by. Eventually, round about
1200, the *Tale of Thorvaldur Far-Farer* was written up in the
monastery of Thingeyrar (see Ch 13), which overlooks the
farm of Stóra-Giljá and the Goldstone itself. The author was
a monk called Gunnlaugur Leifsson; he was considered the
most lettered man of his day, and wrote a (now lost) Latin
history of King Olaf Tryggvason of Norway. He wrote the
Tale in Icelandic, as an edifying yarn—an early mini-saga, in
effect; for Gunnlaugur the monk and his northern audience,

the *Tale of Thorvaldur Far-Farer* and that first Christian mission to Iceland was essentially the story of a local boy who made good.

Thangbrand the Missionary

In the year 991 a formidable young Norwegian princeling burst on to the stage of history at the head of a Viking fleet of ninety-three ships bent on ravaging the south-east of England, according to the *Anglo-Saxon Chronicle*. His name was Olaf Tryggvason, a great-grandson of King Harald Fine-Hair and a pretender to the throne of Norway. That summer he faced and defeated the gallant Ealdorman Byrhtnoth at the Battle of Maldon in Essex—a heroic encounter that was immortalized in one of the finest poems in Old English—and was then paid Danegeld of 10,000 pounds of gold and silver to go away and leave England in peace.

Three years later he was back in England and took part in the vehement siege of London in 994 with Svein Fork-Beard, newly-crowned King of Denmark. This time the Danegeld required to buy him off was 16,000 pounds of silver, plus free winter quartering in Southampton for his army; and during that winter Olaf Tryggvason, most ruthless of Viking warriors, was converted to Christianity. The *Anglo-Saxon Chronicle* relates that he received instruction from the Bishop of Winchester, and that the King of England, Æthelred the Unready, stood sponsor at his baptism in Andover. Thereupon Olaf Tryggvason left England, this time for good. He had achieved a war-chest with which to finance his challenge for the crown of Norway, and a Christian crusade with which to bolster it. The crown fell into his hands with unexpected ease, and he wore it for five violently evangelistic years (995–1000), during which Norway was bludgeoned with merciless ferocity into accepting Christianity, on pain of mutilation or death.

Not content with forcibly converting his reluctant countrymen, Olaf Tryggvason also had designs on those lands which had been colonized from Norway: the Orkneys and Shetland, the Faroes, and, above all, the one that had got away—Iceland. In 996 he sent one of his disciples, an Icelandic convert called Stefnir Thorgilsson, on a mission to Iceland accompanied by a retinue of nine priests. Stefnir was a descendant of a prominent settler who had himself been a Christian, Helgi *bjólan* of Kjalarnes (see Ch 4); but his lineage availed him little, and the people spurned his preaching. Enraged by this indifference, Stefnir adopted Olaf Tryggvason's own uncompromising tactics, destroying pagan shrines and idols, but this only stiffened the Icelanders' opposition. In their undogmatic way they had always tolerated divergence of religious faith; but now a new law was introduced at the Althing whereby those who blasphemed or insulted the gods were to be prosecuted by their kinsmen for 'family disgrace' (*frænda skömm*). Stefnir Thorgilsson was promptly banished, and fled back to Norway.

King Olaf was undeterred by this failure, and in 997 he sent a second and much more determined mission to Iceland, led by a turbulent German priest called Thangbrand, the son of Count Willibald of Saxony. This mission enjoyed some initial success at least, according to *Íslendingabók*:

> King Olaf sent to this country a priest called Thangbrand, who taught people Christianity and baptized all those who accepted the faith. Hallur Thorsteinsson of Síða received baptism early, as did Hjalti Skeggjason from Thjórsárdalur and Gissur the White, the son of Teitur, the son of Ketilbjörn the Old from Mosfell, and many other chieftains; but there were more of those who spoke against it and rejected it.

The three chieftains named by Ari the Learned in *Íslendingabók* as early converts were to play a crucial part in the eventual Conversion of Iceland (see Ch 10). Hallur Thorsteinsson of Síða (Síðu-Hallur) was the leading man in the east of Iceland, where Thangbrand first made land; he lived in Álftafjörður at a farm called Thvottá (Wash River), which is said to have got its name from the stream in which Síðu-Hallur was baptized. An area in the home-field at Thvottá, which is now protected as a historic site, is traditionally the spot where Thangbrand pitched his tent to celebrate the feast-day of the Archangel Michael, and where Síðu-Hallur agreed to accept baptism on condition that St Michael became his personal guardian angel. Síðu-Hallur was a descendant of one of the early settlers, Hrollaugur, the son of the Earl of Möre (see Ch 3).

Gissur the White—Gissur Teitsson of Skálholt—was another highly important catch for Thangbrand, not least because he could claim distant kinship with King Olaf Tryggvason. He was the grandson of Ketilbjörn the Old, the original settler of the fertile lands around Mosfell (see Ch 3), and his father, Teitur, had built the manor farm of Skálholt. Gissur was now the *goði* for the district, a position of considerable power and authority, but one which involved certain pagan priestly duties, like the swearing of public oaths. His conversion to Christianity would disqualify him from carrying out his official duties as a priest-chieftain.

The third man named by Ari the Learned, Hjalti Skeggjason of Thjórsárdalur, was Gissur's son-in-law.

The 'many other chieftains' referred to by Ari included Hallur Thórarinsson of Haukadalur (995–1089), who could remember that day in 998 when he was baptized at the age of three by Thangbrand. Hallur fostered Ari at Haukadalur (see Ch 12), and was one of Ari's most important informants about the events leading up to the Conversion.

Another eminent figure to receive baptism at Thangbrand's hands was the sage Njáll of Berthórshvoll, the eponymous hero of *Njáls Saga*. According to the saga, Njáll had already made up his own mind about Christianity before Thangbrand's arrival:

> Njáll heard many people say that it was monstrous to forsake the old beliefs. But Njáll replied: 'In my opinion the new faith is much better; happy the man who receives it. And if the men who spread this faith come out to Iceland, I shall do all I can to further it.'
>
> He said this on many occasions; and often he would leave the company of others and meditate aloud.

By an irony of history, another leading man who received baptism from Thangbrand, according to *Njáls Saga*, was Flosi Thórðarson, Síðu-Hallur's son-in-law, the powerful and influential *goði* of Svínafell in south-eastern Iceland. It was Flosi who would lead the Burners who destroyed Njáll and his family in their home in the terrible climax of *Njáls Saga* (see Ch 16).

Another leading chieftain who was probably baptized at this time was Snorri the Priest of Helgafell (see Ch 5). There is no documentary evidence of when Snorri *goði* was converted, but he was clearly one of Gissur the White's most important supporters during and after the Conversion crisis at Thingvellir. Yet another *goði* to be converted was Thóroddur Eyvindarson of Hjalli, in Ölfus; his alliance with Gissur the White would soon be cemented when Gissur married his daughter (see Ch 11).

The public conversion of such powerful *goðar* created a serious constitutional problem: they would be unable to subscribe to the oaths with which the Althing was hallowed, or to fulfil all their traditional obligations to their pagan constituents. It has been suggested that the Christian *goðar* must have founded their own breakaway Assembly— or at least that they must have planned to do so. They certainly could no longer operate under the old dispensation. The threat to the integrity of the state was a very real one.

But that was the limit of Thangbrand's success in trying to convert the Icelanders to Christianity, because 'there were more of those who spoke against it and rejected it', as Ari says. Thangbrand was clearly not the ideal missionary to make friends and influence people. According to Snorri Sturluson in *Heimskringla*, 'He was an ungovernable man and a great manslayer, but a good cleric and a doughty warrior.'

Thangbrand's temper was clearly not improved by the sort of reception he received in some parts of the country. *Njáls Saga*, which has a section about the mission (Chapters 100–105), tells of several attempts on his life:

A man called Sorcerer-Héðinn lived at Kerlingardalur. The pagans there hired him to put Thangbrand and his followers to death. He went up on to Arnarstakksheiði and held a great sacrifice there. While Thangbrand was riding westwards, the ground suddenly burst open under his horse. Thangbrand leapt off the horse and reached safety on the brink of the chasm, but the horse and all the gear were swallowed up in the earth and never seen again.

Then Thangbrand praised God.

When Thangbrand went to the west of the country to visit a celebrated old sage called Gestur Oddleifsson, who lived at Hagi on Barðaströnd, a crowd of two hundred pagans was waiting for him:

It was reported that a berserk was also expected. His name was Ótryggur, and everyone was terrified of him. It was even said of him that he feared neither fire nor sword.

The pagans were particularly afraid of him. Thangbrand asked whether the people wanted to accept the new faith, but all the pagans opposed it strongly.

Thangbrand said, 'I shall give you a chance of testing which is the better faith. We shall kindle three fires. You pagans are to hallow one of the fires, I shall hallow the second, and the third fire is to remain unhallowed. If the berserk is afraid of the fire that I hallow, but walks unscathed through your fire, then you shall accept the new faith.'

'That is fair,' said Gestur. 'I accept on behalf of my household and myself.'

When Gestur had spoken, there was loud approval from many of the others.

Then news came that the berserk was approaching the house. The fires were lit and kindled to a blaze. The men took their weapons and jumped on to the benches to await his arrival. The berserk came rushing fully armed into the hall; he strode at once through the fire which the pagans had hallowed, but when he came to the fire which Thangbrand had hallowed he did not dare walk through it, and said that he was burning all over.

He brandished his sword to swing at the benches, but the sword caught in a cross-beam as he swung it upwards. Thangbrand struck him on the arm with a crucifix and, miraculously, the sword dropped from the berserk's grasp; then Thangbrand plunged a sword into his chest . . .

Thangbrand also killed a man called Veturliði and his son Ari. Veturliði was a poet, and had presumably composed a lampoon about him—and that was quite enough to rouse Thangbrand's ire. Another pagan, a man called Thorkell of Stafafell, challenged Thangbrand to a duel. Thangbrand defended himself with a crucifix instead of a shield—'but even so he managed to defeat Thorkell and kill him'.

After evangelizing over much of the country, Thangbrand and his followers headed for Thingvellir. But they had to fight off an ambush at which more blood was spilt, and by the time they reached the Althing tempers were running high, and Thangbrand was refused a hearing. One of his new converts, the hot-headed Hjalti Skeggjason, only inflamed opposition further by insulting the gods with a snatch of blasphemous doggerel at the Law Rock, for which he was prosecuted and sentenced to three years' outlawry.

Soon afterwards, Thangbrand's aggressive mission came to an end. According to Ari the Learned in *Íslendingabók*, 'When Thangbrand had been here for a year or two he left the country, having killed two or three men who had slandered him.'

To add insult to injury, Thangbrand's ship, the *Bison*, was wrecked that summer. A woman called Steinunn, the mother of Refur the Poet, rubbed it in with relish:

> It was Thór's giant-killing hammer
> That smashed the ocean-striding *Bison*;

It was our gods that drove
The bell-ringer's boat ashore.
Your Christ could not save
This buffalo of the sea from destruction;
I do not think your God
Kept guard over him at all.

Thór seized the great ship;
He shook its frame
And beat its timbers,
And hurled it on the rocks;
That ship will never
Sail the seas again,
For Thór's relentless thrashing
Smashed it into fragments.

When Thangbrand had repaired his ship (which the pagans mockingly renamed the *Iron Basket*) he sailed back to Norway to report to the king:

He told King Olaf Tryggvason of the ill-treatment he had suffered at the hands of the Icelanders, and said that they were so steeped in sorcery that the earth had burst open under his horse and swallowed the animal.

The king was so enraged that he ordered all the Icelanders in Norway to be seized and thrown into dungeons, and said that he would have them all put to death.

At that point Gissur the White and Hjalti Skeggjason arrived in Norway; they offered to go surety for their countrymen, and pledged him their help in another attempt to get Christianity adopted in Iceland. The king was mollified, and accepted their offer. He gave all the Icelanders a reprieve, but he kept four men hostage in Norway—the sons of four of the most eminent pagan chieftains in Iceland, including Kjartan Ólafsson, the hero of *Laxdœla Saga*.

And so the scene was set for the climax of the struggle between the Hammer and the Cross in Iceland.

CHAPTER 10

The Conversion

Þá vas þat mælt í lögum, at allir menn skyldi kristnir vesa ok skírn taka, þeir es áðr váru óskírðir á landi hér.

It was then decreed that everyone in Iceland should be Christian, and that those who had not yet been baptized should receive baptism.

(*Íslendingabók*)

Traditionally, the date for the Conversion of Iceland to Christianity has always been the year 1000. But now scholars like Ólafía Einarsdóttir have proved conclusively that tradition has always misconstrued the chronological context provided by Ari the Learned in his *Íslendingabók*, and that the actual date was 999. It is a pity, in a way, because 'the year 1000' has such a fine millennial ring for an event as momentous as the Conversion—a Conversion, what is more, that was brought about not by bloodshed, not by persecution, not by duress, but by arbitration and shrewd political common sense. Still, 'the year 999' has a certain ring to it, too.

The annual session of the Althing began that year in the tenth week of summer, a week later than usual, late in June. On the very day that the session was being hallowed by the Supreme Chieftain, a ship from Norway made land at the Westmann Islands, just off the south coast. On board were Gissur the White and his son-in-law, the outlawed Hjalti Skeggjason, who had returned to Iceland in defiance of the law. Also on board were an Icelandic-born priest called Thormóður (of whom nothing more, alas, is known), and various friends and fellow-travellers all determined on a resolute attempt to persuade their countrymen to turn their backs on the old religion and accept Christianity instead.

With them they carried the hopes of the Icelanders held hostage in Norway, and the threats and blandishments of King Olaf Tryggvason.

From the Westmann Islands they were ferried to the mainland and took horse for Thingvellir, 150 kilometres away. Near the warm lake of Laugarvatn, a few kilometres east of their destination, they thought it prudent to leave Hjalti Skeggjason behind in the care of some friends, for he had not yet purged the contempt he had committed at the Althing the previous year. From there, Gissur the White rode over the high moorland of Lyngdalsheiði with the rest of his company until he reached the great lake of Thingvallavatn. They paused there at an inlet on the north-eastern shore known as Vellankatla (Boiling Cauldron), where water comes bubbling out from a spring under the lava; and from there, Gissur sent word to those of his supporters who were already at the Althing to come and meet him, for he had learned that pagan opponents intended to try to bar the way by force. As they all gathered at Vellankatla, Hjalti Skegg- jason himself arrived hot-foot from Laugarvatn, insistent on taking part in any showdown, banishment or no; and now they set off, all together, for Thingvellir, riding in a long column. The pagans rushed to arms, and for a time a pitched battle that would have involved the whole Althing seemed inevitable; but wiser counsels prevailed, apparently, and no violence ensued.

Next day, Gissur the White and Hjalti Skeggjason were allowed to go to the Law Rock and urge their cause: 'And it is said that they spoke wonderfully well.'

Íslendingabók tells us nothing more about the speeches they made at the Law Rock. We can only surmise that they were as much political as evangelistic: Gissur and Hjalti were not so much missionaries as emissaries of the King of Norway. Their listeners can have been left in little doubt of the menacing reality of royal power, and the starkness of the choice that faced them. Iceland was at the crossroads between the past and the future, between the traditional conservatives of the old religion and the thrustful progressives of the new;

and over them all hung the danger of Norwegian intervention if matters did not turn out to Olaf Tryggvason's liking.

It was a grave crisis, and everyone knew it; but not all the Christian eloquence of Gissur and Hjalti could resolve it, because after the speeches at the Law Rock, the pagans and the Christians solemnly 'declared themselves out of law with each other', as Ari puts it. They refused to abide by the same laws, the same constitution: in effect, the Christians were trying to create a state within a state—to partition Iceland, spiritually if not geographically, into two law-communities, two commonwealths.

To this purpose the Christians appointed one of their number, Síðu-Hallur Thorsteinsson—Thangbrand's first convert in Iceland—to draw up a new code of laws for the Christians to follow, and to become Law-Speaker of their own separatist assembly. In many sagas, Síðu-Hallur is consistently portrayed as a man of great goodness and sagacity, and it was in this unique constitutional crisis that he displayed his outstanding qualities of statesmanship: he refused the offer of secessionist office, and with the consent of his party he held a meeting with the properly elected Law-Speaker of the Althing and asked him to arbitrate on the issue that faced them. His name was Thorgeir Thorkelsson; he was the *goði* of Ljósavatn (Lightwater)—and he was a pagan.

It seems on the face of it an extraordinary decision—to hand over the fate of the Christian party to a man who was a pagan and who represented in his office all the traditional paganism of the state. But Thorgeir had been Law-Speaker of the Althing for the past fifteen years, having been re-elected for term after term. He was a man of great experience, a highly-respected lawyer, a man accustomed to taking the chair at difficult meetings of the Legislature. There was no one in Iceland better suited, by training or temperament, to resolve the dilemma that threatened the integrity of the state.

Ari relates that Thorgeir the Law-Speaker withdrew to his tented booth and covered himself with his cloak, and remained like that, silent and abstracted, for twenty-four hours. There has been much argument about what he was actually doing when he retired under his cloak; some scholars think he was communing with the old gods, or with the land-spirits, or practising some sort of shamanism, but it is just as likely that he was simply concentrating fiercely on the immensely important decision he had been deputed to make—how to work out some acceptable compromise that would allow Christians and pagans to live together in amity in Iceland.

On the following morning he sat up and sent word for everyone to gather at the Law Rock; and when they were all assembled, Thorgeir the Law-Speaker rose to deliver one of the most significant orations in the whole Iceland Saga.

He did not proselytize. He did not theologize. Instead, according to Ari, he addressed himself to the problem of safeguarding the unity of the state:

> He said he thought that an impossible situation would arise if men did not all have one and the same law in Iceland; and he urged them in every manner not to let that happen, saying that it would lead to such discord that fighting would break out which would surely destroy the nation . . .
>
> 'And now it seems to me good sense,' he said, 'that we should not allow those to prevail who are eager for conflict, but that we should seek a middle course that would allow both sides to have something of their case, and that we should all have one law and one faith; because if we sunder the law, we shall also sunder the peace.'

It was a classic appeal for moderation on both sides, an exemplary exercise in conciliation that offered the promise of concessions in exchange for compromise; and when he had concluded his speech, both sides bound themselves to abide by his sole arbitration and to accept one law—the law that Thorgeir the Law-Speaker now pronounced:

> It was then decreed that everyone in Iceland should be Christian, and that those who had not yet been baptized

should receive baptism.

But the old laws should stand [allowing] the exposure of unwanted infants, and the eating of horse-flesh. Also, people could make sacrifices in private if they wished to, but sacrificing would be subject to a sentence of outlawry if it were done in public, before witnesses.

The concessions to paganism were a matter of economics as much as of ethics. Exposure of children at birth as a crude method of controlling population growth was never a common practice in Iceland, although it is mentioned in a few of the sagas—usually with a hint of disapproval; but for some poor families it may have been thought unavoidable. The eating of horse-flesh was specifically associated with temple-worship and sacrifices, particularly sacrifices to the god Freyr; but it was also part of the staple diet of many Icelanders, and it would have been considered too drastic to ban it outright.

As it happened, these concessions to paganism proved to be only temporary, and after a few years they were abolished.

So thus it was, without any further ado that we know of, that Christianity was adopted as the official religion of all Icelanders—nominally, at least.

Becoming Christian made baptism obligatory. The triumphant Christian party was eager to hold mass baptisms there and then at the Althing; but the pagans objected that the water of the River Öxará was too cold, and insisted on being baptized instead in the hotsprings of Laugarvatn on their way home. *Kristni Saga* also relates that the magnificent horse-shoe-shaped waterfall of Goðafoss (Falls of the Gods) in the north of Iceland got its name from the fact that Thorgeir the Law-Speaker pitched into its tumbling waters the carved effigies of his pagan gods on his way home to Ljósavatn.

Yet another example of the pragmatism that triumphed on that day at Thingvellir occurs in *Kristni Saga*. During the debate that followed the addresses by Gissur the White and Hjalti Skeggjason, it is said that a breathless messenger came running into the arena with the news that a volcano was erupting in Ölfus, spewing burning lava that was threatening the home of one of the leading Christians, Thóroddur Eyvindarson, the *goði* of Hjalli. 'It's not surprising that the gods are angry at all this blasphemous talk!' cried the pagans; whereupon Snorri *goði* of Helgafell commented drily, 'At what were the gods angry when all the lava on which we are now standing burned?'

Scientific research has now identified two Eldborg craters in the Svínahraun lava-field which erupted around the year 1000. This so-called 'Conversion Lava, (*Kristnitökuhraun*) was some distance from Hjalli; but it made a good story!

The Church at Thingvellir
The little church at Thingvellir is one of the humblest churches in Iceland; but for many Icelanders it is perhaps the most important, for it is directly descended from the first 'state' church to be built after the Conversion.

Snorri Sturluson in his *Ólafs Saga Helga* (*St Olaf's Saga*— part of *Heimskringla*) tells us that King Olaf Haraldsson of Norway (1014–30), later to be canonized as St Olaf, the patron saint of Norway, sent to Iceland a shipload of timber for the building of a church at Thingvellir, and a great bell to go with it. This would have been around the year 1016—a reminder that the new king of Norway was taking a close interest in Icelandic affairs. A few years later his half-brother, King Harald Sigurðsson—Harald Hardraade, who would die at Stamford Bridge during the abortive Norwegian invasion of England in 1066, just before the successful Norman invasion—sent a smaller bell for the same church at Thingvellir. These bells were later melted down, and a new bell for the Althing was cast from their metal in 1593. This bell at Thingvellir, 'Iceland's only possession', is used to powerful symbolic effect in Halldór Laxness's mighty trilogy of historical novels, *Íslandsklukkan* (*Iceland's Bell*).

St Olaf's church at Thingvellir was by no means the first to be built in Iceland after the Conversion; the sagas record the building of several churches by former pagan *goðar* soon after the year 999, as the priest-chieftains of the old order consolidated their positions in the new power-structures of the land. Gissur the White soon built a church on his ancestral lands at Skálholt, which would become the mother church of Iceland as the seat of the first Icelandic bishopric in 1056 (see Ch 11). At Borg in Borgarnes, in the year 1003, Thorsteinn Egilsson, son of the doughty warrior-poet Egill Skallagrímsson of *Egils Saga* (see Ch 14), built a church in whose graveyard Kjartan Ólafsson, the hero of *Laxdæla Saga*, was laid to rest in the same year. At hallowed Helgafell (see Ch 5), Snorri the Priest built the first church on Snæfellsnes, where Guðrún Ósvífursdóttir, the heroine of *Laxdæla Saga*, lies buried.

There was no formal Church organization in existence in Iceland at the time, and all these early churches were built under lay patronage by chieftains as a facility for their constituents and adherents, and to enhance their own status and prestige. *Eyrbyggja Saga* records that Gissur the White sent Snorri *goði* a priest to conduct services in the new church at Helgafell; and it also describes the incentives that were used to induce chieftains to build churches on their land: 'The priests promised that those who built churches would be granted as many places in Heaven as there was standing-room in their churches, and this proved a great inducement to church-building.'

These early vernacular churches were probably small turf-and-stone structures like the delightful little seventeenth-century chapel at Núpstaður, under the precipitous cliffs of Lómagnúpur on the south coast, which has been elegantly restored by the National Museum of Antiquities. The original Thingvellir church, however, would have been a stave-church in the Norwegian style (so called because the walls consisted of vertical tree-trunks split into two, like the Urnes church in the district of Sogn in Norway). It would have been intended to show Icelanders the proper style for churches and church services; and although it was a gift to the Althing, to the people of Iceland, it was also a symbol of Norwegian patronage, for St Olaf was as ambitious as his royal namesake Olaf Tryggvason had been to bring Iceland into Norway's imperial sphere by means of the Church.

The little church at Thingvellir was rebuilt several times over the centuries, most recently in 1859: it was in the 1859 church that King Christian IX of Denmark was housed when he came to Iceland in 1874 to celebrate at Thingvellir the millennium of the Settlement and to grant the Icelanders their first, limited measure of domestic self-government (see Ch 2).

In 1970 the Thingvellir church was restored by the National Museum to something like its 1859 condition, albeit with a rather alien copper roof. The simple interior, wood-panelled and with an arched ceiling, was repainted in its pristine colour-scheme of pastel greens and blues. The old pulpit, dating back to 1683, was handsomely restored. And the old altarpiece, a humble painting of the Last Supper made by a local craftsman in 1834, was found and returned to its rightful place.

And thereby hangs a tale as fascinating as any saga: a tale about an intrepid Victorian traveller called Mrs Mary Disney Leith.

Mrs Disney Leith (1840–1926) might well have stepped straight from the pages of a romantic novel. She was born three years after Queen Victoria came to the throne: Mary Charlotte Julia Gordon, the archetypal Victorian heiress. Her father was a baronet, her mother was the daughter of an earl. Her home was a magnificent seventeenth-century Jacobean manor house called Northcourt, in the village of Shorwell on the Isle of Wight: eighty rooms, fifteen acres of manicured parkland, and servants to attend to her every need. When her father died, he left her a fortune of £120,000. Mary Gordon was rich and beautiful, tiny and talented; and her cousin and childhood playmate, three years her senior, was destined to be a famous poet: Algernon Swinburne.

They grew up more or less together: he precociously intellectual but emotionally handicapped (he became a notorious alcoholic and pervert), she a tomboy determined to do everything he could do, only better. She studied music and became an accomplished pianist and church organist. Her grandmother had been a talented artist, so Mary Gordon became a painter, too. And she rode horses like a demon, thundering all over the Isle of Wight with Swinburne by her side. When Swinburne took to writing, Mary Gordon started writing too—and had her first novel published by the time she was nineteen.

And then, at the age of twenty-five, quite late but almost abruptly, she got married—but not to Swinburne, with whom she was in love, for he would have been regarded as a highly unsuitable match. Her husband was a veteran Scottish war-hero, Colonel (later General) Disney Leith of Aberdeen-shire: a black-bearded giant of a man, six foot six inches tall, who towered over his tiny bride by a foot and a half and was almost twice her age. He had lost an arm in India leading the heroic 'Forlorn Hope' assault on the fortress of Moultan, in the Punjab, during the second Sikh War in 1849.

For the next twenty-five years she lived the life of a devout and devoted Victorian chatelaine between great houses in Scotland and the Isle of Wight. She bore her husband six children—two sons and four daughters. But behind the strict façade of formal Victorian life she was unceasingly active in her imagination. She wrote nearly a dozen novels, and much poetry, and she developed a passion for a country she had never seen but had come to know through the writings and translations of Swinburne's friend, William Morris: the Land of the Sagas, Iceland. In her remote Scottish estates she taught herself Icelandic with the help of an Icelandic-Latin dictionary. She translated pious sagas of medieval Icelandic bishops, and dreamed of the day when she would visit Iceland herself.

In 1892 General Disney Leith died; and widowhood at the age of fifty-two seemed to give Mary Disney Leith a new lease of life. It was not long before she was fulfilling her cherished ambition of visiting Iceland. In 1894 she set off with her family and sailed from Leith on board the ss *Laura*, bound for Reykjavík.

It was the first of no fewer than eighteen visits: always travelling on horseback, intensely curious, intensely observant, intensely game. She wrote up her diary every night, dreaming of the heroic past of the sagas, affectionately describing and sketching this strange world of hospitable, cultivated peasants that was so totally different from her own aristocratic world of landed gentry.

There have been some 500 travel books written about Iceland, and of these, about 150 were by British travellers. Mrs Disney Leith was no exception; in 1897 she published a journal of her first impressions, *Three Visits to Iceland*. In it she described her first visit to Thingvellir and its little church, with a photograph of the old altarpiece: 'The altar is very tiny, but very neat, railed in; and above it is a very quaint, rude small painting of the Last Supper, with two texts relating to it inscribed in old Icelandic black-letter.'

This altarpiece had been painted on a panel of driftwood by a local farmer, Ófeigur Jónsson of Heiðarbær, in 1834. He was a good craftsman, an excellent smith in both metal and wood, a painter and decorator, a man of many skills and talents.

In the 1890s, however, the congregation of Thingvellir church felt that Ófeigur's 'Last Supper' was too naïve and primitive for their taste. A new fashion was sweeping Iceland—glossy biblical illustrations by the Danish painter Niels Anker Lund (1840–1922); no fewer than twenty-five of them are still extant in churches in Iceland. In 1896 or 1897, Thingvellir acquired an Anker Lund ('Christ Healing the Blind Man') at the princely cost of 300 *krónur*. When Mrs Disney Leith came to Iceland in 1899 she found the discarded old altarpiece going for a song, and promptly bought it for ten *krónur*.

She had a special personal reason for the purchase. In the previous year her younger son, Robert Thomas Disney Leith, had died of fever while on military service in India; he had seen and admired the old altarpiece during that first family visit to Iceland in 1894, and now she bought it for dedication to his memory in the church in which her family had always worshipped. And so the altarpiece travelled from its unassuming Lutheran home in Iceland, to be placed reverently amidst the rich Anglican sonorities and medieval treasures of St Peter's Church, Shorwell, on the Isle of Wight.

When the Thingvellir church was renovated in 1970, I was asked by the Director of the National Museum of Antiquities, Thór Magnússon, to try to discover the whereabouts of the missing altarpiece; no one in Iceland seemed to know where it had gone. With the help of Mrs Disney Leith's granddaughter, the Honourable Mildred Katherine Leith, who had accompanied her grandmother to Iceland six times as a child, I was able to trace it to the Isle of Wight. The congregation of Shorwell Church most generously agreed to return the altarpiece to Thingvellir, in exchange for a replica made by the National Museum. And so, in 1974, the Thingvellir altarpiece came home. It was a happy ending to an enchanting little modern saga.

CHAPTER 11

Skálholt: the First Bishopric

The Icelanders have no other king than their laws. Sinning is forbidden, and the wages of sin are death. The largest town in Iceland is called Skálholt.

(Adam of Bremen)

In 1957 a small crozier-head in bronze, shaped like the letter T (a Tau-cross, as it is called), was found by chance at Thingvellir when a trench was being dug to take underground cables. It was lying buried some half a metre below the surface. Because of its style it has been confidently dated to the middle of the eleventh century, which made it about 900 years old when it was discovered—the oldest crozier of Scandinavian make in existence. The head of the staff, made of cornel wood, was still in the socket.

How did a bishop's crozier come to be lost at Thingvellir? Bishops are not normally prone to such carelessness. But immediately after the Conversion of Iceland, times were far from normal. There was no major social upheaval, in that the changeover from pagan *goði* to Christian chieftain and churchman seems to have gone remarkably smoothly. But the Church itself had to be built up from nothing; and to that end, the Archbishop of Hamburg/Bremen sent a succession of missionary bishops to Iceland, for the see of Bremen had overall responsibility for church affairs in the North at that time.

The most significant of the early bishops who came to Iceland was an Englishman, a Benedictine monk called Rudolph (Hróðólfur), a kinsman of the saintly English king Edward the Confessor. He arrived in Iceland in the year 1030 and made his base at the farm of Bær, in the heart of the

Borgarfjörður district. Today it is an unassuming little place, just a scatter of houses with a community centre, a petrol service station, and a brand-new church; but its place in the Iceland Saga is assured because it was at Bær that Bishop Rudolph established the first known school in Iceland. Rudolph stayed at Bær for nineteen years; he returned to England in 1049 and was appointed Abbot of Abingdon by his royal kinsman, but he left three monks at Bær to carry on the work he had started. They seem to have founded some sort of cloister or monastic community there, but it did not last for very long.

Before the Conversion, Icelanders had known no form of writing, no alphabet, other than runes. Although runes could easily have been used for writing books, there is no evidence that they ever were—their chief use was for monumental inscriptions. It was missionary bishops like Rudolph who brought the Roman alphabet to Iceland. What is more, the basic script they brought with them had two letters that did not exist in Latin: the letters for the sound of *th* (both hard and soft)—ð (eth) and þ (thorn). These Anglo-Saxon letters no longer appear in modern English, but are still part of the Icelandic alphabet. Thus, when the Icelanders came to write their own books and sagas in the vernacular, it was the basic English insular minuscule script that they used.

Various other foreign bishops who worked in Iceland in the first decades after the Conversion are known by name. One was an Englishman called Bernhard the Book-Learned (*bókvísi*), who was sent by St Olaf of Norway to superintend the church at Thingvellir. Another was an Irishman called John (Johannes Scotus, Bishop of Mecklenburg, who was later martyred in Wendland in 1066). There was also another Bernhard, a German, who stayed for some twenty years at Stóra-Giljá, the family home of Thorvaldur Far-Farer (see Ch 9), and was renowned for consecrating local springs and wells and boulders and bells.

Apart from a brief list of names in *Íslendingabók*, the main source of information about these early itinerant bishops is a book with the charming title of *Hungrvaka* (*Appetizer*), which was written about 1200, at the dawn of the saga-writing age. It is a synoptic history of the first five bishops of Skálholt, designed not only to tell the story of how Christianity grew up in Iceland, but also to encourage young people to read books written in their native language, on law, history, and genealogy.

Hungrvaka says that in addition to the official missionary bishops there were various 'imposters' and 'heretics'; some were simply adventurers who were chancing their luck in a pioneer society where there was not yet any firmly established church structure or authority, while others seem to have been freelance missionaries from the Orthodox Church of Poland, trying to gain a foothold in Iceland. Either way, they were considered not only a nuisance but a threat:

> They preached a less rigorous Christianity, and thus became popular among the wicked, until Archbishop Adalbert of Bremen sent letters to Iceland forbidding all men to accept their teaching, and said that some of them were excommunicated and that they had all gone to Iceland without his leave.

It is tempting to suppose that the bronze crozier-head found at Thingvellir had belonged to one of these maverick bishops, and was broken and lost during a scuffle at the Althing when their right to preach there was forcibly called into question.

Bishop Ísleifur: the First Icelandic Bishop

The universal Catholic Church brought Iceland into the mainstream of European literature and learning. Iceland ceased to be a remote outpost of civilization, a place of refuge. But the Church that grew up in Iceland was remarkable for its intensely national character; Europeanism was quickly and eagerly absorbed, but equally quickly was translated into Icelandic, both literally and metaphorically. And this was because its leaders and its most prominent teachers were native Icelanders. Young Icelanders went

Mount Hekla, the most celebrated volcano in Iceland. It was an eruption in 1104 that devastated the valley of Thjórsárdalur and preserved the Settlement Age farms under a deep shroud of volcanic ash.

The Commonwealth Farm in Thjórsárdalur: back view of the modern reconstruction of the excavated farm of Stöng, showing the two side-chambers off the main long-house.

abroad to study and become priests, but they came back still Icelandic at heart. They belonged to families which cherished their traditions and their ancestry, and came home to organize their own schools. It became fashionable to be educated, not only in strictly religious studies but also in all the other branches of learning—science, mathematics, geography, history, astronomy, grammar and poetics. These were the young people to whom books like *Hungrvaka* were specifically addressed.

The man who blazed the trail for the future of the native Church was Gissur the White of Skálholt, the chieftain who had led the Christian coup at the Althing. One of his political allies at the time was Thóroddur Eyvindarson, the *goði* from Hjalli in Ölfus, whose daughter Thórdís became Gissur's third wife. In the year 1005, Gissur and Thórdís had a son called Ísleifur. He was the only son of their marriage, and like all late offspring he must have been the apple of his father's eye. Yet when Ísleifur was only five or six years old his father travelled with him to the renowned convent school of Herford, on the river Weser in Westphalia (now in West Germany), and handed him over to the abbess Godesti there to be educated for the Church. It must have meant a huge personal sacrifice; but Gissur the White knew which way history was heading. He knew what power-politics were about, and he knew that the Church would soon become a power in the land. By sending his child to be educated abroad for the priesthood, Gissur was taking a significant dynastic stake in the future—knowing also that he probably would not live to see his son again.

Around the year 1030, Ísleifur Gissurarson returned home as an ordained priest. Gissur was dead by then and lay buried in the little church he had built at Skálholt soon after the Conversion. Ísleifur inherited the family estate and the once-pagan office of *goði* that his father had enjoyed, thus becoming the first Icelandic chieftain in holy orders: the first trained cleric to emerge from the native aristocracy.

At Skálholt, Ísleifur established a proper parish ministry, and a proper school for ordinands:

And when the chieftains and other good men saw that
Ísleifur was much more able than those other clerics who
were to be found here in Iceland, many of them sent their
own sons to him for their education and had them
ordained as priests.

(Íslendingabók)

Two of Ísleifur's pupils later became bishops. One was his
cousin, Kolur Thorkelsson, who was appointed Bishop of Vík
(Oslo) in Norway—a remarkable tribute to the learning of
the young Icelandic Church. The other was Jón Ögmundarson, who in 1106 was appointed the first bishop of the
northern see of Hólar (see Ch 13).

In those early days the doctrine of celibacy for the clergy,
which had sprung up at the monastery of Cluny in France in
the tenth century, had not yet reached Iceland; and Ísleifur
Gissurarson needed a wife. On the advice of his kinsmen (as
was the custom when marriage contracts were to be arranged)
the choice fell upon a girl called Dalla, the daughter of a
prosperous farmer from Ásgeirsá, up north in Víðidalur. A
charming story about the courtship is told in the *Tale of
Bishop Ísleifur*, which is preserved in the great codex of saga
material called *Flateyjarbók*. According to this late source,
when Ísleifur made a formal visit to present his proposal of
marriage, Dalla's father insisted that Ísleifur would have to
come and live in the north if he wished to marry Dalla;
Ísleifur, however, felt that he could not abandon his parish
work at Skálholt, and took his leave. As was right and proper
in those days, Dalla herself had not been present when her
marriage prospects were being discussed—she was outside,
busily at work on top of a hayrick. She saw Ísleifur departing,
and when she was told who he was, and what his errand had
been, she sent messengers to bring him back: 'It is my
ambition to have the best husband in Iceland, and to have by
him the best son ever born in Iceland.'

And so Ísleifur and Dalla married, and settled at Skálholt,
and did Iceland proud with the sons they had; for one of them
was the great Bishop Gissur Ísleifsson, who was to succeed his

father at Skálholt in 1082, and another was Teitur Ísleifsson, who founded another Icelandic school at Haukadalur and there tutored the young Ari Thorgilsson, the future author of *Íslendingabók* (see Ch 12).

In his late forties, Ísleifur was unanimously elected Bishop of Iceland, presumably at the Althing in 1053. He was the obvious choice—probably the only choice, indeed. He set off for the Continent to seek consecration. On his way to Rome he visited the court of the Holy Roman Emperor, Henry III, to whom he presented a live polar bear from Greenland—a spectacular novelty for the courts of Europe in those days, and every bit as newsworthy as giant pandas from China nowadays. Early next spring he was received by the Pope, Leo IX, who approved his election and sent him with papal missives to Archbishop Adalbert in Bremen for consecration. After some delay, Ísleifur was duly consecrated bishop on Whitsunday, 26 May 1056.

Apart from the Icelandic sources about Ísleifur, we have a contemporary account of his consecration written by a German cleric called Adam of Bremen, who around 1075 compiled in Latin a monumental *History of the Archbishops of Hamburg/Bremen*. He called Ísleifur a most saintly man: 'The Icelanders respect their bishop as though he were a king, and the whole nation obeys his command . . . Sinning is forbidden, and the wages of sin are death.'

Alas, this was no more than wishful thinking. Ísleifur's episcopacy, which lasted twenty-four years, was by no means an easy one. The see he established at Skálholt had no revenues, and was always short of money and resources. There was famine, and times were hard. Contrary to Adam of Bremen's pious comment, sinning was rampant and morality, both private and public, was lax, according to *Hungrvaka*: 'He suffered much, and in many ways, during his period of office because of the people's disobedience.'

On one occasion he had to censure the Law-Speaker, no less, for marrying both a mother and her daughter, although we are not told whether the marriages were concurrent or consecutive. Lawlessness and violence abounded, no less than in pagan times. Ísleifur's personal piety and goodness were always manifest, however; he healed the sick with the laying on of hands, and he could make spoilt beer drinkable by blessing it. On his deathbed in July 1080, when asked who his successor should be, Ísleifur's sense of disappointment and frustration over his twenty-four arduous years came to the surface: 'He said they would find it hard to get a bishop in Iceland if they did not promise to show his successor more honour and obedience than they had shown him.'

Bishop Gissur Ísleifsson

Ísleifur's successor was his eldest son, Gissur—and he had clearly taken his father's dying words to heart. From his description in *Hungrvaka*, he was exactly the sort of son that his mother Dalla had dreamed of having:

> Gissur was a tall, well-built man with bright eyes set well apart, noble in bearing and the kindliest of men, power-ful both physically and intellectually, and well skilled in all manly accomplishments. During his father's lifetime he had been a merchant and had travelled widely, consorting with men of rank and title wherever he went and held in high esteem by them. Harald Sigurðsson [Harald Hardraade] was King of Norway at the time, and he told Gissur that he considered him eminently fitted for any rank he might choose.

Like his father, Gissur had been educated in Germany and ordained to the priesthood. But his life-style was much more that of a secular chieftain. At his father's death, the people of Iceland begged him to become their next bishop, but Gissur declined at first: 'But in the end he agreed to accept the burden of office, when all the chieftains had promised that they would keep all God's commandments in accordance with his preaching.'

Bishop Gissur proved to be a highly successful leader and politician, and quickly won the people's admiration and respect: 'Everyone would sit or stand as he requested, whether young or old, rich or poor, man or woman, and it would be true to say that he was both king and bishop over Iceland as long as he lived.'

It was as a social and political reformer that Gissur made his mark. His major achievement was to place the Church on a secure and well-organized footing. Gissur handed over the whole Skálholt estate and its revenues to the Church in perpetuity as an episcopal see; and in 1096 he steered through the Althing a new law that introduced the principles of tithes to Iceland—the first country in northern Europe to do so. Tithes were to be levied from all self-supporting farmers, and were to be divided four ways: a quarter to the bishopric, a quarter to the priests, a quarter to the poor, and a quarter to the church buildings. Since nearly all church buildings in the country were owned by the chieftains, who also supplied the churches with priests, the new law was of great financial advantage not only to the bishopric but to the chieftains who maintained feudal rights over the churches on their estates. No wonder the chieftains at the Althing were happy to pass the measure!

From now on, Skálholt became the spiritual and cultural and intellectual capital of the nation. Gissur built a new church to replace the church built by his grandfather, and encouraged secular chieftains to come to Skálholt to be educated and ordained as priests.

Adam of Bremen wrote that 'The largest town in Iceland is called Skálholt.' It was never a town in the literal sense of the term; but large it certainly became. In the middle of the twelfth century, Bishop Klængur Thorsteinsson (1152–76) added immeasurably to the prestige of Skálholt by building there a magnificent timber cathedral that matched any other building in Scandinavia for size. Klængur's medieval cathedral was an act of sheer extravagance, a noble stave-church built with two ship-loads of Norwegian timber. There was even concern that he would bankrupt the bishopric altogether—especially when the consecration was celebrated with unparalleled pomp and ceremony, and a dinner for more than 800 guests. The cathedral and its associated school became the nearest thing to a town that Iceland was to possess for centuries, a busy self-sufficient seminary of the soul and the body politic, housing some two hundred people. For seven centuries, Skálholt was a powerhouse of learning and literature, until the see was transferred to Reykjavík in 1797 (see Ch 2); after that, all the grandeur of the past became just a memory. The last timber cathedral on the site, dating from the seventeenth century, was dismantled, and all of its timbers and most of its church treasures were sold off by auction, and nothing remained at Skálholt except a dilapidated little parish church.

Bishop Páll's Coffin

Exactly 900 years after the consecration of Ísleifur Gissurarson as Iceland's first bishop in 1056, the foundation stone of a new memorial church was laid at Skálholt. As part of the preparation for this project, a team of archaeologists led by the late Dr Kristján Eldjárn (then Director of the National Museum, later to be elected President of Iceland, 1968–80) explored the whole area of the medieval church and churchyard. They found clear and unexpected evidence of the prodigious size of Bishop Klængur's church, which had burnt down in 1309; it was fifty metres long, nearly twice the length of the memorial church that was to be built there.

While the excavation of the cathedral foundations was in progress, one of the volunteer helpers at the dig jarred his spade on what seemed to be a huge boulder at a depth of some two feet; the volunteer was the brilliant young Icelandic playwright, Jökull Jakobsson (1933–78), who later liked to claim that it was the greatest theatrical stroke of his career. As Jökull scraped away the soil round the stone to try to free it from the ground, he realized that it was even larger than he had thought; it was obvious, moreover, that it had been deliberately shaped by a mason or sculptor. Dr Eldjárn and his colleagues were summoned to the spot, and identified it as the corner of a stone coffin. A few hours later it stood clear: it was a magnificent sarcophagus carved from a solid block of sandstone, unadorned but handsomely shaped.

A few days later, on 30 August 1954, the lid of the coffin

was raised at a formal ceremony at Skálholt. Inside lay the skeleton of a middle-aged man of medium height. At his right shoulder lay the head of a bishop's crozier with a carved crook of walrus ivory; the motif shows a lioness breathing life into her new-born cubs. There was no episcopal ring on his hand, however, and the probable explanation is that it had been stolen by grave-robbers, for the crozier itself had been crudely scraped with a knife as if to see whether it was made of precious metal. The skull rested on a stone pillow, and dust from the underside of the coffin lid had settled over it, giving it a golden hue.

For anyone who knew the sagas as intimately as Dr Eldjárn did, there could be no doubt about the identity of the skeleton: Bishop Páll Jónsson (1196–1211), one of the greatest of the chieftain-bishops of the golden age. A saga was written about him (*Páls Saga Biskups*) soon after his death, by the same anonymous author who wrote *Hungrvaka*: 'He had a fine stone coffin made, in which he was laid when he died.'

Páll Jónsson was the only Skálholt bishop to be buried in a sarcophagus. Through his saga we also know about his crozier, the only medieval crozier of specifically Icelandic make that has survived, because we are told that all the ecclesiastical carvings at Skálholt were done by a woman called Margrét the Skilful (*hin haga*), who is described as the finest craftswoman of her time.

He was an extraordinary man, and an extraordinary bishop, this Páll Jónsson. He was born to wealth and education, the illegitimate son of the most powerful chieftain in Iceland, Jón Loftsson of Oddi, grandson of the historian Sæmundur the Learned (see Ch 12). Jón Loftsson's mother had been a princess of the Norwegian blood royal—Thóra, the illegitimate but formally acknowledged daughter of the amorous King Magnus Bare-Legs of Norway (1093–1103). Jón Loftsson was enormously proud of his royal ancestry, which added to the prestige conferred by his huge wealth; indeed, he was known to his contemporaries as the uncrowned king of Iceland, *princeps patriae*. The only rival to his unofficial authority in Iceland was the Bishop of Skálholt, a saintly, ascetic man called Thorlákur Thórhallson (1178–93), who was declared a saint by the Althing although not by the Pope (in 1985, however, he was recognized by the Vatican as a saint). Bishop Thorlákur challenged the right of lay chieftains like Jón Loftsson to own churches and their revenues, as they had done since the Conversion; Jón Loftsson, who owned several churches, resisted the bishop's claim, and won. But there was another and more intimate reason for the hostility between Jón Loftsson and Bishop Thorlákur. The bishop did everything he could to raise the standard of morality both of clergymen and laymen, amongst whom concubinage was prevalent. It so happened that Bishop Thorlákur's own sister, Ragnheiður, was Jón Loftsson's mistress. One of the children she bore him was Páll Jónsson.

As a young man, Páll Jónsson was groomed for chieftaincy. He was educated in England, where he took minor orders as a deacon, but he had no intention of making a career in the Church. He was the traditional Icelandic gentleman scholar *par excellence*, one of the best educated men of his day, a fine singer, and a skilled composer of Latin verse.

When Bishop Thorlákur died in 1193, the lay chieftains looked for a successor amongst one of their own—someone who would not disturb the old order by making too many demands on the traditional office of chieftaincy and its perquisites. Their choice fell upon the reluctant chieftain of Oddi, the illegitimate son of Jón Loftsson and the late bishop's sister; and one of Páll Jónsson's first tasks as bishop was to grant permission for his uncle Thorlákur to be invoked as a saint.

However bizarre or even cynical Páll's election as bishop might have seemed, his episcopacy was regarded as highly successful. He did a great deal to beautify the cathedral at Skálholt and to encourage cultural activity. It was under his patronage at Skálholt that *Hungrvaka* was written. He was admired for his many accomplishments and for his princely hospitality, and when he died in 1211 he was universally mourned. According to *Páls Saga*, the earth shook and the skies wept at his death. By an extraordinary coincidence, on the very day that his coffin was opened again, on 30 August 1954, the heavens opened again in a cloudburst so sudden and so torrential that no one who attended the ceremony will ever forget it.

His coffin now lies in the crypt of the new memorial church at Skálholt. The crypt is approached through an underground passage which once led from the medieval cathedral to the complex of school buildings that have now all disappeared without trace. The new church above it is a neo-Romanesque building with a grey tiled roof and a severely austere interior, a monument to modernity. The altarpiece is a towering, impressionistic mosaic of Christ by the late Nína Tryggvadóttir (1913–68), the stained-glass windows are abstracts by Gerður Helgadóttir (1928–75). The floor is parquet, the bells are all rung by electricity. Amidst all these *objets d'art*, however, the most telling objects, to my mind at least, are the relics from the past: the chandelier and the candlesticks, the seventeenth-century side-altar—and, above all, a sturdy old pulpit adorned with representations of Jesus and the Apostles. That pulpit is a poignant reminder of one of Skálholt's most memorable bishops, the man who built the timber cathedral that stood there from 1650 until the end of the eighteenth century: Bishop Brynjólfur Sveinsson (1639–74).

Bishop Brynjólfur

In the seventeenth century, Bishop Brynjólfur Sveinsson stood head and shoulders above all his contemporaries, a great leader of men, intellectually formidable and physically impressive. He was a big, thunderous man, with a mop of red hair and a magnificent red forked beard that flowed over his chest and shoulders. He had a sonorous pulpit voice, an autocratic and majestic manner, a stern face—and a heart of gold. But for all his outstanding qualities as a churchman and a scholar, it is the personal tragedy of his life that has made him unforgettable in the hearts of all Icelanders.

He became bishop reluctantly, and only at the insistence of the King of Denmark (Iceland had by then become a Danish colony). He had intended to devote himself entirely to scholarship, for he was highly educated and exceptionally well versed in Greek and Latin and Disputation as well as in the saga literature of Iceland, and he was a keen collector of saga manuscripts. But when the call to Skálholt came in 1639 he threw himself into the task with boundless drive and determination. He proved himself an exemplary manager of church affairs, and did much to raise the education and moral standards of the clergy. He spared no effort or expense in the building of his new cathedral, using only the finest craftsmen and the choicest of imported timber; and once again, after centuries of decline, Skálholt and its school became the cultural powerhouse of Iceland.

As a churchman his preaching from the painted pulpit in Skálholt cathedral was fiery, but his Protestantism was unbigoted. He was proud of the fact that he was descended on his mother's side from the last Catholic bishop, Jón Arason, who had been summarily executed with two of his sons at Skálholt in 1550: 'The medieval church,' he used to say, 'had indeed a scabby head, but Luther took a curry-comb to it and scraped off hair and scalp and all.' In an age notable for its hysterical persecution of suspected witches, Brynjólfur Sveinsson was a humane and steadying influence; in an age of economic decline, his administration of the diocese gave Skálholt a soundly-based prosperity.

He lived his life with tremendous relish. He enjoyed his position, and his name—Brynjólfur, a compression of the words *brynjaður úlfur*, 'mail-clad wolf'—and he would mark his books with the monogram LL, standing for *lupus loricatus*.

Brynjólfur was always helping young people who showed promise but lacked means; for instance, he paid for the education of a promising young Icelander whom he met in Copenhagen called Hallgrímur Pétursson (1614–74), who was to become Iceland's greatest hymn-writer. But another of his young protégés was to bring him nothing but tragedy and bitter sorrow. His name was Daði Halldórsson, a personable youngster who was the son of his oldest friend, the pastor at nearby Hruni. The bishop educated him at Skálholt, and gave him advancement by making him his personal attendant; and therein lay the seeds of the tragedy.

Bishop Brynjólfur had seven children. Of these, only two survived infancy—a son, Halldór, and a daughter, Ragnheiður. Ragnheiður meant the world to her father: a strikingly beautiful and intelligent girl, highly educated and exceptional in every respect. In 1658, when she was seventeen years old, her father appointed young Daði Halldórsson to be her tutor. Not surprisingly, perhaps, these two attractive young people were soon on rather more than a strict teacher-pupil relationship, and in the spring of 1661 rumour started going the rounds in the big household at Skálholt that they were having a love affair.

Bishop Brynjólfur was thunderstruck when the rumour reached his ears, and he refused to believe that his beloved daughter could have been so wicked. He asked her point-blank if she had had carnal knowledge of the young man. Ragnheiður denied the charge vehemently. Her father wanted to clear any slur that might attach itself to her, and to that end, for the sake of her honour and the honour of his office, he asked her to swear to her innocence before the church council at Skálholt. Ragnheiður was horrified at the suggestion, and begged her father to spare her this humiliation; but Brynjólfur insisted on putting public honour before private feelings, and on 11 May 1661 Ragnheiður Brynjólfsdóttir swore the oath:

> I swear to Almighty God with my hand on the Holy Book that I, Ragnheiður Brynjólfsdóttir, am still at this moment a maiden as pure and untainted of lechery or fornication as when I came into this world from my mother's womb. May God have mercy on me, for this oath is true, or else punish me if I lie.

And that, as far as the bishop was concerned, was surely that. In the autumn of that year, Ragnheiður went on an extended visit to her kinsfolk at Bræðratunga; and then, one evening in February, messengers came to Skálholt from

Bræðratunga to tell the bishop that his daughter had given
birth to a son on the night of Saturday, 15 February 1662,
some forty weeks after taking the oath of purity. The bishop
seems to have had no inkling that she was expecting a baby;
he sat in stunned silence, then groaned a quotation from the
Pharaoh Psammetichus, founder of the Saïte dynasty in
ancient Egypt: *Mala domestica majora sunt lacrymis*—
'Family misfortunes lie too deep for tears.'

Had Ragnheiður compounded her sin by perjury? Had she
lied about her virginity on that fateful day in May 1661?
Ragnheiður herself claimed afterwards that she had only
given herself to Daði for the first time that very night, in a fury
of shame and bitterness about the ordeal her father had
forced her to endure, and that the child had been conceived
then, nine months earlier. Most Icelanders would like to
believe her; but her father's rage and mortification were
boundless. Most of his anger he turned against his protégé,
Daði, the attractive scoundrel who, he believed, had seduced
his daughter (and soon afterwards, to make matters even
worse, a serving-girl at Skálholt also had a baby by him). Daði
was banished from Skálholt, and made to pay such swingeing
damages that he was financially ruined for life.

The baby boy, Thórður, was taken away from his mother
and put into fosterage. Ragnheiður was never to see him
again. She was brought back to Skálholt, where she was
forced to do public penance, kneeling half-naked on the floor
in the middle of the great cathedral her father had built so
lovingly.

Grief-stricken and broken in spirit, the poor girl languished
at Skálholt for a year. Her only consolation was a manuscript
copy of the *Passion Hymns* of Hallgrímur Pétersson, her
father's other protégé, which he sent her 'as a token of dear
friendship in the love of Christ'. By now she had tuberculosis,
the scourge of Iceland in those days, and on 23 March 1663
she died. She was twenty-two years old.

Three years later, Brynjólfur's son, Halldór, also died, at
Yarmouth in England. Having failed as a scholar he had
become a merchant seaman and spent some years in Norfolk,

where he became friendly with Sir Thomas Browne's household; in December 1666, tuberculosis killed him, too.

Now Bishop Brynjólfur's only surviving descendant was his grandson, Thórður, the illegitimate boy whose conception had caused so much grief and sorrow. In 1667, Brynjólfur made the child his sole lawful heir—thus making him the richest little boy in Iceland; and on to this ill-begotten child he poured all of his troubled love. Thórður became the centre of his universe, especially after his wife died in 1670.

But sorrow had not wreaked its full revenge, even yet. In July 1673, when the boy was only eleven years old, he too died at Skálholt, of tuberculosis.

Bishop Brynjólfur's tragedy was complete. In failing health he handed over the bishopric to a colleague and successor, and on 5 August 1675 he died.

CHAPTER 12

The First Historians

En hvatki es missagt es í fræðum þessum, þá es skylt at hafa þat heldr, es sannara reynisk.

But if anything is mistaken in this book, one should prefer whatever proves to be more accurate.

(*Íslendingabók*)

The place-name of *Oddi* simply means, in Icelandic, 'Point': a point of land, now smothered in black volcanic sand and studded with clumps of purple thyme, which lies in a triangle between the rivers Rangá and Thverá in the southlands. In early times, Oddi was one of the most renowned and prosperous manor farms in all Iceland. It was the family home of the Oddaverjar, the Men of Oddi, who dominated Icelandic politics in the twelfth century; it was also one of the great centres of culture and learning in the Iceland Saga.

There has been a church at Oddi since earliest Christian times. Legend has it (no doubt fuelled by the meaning of the place-name) that the siting of the first church, which was dedicated to St Nicholas, was inspired by the vision of a spear that was hurled down from the heavens, and where the spear-point stuck, the church was built. The present church, a substantial building erected in 1924 and extensively refurbished in 1953, has some interesting old pieces in its possession: a curious dove-and-globe baptismal font made by the celebrated craftsman Ámundi Jónsson of Vatnsdalur in Fljótshlíð some two hundred years ago; a bronze crucifix in the Romanesque style; and a beautiful silver-gilt chalice thought to date from around 1300, with eight panels depicting Jesus and some apostles and kings.

Many famous men have been pastors there, including the

poet Matthías Jochumsson (1835–1920) who wrote the hymn '*Ó, Guð vors lands*' ('God of our Land') which is now Iceland's national anthem. But its chief claim to historic fame is that it was home to three exceptional men who helped to mould the early history of Iceland: Sæmundur the Learned (*hinn fróði*), the first Icelandic historian we know by name; his grandson, Jón Loftsson, the 'uncrowned king' of Iceland in the twelfth century, and the father of Bishop Páll Jonsson (see Ch 11); and the young prodigy whom Jón Loftsson fostered at Oddi as a boy, the great historian and saga-writer, Snorri Sturluson (see Ch 14).

Sæmundur the Learned

Sæmundur Sigfússon (1056–1133) was born at Oddi in 1056, the year in which Iceland's first bishopric was established at Skálholt. He was educated abroad, either in Paris or, as some scholars now think, in Franconia in Germany. He returned to Iceland in his early twenties to take holy orders, and succeeded his father as the priest of Oddi and *goði* for the district. He rebuilt and enlarged the old church, and through good management greatly enhanced the prosperity of the estate and lifted it to its position of eminence.

Sæmundur never became a bishop, but he was an immensely influential figure in ecclesiastical circles. He was a close and lifelong friend of Jón Ögmundarson, the first Bishop of Hólar (see Ch 13), and was the power behind the scenes when the tithe law was pushed through the Althing of 1096 (see Ch 11). He was considered the most intellectually formidable man of his generation. Indeed, such was his erudition that he was given the nickname *hinn fróði*, 'the Learned', which was bestowed only on men renowned for their knowledge of the history and traditions of the ancient north.

It is as a writer of history that Sæmundur the Learned is most celebrated; yet not a word of anything he wrote has come down to us. His reputation rests solely upon the testimony of later writers, especially Ari the Learned, who credited him with being the first Icelander to write historical works, and cited him as an authority. It seems certain that Sæmundur wrote, in Latin, a now lost *History of the Kings of Norway*, which later historians all quarried for information. Less certainly, but equally plausibly to my mind, he is credited with penning genealogical and chronological notes about aspects of Iceland's early history and the first settlers.

Although nothing of Sæmundur's work has survived, it was cited directly or indirectly so often by later writers that he can assuredly be considered the first Icelandic historian. In that respect he was the grandfather, at least, of Icelandic historiography; the title of 'father' more properly belongs to his younger contemporary, Ari the Learned, for Ari was the first to write history not in Latin but in the vernacular, in Icelandic.

Such was Sæmundur's prodigious reputation for scholarship that he quickly became a legend, a living parable of the importance of learning as an end in itself. Anything and everything associated with ancient lore came to be associated with his name. This is why the *Poetic Edda* used to be referred to as *Sæmundur's Edda*; when the only surviving vellum manuscript of the *Edda* came into the hands of Bishop Brynjólfur Sveinsson of Skálholt (see Ch 11), he had no hesitation in ascribing its authorship to Sæmundur, and giving it a title to that effect: *Edda Sæmundi multiscii* (*Edda of Sæmundur the Learned*). It was this priceless manuscript, incidentally, that Bishop Brynjólfur sent to Denmark as a gift to the king, and which recently returned to Iceland as *Codex Regius* (see Ch 1).

In popular tradition, Sæmundur became known as a magician, the medieval equivalent, perhaps, of a scientist. Within a century of his death, stories were being written about his prowess as a wizard and a master of astrology, and he soon became a hero of folk-tale. Dozens of stories accrued round his name, in which he used his superior knowledge and wisdom to outwit the Devil.

During his studies abroad, it was said, Sæmundur was supposed to have attended the 'Black School' in Paris, where the Evil One was master and where pupils were taught the

Black Arts. The school itself was underground, and no daylight ever penetrated. No teacher was visible; but whatever the pupils wanted to know each evening was provided for them next morning in books with crimson letters that glowed in the dark. A hairy grey hand would appear through the wall with food every day. The course lasted three years, and no student was allowed to leave the building or glimpse the daylight throughout the time he was there. The Devil charged no fees, but it was understood that he would take the hindmost pupil to leave the building each year. When it came to the turn of Sæmundur's class, no one was eager to be the last one out; but Sæmundur nevertheless volunteered, to everyone's relief. He put on a huge sleeveless cloak. As the class filed up through the tunnel towards the door, a brilliant shaft of sunlight struck them, casting deep shadows. The Devil was waiting for Sæmundur to come out last; but as he reached out to seize him, Sæmundur said, 'I am not the last— do you not see the one behind me?'—and he gestured towards the shadow flapping on the wall behind him. The Devil grabbed at the shadow, while Sæmundur slipped past him and the door slammed at his heels. From that day onward Sæmundur always lacked a shadow, for the Devil refused to give it back.

The most telling of all the many folk-tales about Sæmundur and his brushes with the Devil concerns a contract that he made with the Evil One to get him to Iceland in a hurry. It is told in Jón Árnason's monumental collection of *Icelandic Folk-Tales* (*Íslenzkar þjóðsögur og Ævintýri*):

When Sæmundur and his companions graduated from the Black School, the living at Oddi fell vacant, and they each petitioned the king to be appointed to it. The king knew well enough the kind of men they were, and declared that he who reached Oddi first would get it.

Sæmundur summoned the Devil at once and said to him: 'Swim with me to Iceland, and if you get me ashore without wetting so much as the hem of my cloak, you may have me for your own.'

The Devil agreed. He changed himself into a seal, and set off with Sæmundur on his back. All the way across the ocean, Sæmundur read the Psalter. It did not take them long to come within sight of the coast of Iceland; and then, without warning, Sæmundur struck the seal on the head with the Psalter. The seal sank, and Sæmundur himself went into the sea and swam ashore. So the Devil missed his bargain, and Sæmundur got Oddi.

This folk-tale is immortalized by a sculpture by the veteran artist Ásmundur Sveinsson that stands on the lawn in front of the main University building in Reykjavík. It depicts Sæmundur raising his Psalter to strike, just as the seal is turning its head to look at him with a grin of premature triumph. For Icelanders, the ultimate defence against the darkness and the powers of darkness has always been the light of learning, as personified by Sæmundur Sigfússon of Oddi.

Ari the Learned

Ari Thorgilsson (1068–1148), the author of *Íslendingabók*, was born in the renowned saga manor farm of Helgafell (see Ch 5). He was the great-grandson of one of the most striking heroines in saga literature, Guðrún Ósvífursdóttir of *Laxdæla Saga*. His father, Thorgils Gellison, was drowned at sea while Ari was a small child, and Ari was then brought up at Helgafell by his grandfather, Gellir Thorkelsson. And what an upbringing for a child destined to become a great historian! Gellir Thorkelsson was the son of Guðrún and her fourth husband, and would have told the little boy countless tales of the life and loves of the most sensational saga heroine of them all.

Gellir Thorkelsson died at the age of eighty: sprightly to the last, he was on his way home from a pilgrimage to Rome. The estate of Helgafell passed to Ari's uncle, and the following year, in 1075, at the age of seven, Ari was sent away for schooling at Haukadalur, from which he graduated as an ordinand fourteen years later, in 1089.

Along with Skálholt and Oddi, the estate of Haukadalur

was one of the three great educational centres in the south of Iceland. It lies at the head of the valley of Haukadalur (Hawksdale); it's a lovely site, wide and green, and it used to be choice farming land until erosion soured its fruitfulness. Today the farm is abandoned, but there is still a charming country church there, originally built in 1842 but dismantled and totally rebuilt in 1939, which boasts a fine sculpted altar-piece depicting the Crucifixion, fashioned from pear-wood by the sculptor Ásmundur Sveinsson. The church is a symbol of a determined attempt to regenerate the wasted acres of Haukadalur; in 1938 the site was purchased by a wealthy Danish philanthropist, Kristian Kirk, who not only restored the old church but financed an extensive programme of tree-planting. When he died, he bequeathed the estate to the Forestry Commission, which has planted more than 600,000 trees there in order to re-create the woodlands that used to clothe the upper reaches of the valley in early Settlement days.

A few kilometres down the valley lies a seething silica basin of hotsprings. It is a magnet that draws every visitor from far and wide, for this is the site of the Great Geysir, the Great Gusher, which has given the word 'geyser' to the English language. Geysir is now a sort of geothermal park, an area of spectacularly intense activity: little mud-pots boiling away wickedly, translucent pools of exquisitely delicate colouring, venomous jets of steam hissing furiously at your feet, and dominating the whole lunar scene, the two most celebrated geysers in Iceland—Strokkur (The Churn), which spouts a tall column of boiling water every few minutes, and the Great Geysir itself, which has been quiescent for some time but is persuaded to 'perform' by the application of several kilos of soap every Saturday in the tourist season. It is an awesome sight—but it was not there in Ari's day. The Icelandic *Annals* for the year 1294 record a series of earthquakes in the area, during which 'large hotsprings appeared near Haukadalur, while others that had been there before disappeared'.

History in Haukadalur really began in the year 1025, when a man called Hallur Thórarinsson inherited the estate. He was thirty years old, a man of cosmopolitan experience, a merchant who had had close contacts with King Olaf Haraldsson (St Olaf) of Norway, and who was cited by Snorri Sturluson himself as an authority on St Olaf's reign (1014–30). He was not 'learned' in the conventional sense, in that he could neither read nor write, but he was blessed with a remarkable memory: he could remember being baptized at the age of three by the German missionary Thangbrand shortly before the Conversion of Iceland (see Ch 9). Hallur was nearly eighty years old when young Ari went to school at Haukadalur in 1075; his lively knowledge of European and Icelandic affairs, reaching right back to the turn of the century, was a vital factor in Ari's education.

The man who started the school at Haukadalur was another of Hallur's fosterlings: Teitur Ísleifsson, son of the first bishop of Iceland and brother of the second (see Ch 11). Like them, he was educated abroad. Teitur was Ari's tutor at Haukadalur, 'the wisest man I have known', according to Ari; and Snorri Sturluson would write: 'He taught Ari the priest, and passed on to him much learning, which Ari wrote about later.'

This education at the school for scholars in Haukadalur laid the basis of the historical erudition that would make Ari the Learned Iceland's first literary giant, the first historian to write in the vernacular. His only surviving work, *Íslendingabók* (*Book of Icelanders*), written in the 1120s, was the prototype of Icelandic historical writing:

> The priest Ari the Learned, the son of Thorgils Gellison, was the first man in this country to write down lore, both old and new, in the Norse language . . .
> I think his whole account most remarkable.
> (Snorri Sturluson: *Heimskringla*)

Íslendingabók is a very slim volume indeed, covering only a dozen printed pages. It is severely concise. It gives a very brief description of the Settlement of Iceland, naming only five of the original settlers—one outstanding individual for each of the four Quarters of Iceland, and the First Settler himself,

Ingólfur Arnarson. Ari traces the evolution of the Althing, and lists all the Law-Speakers in order to establish a skeletal chronology for Iceland's early history; but above all he gives a longish account, both vivid and carefully documented, of the Conversion and the growth of the Church. This in itself is hardly surprising, for Ari says in his Foreword that the book was written at the request of the two bishops of Iceland, and it seems to have been designed to provide an authoritative account of the place of the Church in Icelandic society. From the Foreword it is also clear that our version of *Íslendingabók* is a second, and shorter, edition, for Ari declares that he made some emendations at the suggestion of the bishops and with the advice of his fellow-scholar, Sæmundur the Learned, to whom he submitted the book for criticism.

The copy of *Íslendingabók* that has come down to us is not Ari's original manuscript. It only survives in two paper copies that were made by a clergyman in the seventeenth century— and even those had not been copied from the original, but from a vellum copy. Both Ari's original, and the manuscript from which the paper copies were made, have long since disappeared without trace, like so many others of the medieval manuscripts of the Iceland Saga.

Ari's towering reputation as the father of Icelandic history must rest on more than just *Íslendingabók*. Scholars are now convinced that *Íslendingabók* is a summary not only of Ari's history of Iceland, but of his other historical works. Ari the Learned, they believe, was the original author of the seminal work on Iceland's origins—*Landnámabók*, the *Book of Settlements*.

Very little is known about the life and career of Ari the Learned after he left Haukadalur as a newly-ordained priest. There is a possibility that he got the living at Staðastaður, a church on the southern arm of Snæfellsnes, for Ari was a Snæfellsnes man and we know that his grandson, at least, was the incumbent at Staðastaður. It is no more than a surmise, albeit a plausible one, that Ari himself served there; but that was enough to inspire the people of Snæfellsnes to erect a memorial stone to Ari the Learned at Staðastaður in 1981, inscribed with Ari's own celebrated proviso in the Prologue to *Íslendingabók*: 'But if anything is mistaken in this book, one should prefer whatever proves to be more accurate.'

Wherever it was that Ari the Learned lived after he left the school in Haukadalur in 1089 until his death at the ripe old age of eighty in 1148, he apparently played no noteworthy part in the public affairs of Church or State. But he clearly was not being idle, and it is tempting to suppose that he may have been attached to the bishopric of Skálholt, perhaps as the bishop's amanuensis; for Bishop Gissur Ísleifsson was the brother of his tutor at Haukadalur, and it was Bishop Gissur who had ordained him to the priesthood. Bishop Gissur, we know, spent much of his time traversing the country, organizing the parishes of the fledgling Church; and if Ari had accompanied him on these extensive visitations it would have provided him with a unique opportunity to amass historical, genealogical and topographical notes for later use. He may even have been commissioned to make a special survey of this kind, to go with the passing of the tithe law in 1096 (see Ch 11).

Be that as it may, Ari the Learned was undoubtedly applying his intellectual energies to scholarship in one capacity or another, to the 'learned works' (*fræði*) for which he was to become renowned—and that, scholars now agree, can only mean *Landnámabók*.

Landnámabók tells the stories of some 430 of the principal settlers—their land-claims, their farmsteads, their adventures, their ancestors in the old country and their descendants in the new. It is a systematic but not exhaustive account of the way in which the virgin land was colonized, district by district, Quarter by Quarter; and because the history of Iceland was the history of all Icelanders, rather than the preserve of an élite royal dynasty, *Landnámabók* contains a wealth of memorable characters and dramatic incidents that would form the basis for later saga-writers. It was a functional book, just as the *Domesday Book* in England in 1086 was functional; but whereas the *Domesday Book* was a bureaucratic register of land and farm ownership prepared by the Norman conquerors of England specifically for taxation purposes, in order to assess the realizable wealth of England, *Landnámabók* was essentially a historical register of Iceland's settlers. The study of genealogy had immense significance in a country whose fabric was closely woven on the loom of family kinships, and it was assiduously cultivated in schools as a special branch of learning.

It is almost as if the Icelanders felt a special mission to preserve the past of their own country and those of their Scandinavian kinsmen. Saxo Grammaticus, the Danish historian who wrote a Latin account of his own nation's story around the year 1200 (*Gesta Danorum*), had this to say of these 'industrious Icelanders':

> They are happy to spend their whole lives promoting knowledge about the deeds of other peoples. They take pleasure in learning and recording the history of all peoples, and they take just as much pride in describing the exploits of others as in performing them themselves.

The original version of *Landnámabók* (proto-*Landnámabók*, as scholars call the version they believe was compiled by Ari the Learned) is not strictly history in the modern sense of the term. Two centuries had already elapsed between the end of the Age of Settlement and the *Book of Settlements*, and much could have become distorted in that time. A landscape as varied and dramatic as Iceland's landscape inspires the imagination and encourages composition—not just the composition of books but the composition of ideas. Landscape provides a context for identity, and it was through the landscape of Iceland, vividly peopled and rationally explained, that *Landnámabók* gave the Icelanders their own sense of identity, on their own terms.

CHAPTER 13

Hólar: the Northern Bishopric

Hér mátti sjá um öll hús byskupsstólsins mikla iðn og athöfn.
Sumir lásu heilagar ritningar, sumir rituðu, sumir sungu,
sumir námu, sumir kenndu.

There was great industry to be seen in every building at the see:
some were reading holy scripture, some were writing, some
were singing, some were learning and some were teaching.

(*Jóns Saga Helga*)

On a green eminence in the lovely, mountain-girt valley of
Hjaltadalur that sweeps down towards Skagafjörður in the
north of Iceland, the white bell-tower of the cathedral church
of Hólar stands tall and proud as a beacon. The church itself is
the oldest in Iceland, built in the 1750s of red sandstone and
basalt, quarried from the mountain Hólabyrða that superin-
tends the site, although it is whitewashed now. There is an
agricultural college there now, too, a nest of neat white red-
roofed buildings. Serenity surrounds the place, and a gentle
air of busy-ness—the business of husbandry and the cultiva-
tion of young minds in its famous school. For many centuries,
Hólar has been regarded with profound affection by the
people of Iceland, especially northern Iceland. It used to be
Iceland's other bishopric; and long before modern Akureyri
developed as a major town, Hólar was the real capital of the
north, another cultural and spiritual powerhouse to rival the
renown of Skálholt itself as the home of the northern bishops
until 1798.

The bishopric was founded in 1106, exactly fifty years after
Skálholt; and it was the second bishop of Skálholt, Gissur
Ísleifsson, the great church administrator, who was respon-
sible for it. The people of the north had complained that

Skálholt was too far away for them, and in response to their appeals Bishop Gissur relinquished a quarter of his own diocese with all its revenues to establish a northern diocese at Hólar.

The first bishop appointed to the new see was a southerner called Jón Ögmundarson, who turned out to be an inspired choice. He had been trained at the school at Skálholt by the first bishop, Ísleifur Gissurarson, and then studied in Norway and Denmark; he had been to Rome, and had become imbued with the stern ideals of the monastic movement centred on the Abbey of Cluny. He was shrewd and tough-minded, dedicated to raising the intellectual and moral standards of both the clergy and the laity in his diocese. To that end he founded a school at Hólar which would have a tremendous effect on Iceland's cultural growth.

The story of his life and work at Hólar is told in a rather flowery biography, *Jóns Saga Helga* (*Saga of St Jón*), which was written early in the thirteenth century by a monk at the nearby monastery of Thingeyrar to celebrate the promotion of Bishop Jón to a sort of minor canonization that did not require, and never received, recognition from the Vatican.

Jón Ögmundarson was fifty-four years old when he was appointed bishop, and he threw himself into the task with tremendous energy. He built a cathedral, a huge timber stave-church in the Norwegian style, to replace the existing stone-and-turf chapel, and this cathedral stood for nearly three centuries, challenging even Skálholt for size. The builder was the most renowned craftsman in Iceland, Thóroddur Gamlason. But Bishop Jón's chief work, his most enduring monument, was the school that he founded at Hólar, the first school in the north. *Jóns Saga Helga* provides a charming picture of the activities at this school in Bishop Jón's days:

> There was great industry to be seen in every building at the see: some were reading holy scripture, some were writing, some were singing, some were learning and some were teaching. There was never any envy or discord amongst them, no strife or disputation; each

wanted only the best for the other, and obedience and humility reigned.

And when the signal for service was sounded, they would all hurry from their cells to the church, like busy bees bringing with them to the hive of Holy Church the sweet honey they had gathered in the delicious wine-cellar of holy scripture.

To be headmaster of his new school, Bishop Jón brought with him from abroad a learned young Swede called Gísli Finsson, who taught Latin and preached in the cathedral. Bishop Jón also had a great interest in music; he himself had an excellent singing voice, and now he appointed as his chaplain a Frenchman from Alsace-Lorraine called Ríkini, who taught singing and versification at the school; it was the first time that the glories of Gregorian chant were heard in Iceland.

Most of those who were to be the leading clerics of northern Iceland for the next generation were trained at Hólar. But it was not just the sons of chieftains who were educated there. *Jóns Saga* mentions a woman student, a 'chaste maiden' called Ingunn Arnórsdóttir, who was so proficient at Latin that she became a teacher there as well, taking classes in Latin grammar; she would listen to their compositions while she played draughts, or embroidered stories from the lives of the saints. Another extra-mural student (quite literally) was the church-builder himself, Thóroddur Gamlason; while he was working on the cathedral structure he would eavesdrop on the Latin class, and picked up the lessons so readily that he became a competent and noted scholar, and is thought to be the 'Thóroddur Runemaster' mentioned in the *Fourth Grammatical Treatise* as an expert on the ancient runic alphabet.

In his campaign to raise standards in the diocese, Bishop Jón demanded that everyone should know by heart the Lord's Prayer, *Credo* and *Ave Maria*, go to church regularly, and praise God seven times a day. Moral laxity was anathema to him. He knew the temptations of the flesh himself: he had been married twice before his appointment as bishop, and had had to get special dispensation from the Pope before being consecrated (his poor wife was relegated to the status of housekeeper). In an attempt to combat immorality and loose living, he tried to ban the popular pastime of singing erotic love-songs at public dances – the medieval equivalent of today's discos:

> This pastime was very popular before the saintly Jón became bishop: a man would sing to a woman in the dance amorous and lascivious ditties, while the woman would reply with love-songs to the man. This sport the bishop banned and prohibited strictly . . . but did not quite succeed in abolishing it.

To root out any vestigial pagan superstitions and practices, he condemned 'witchcraft and the black arts, incantations and magic, and all kinds of sorcery which deceived the eye'. In order to erase the 'bad old days'—literally—he changed the names of those days of the week that had been named after pagan gods: Tuesday (Týr's Day), Wednesday (Woden/Óðinn's Day), Thursday (Thór's Day) and Friday (Frigg's Day). In their place he substituted the more prosaic names that Icelanders still use—*þriðjudagur* (Third Day), *miðvikudagur* (Midweek Day), *fimmtudagur* (Fifth Day), and, as a reminder of Christian observance, *föstudagur* (Fast Day). The Sun and the Moon were considered innocuous enough, so he left Sunday and Monday, and happily he spared the Icelandic name for Saturday, *laugardagur*, which literally means 'Hotsprings Day', or more colloquially, simply 'Bath Night'!

Bishop Jón disapproved of any frivolity that might lead to lewdness. He once caught one of his younger students surreptitiously reading Ovid's licentious poem *Ars Amatoria*; he rebuked the child sternly, saying that frail human nature was sufficiently prone to carnal lusts without such filthy and libidinous incitements. The student was none other than Klængur Thorsteinsson, future bishop of Skálholt and builder of the great twelfth-century cathedral there (see Ch 11).

Bishop Jón's answer to the grosser forms of popular

entertainment like dancing and ballad-singing was to encourage the widespread use of books. We know that the headmaster of the Hólar school used a vernacular book of homilies from which he preached on feast-days in the cathedral. Bishop Jón was assiduous in ensuring a copious supply of edifying books in Icelandic—homilies, saints' lives, and so on—so that people could hear the Word in even the remotest parishes in their mother tongue. He established a brisk manuscript-making industry in the scriptorium at Hólar, with a number of copyists engaged full-time in the task of copying books for sale. It is entirely fitting that when he was lying on his deathbed in April, 1121, one of the last questions he was asked was what the price of a newly completed book should be. Alas, we will never know the answer. According to *Jóns Saga*, the good bishop used the occasion to demonstrate his prescience by announcing that he had had a premonition that the intended recipient had just died, and would have no need of the book now.

The Monastery of Thingeyrar
On the wide pasturelands by the shores of Húnafjörður, where Ingimundur the Old of *Vatnsdæla Saga* had beached his boat when he was looking for a place to settle (see Ch 3), there stands an imposing stone-built church, hard-hewn from the local basalt at enormous cost just over a hundred years ago: the church at Thingeyrar. It was built on the site where Bishop Jón Ögmundarson founded the first monastery in Iceland, in the year 1112, which would have enormous significance in the literary tradition of Iceland and thus has a special place in the cultural annals of the land. Thingeyrar was the first of twelve monasteries founded in Iceland in the twelfth and thirteenth centuries.

The present church is one of the most remarkable in Iceland. It was designed and built and financed entirely out of his own pocket by the farmer of Thingeyrar, a member of the Althing, between 1864 and 1877. It has an apsidal choir, and a barrel-vaulted ceiling painted blue and studded with a thousand golden stars. The altarpiece is a magnificent work, dating from the fifteenth century and made in Nottingham with relief figures in alabaster, which originally came from the monastery; it used to have wing-panels, but they were lost when it was so badly damaged in transit (it was to be sold abroad) that it was returned to Thingeyrar unsold. There is also a splendid canopied pulpit of Dutch make, with a matching font in Baroque style, dating from the seventeenth century. But the pride and joy of the church is the so-called Apostles Collection: a group of little statuettes of Christ and the Apostles, carved from oak in Germany in the late sixteenth century and brightly painted, which stand between the posts of the railing of the gallery. They are replicas; the originals were sold off at the turn of the century, but later presented to the National Museum. However, in 1983, enough money was raised locally to have a superb set of replicas made and ceremoniously installed where they belong.

Just beside the present church there is a confused muddle of grass-grown undulations, including an elliptical configuration measuring about twenty-five metres by twenty. Local tradition calls it the *Lögrétta*; it is a protected patch, and thought to be the remains of an open-air enclosure which was once the site of a district Thing—hence the name, Thingeyrar (Assembly Sandbanks). This Thing gave Thingeyrar strategic significance in early times; and that is why the site was chosen as an ecclesiastical centre by Jón Ögmundarson as he set about organizing the new see of Hólar.

The story of its beginnings is told in *Jóns Saga*, and conjures up an attractive picture of the new bishop, bursting with vigour despite his sixty years and sublimely confident in Divine provision for his diocese:

> Soon after Jón Ögmundarson had been installed in his see, hard times ensued: famine loomed, and the weather was so severe that there was no growth in the ground even by the month of May. So Bishop Jón visited the spring meeting of the Thing at Thingeyrar, and there, with the consent of all those present, he pledged, in

return for a good season, that a church and farm would be built there, with everyone present contributing. After making this vow, Bishop Jón threw off his cloak, and with his own hands he marked out the foundations for the church. In a trice, everything changed: before the week was out, all the ice that had brought on the famine had disappeared, and the earth grew fertile so quickly that within that same week, the pastures were almost ready to take sheep.

It was doubtless this signal token of Divine approval that inspired the foundation of a Benedictine monastery at Thingeyrar as well. Bishop Jón endowed it there and then with a portion of tithes, although it was not until 1133, twenty-one years later, that the first abbot was appointed. The monastery quickly grew rich on the bounty of land and sea—fine grazing, an abundance of salmon and trout and seabirds' eggs, and plenty of valuable driftwood. And as its prosperity grew, so did its literary and intellectual output.

By the middle of the twelfth century, learned literature was flourishing. Icelandic was being used in many branches of scholarship, to such an extent that around 1150 an anonymous scholar wrote a work known as the *First Grammatical Treatise* designed to provide a standard form of spelling for the language, based on the Latin alphabet which had been introduced from England. In this pioneering treatise, the author refers to the kind of books that were already available to the general reader: law-books, books on genealogy (like *Landnámabók*) and history, and translations of sacred writings.

In the second half of the twelfth century, the monks of Thingeyrar were playing a leading part in the composition of sagas as well, especially Kings' Sagas—men like Abbot Karl Jónsson with his contemporary biography of King Sverrir of Norway (see Ch 1), and two erudite and gifted monks, Gunnlaugur Leifsson and Oddur Snorrason, with sagas about King Olaf Tryggvason and King Olaf the Saint. It was Gunnlaugur Leifsson who wrote the saga of Bishop Jón

Ögmundarson, *Jóns Saga Helga*; the original version was written in Latin, because Gunnlaugur was seeking an international audience in his attempt to promote the bishop's sanctity, but it was quickly translated into Icelandic.

Many of the early Sagas of Icelanders are associated with the monastery of Thingeyrar, either actually written in the scriptorium there or classified as 'of the school of Thingeyrar'. The *Tale of Thorvaldur Far-Farer* was certainly written there, by the monk Gunnlaugur (see Ch 9); and so, in all probability, was *Vatnsdæla Saga* (see Ch 3). Also from Thingeyrar came the saga which is conventionally regarded as the oldest of the surviving Sagas of Icelanders, or Family Sagas: it is called *Heiðarvíga Saga* (*Saga of the Heath-Slayings*), and was written late in the twelfth century, around 1190 or so.

Heiðarvíga Saga

Heiðarvíga Saga is not one of the 'fashionable' sagas. It has only been translated into English once, by William Morris and Eiríkur Magnússon in their Saga Library (Vol 2, 1892) where it is appended to their translation of *Eyrbyggja Saga* (*The Story of the Ere-Dwellers*). It is a distinctly primitive saga, but it contains many of the robust themes that were to exercise the minds of later saga-writers, particularly the theme of blood-vengeance and feud.

In the saga we meet the brutal Víga-Styrr Thorgrímsson, the man associated with the Berserks' Lava in *Eyrbyggja Saga* (see Ch 5), and learn why he had such an evil reputation as a killer who never paid compensation for those whom he slew. One of the men he slaughtered without justification or justice left an orphaned boy called Gestur; when Styrr was asked to offer the boy compensation for his father's death, he mockingly offered a stunted grey lamb which could not grow wool. The boy was himself rather stunted in growth, and took the insult to heart. One evening Styrr happened to visit the house where the boy was being fostered; Gestur prepared a pile of damp firewood, and when Styrr complained that the fire was burning low, Gestur dumped the wet twigs on the fire; the house filled with smoke, and Gestur slipped behind Styrr's chair and buried an axe in his head: 'That's my thanks for the grey lamb.'

The central section of the saga deals with another vengeance. The main character now is a phlegmatic young man called Barði Guðmundarson, whose brother, Hallur, had been killed by two Icelanders while he was abroad in Norway. The killers themselves had subsequently lost their lives, so the feud had to be laid on their kinsmen. Barði seemed disinclined to take up the feud, but his mother never let him forget that his brother was still unavenged:

> That autumn Barði happened to sit down in the chair in which his brother used to sit. When his mother came in and saw this, she struck him hard in the face and ordered him to crawl out of the chair at once, and never dare to sit in Hallur's seat while he was still unavenged.

Barði's mother was Thuríður, a daughter of Ólafur the Peacock and granddaughter of Egill Skallagrímsson, a woman in whom the blood of the Vikings still boiled; she is the prototype of the avenging furies who appear in so many of the sagas, egging on their dilatory menfolk to the bloody business of revenge. Years later, when Barði and his brothers had still not made a move to avenge Hallur, Thuríður brought out her goad again. At breakfast one morning, when the rest of the household were given porridge as usual, she served her three sons with huge, unwieldy chunks of the shoulders of an ox. This irritated one of the brothers:

> 'You carve generous portions, mother, yet you do not usually dole out food in such rich measure. This lacks all moderation; have you taken leave of your senses?'
>
> 'That's nothing,' she replied, 'and there's no need for you to be surprised; because your brother, Hallur, was carved up into even larger pieces, and I never heard any of you comment much on that.'
>
> With each portion of meat she had served a stone. They asked her what she meant by it.

Aerial view of Skálholt, and the modern memorial church that replaced the old cathedral. In the background, the hill of Mosfell where the first settler in the district, Ketilbjörn the Old, made his home.

Hólar in Hjaltadalur: seat of the former northern diocese. The modern bell-tower stands beside the eighteenth-century church, flanked by the buildings of the modern school.

'You brothers have swallowed harder things than stones, because you still have not dared take vengeance for your brother Hallur . . .'

When the vengeance did eventually start, it escalated into a full-scale war between kinsmen and supporters of the two sides, which culminated in a pitched battle that raged across the high moorlands above Kjarradalur, in Borgarfjörður— the 'Heath-Slayings' of the title. In the complicated lawsuits that ensued, Barði was helped by Snorri *goði* of Helgafell (see Ch 5). He was outlawed for the killings, but managed to elude his enemies long enough to get safely away from Iceland; he joined the Viking equivalent of the Foreign Legion, the Varangian Guard in Constantinople, and eventually fell gloriously in battle.

Heiðarvíga Saga is considered the oldest of the sagas that have survived; but it is a bit of a miracle that it survived at all. It was immensely popular in the Middle Ages, but by the end of the seventeenth century, when antiquarians were scouring Iceland for old manuscripts, there was only one manuscript of it in existence. It was sent to the Royal Library in Sweden, from which it was borrowed by Árni Magnússon in Denmark for copying. By great good fortune, the librarian in Stockholm could not read Old Icelandic; he did not know where *Heiðarvíga Saga* ended and the next saga began, and he only sent the first part of *Heiðarvíga Saga*—about a third of the whole saga. Árni Magnússon promptly had it copied by his amanuensis, Jon Ólafsson; he then, like so many booklovers, conveniently forgot to return it to Stockholm. It was still in his library when the Great Fire of Copenhagen broke out in 1728, and both it and the copy were among the casualties.

In the aftermath of the disaster it was assumed that *Heiðarvíga Saga* had utterly perished for all time. Jón Ólafsson thereupon rewrote the section he had copied, relying only on his memory. It was a remarkable feat. Where he felt he might be paraphrasing, he wrote in brackets *mm*, for *mig minnir*, 'as I recall'; where he was confident of his memory, he wrote *ss*, for *segir sagan*, 'the saga says'.

Nearly fifty years later, another Icelandic scholar went to Stockholm to study and copy the Icelandic manuscripts in the Royal Library collection; and there he stumbled across the part of *Heiðarvíga Saga* that the Swedes had accidentally omitted to send to Copenhagen. One page of it was missing, however. And then, in 1951, that page turned up, too—it had been used for the binding of another book that was preserved in, of all places, the archives of the National Library in Reykjavík!

Heiðarvíga Saga is a classic story of blood-feud and revenge and all its terrible ramifications; but the story of the manuscripts of *Heiðarvíga Saga* is itself a classic—a supreme example of the hazards of survival with which the saga literature was beset down the centuries. We can only guess at just how much has been lost without any trace at all.

The Wedding at Reykhólar in 1119
Monasteries like Thingeyrar, Munka-Thverá (the former home of Víga-Glúmur, see Ch 6), Möðruvellir in the north and Helgafell in the south, played a vital part in the composition, encouragement and production of saga literature. But from earliest times, the writing of sagas was never a Church monopoly. Certainly, literacy would be achieved through church schools, and the church authorities encouraged as many people as possible to learn to read and write; but the saga writers were just as likely to be educated laymen as trained clerics.

Throughout the twelfth century, while scholars like Ari Thorgilsson the Learned were pioneering the writing of history and genealogy in the vernacular—what one might call 'official' literature—secular saga-entertainment was growing as a popular pastime for the people. It was no doubt given a boost by Bishop Jón's campaign against dancing and ballad-singing. There is intriguing evidence that sagas were being written to be read aloud at special entertainments from quite early on in the century.

In the year 1119 a celebrated wedding-feast was held at the

manor farm of Reykhólar, on the northern shore of Breiðafjörður, at the head of Berufjörður. From the earliest days of
Settlement, Reykhólar was considered one of the most prosperous estates in all Iceland (it is now owned by the state).
Parties at Reykhólar were apt to be memorable affairs, and
the wedding-feast in 1119 was no exception.

The story is told in *Þorgils saga og Hafliða* (*Saga of
Thorgils and Hafliði*), which was written late in the twelfth
century. The feast lasted for seven days and nights. There was
a great deal of drinking, because there was never any shortage
of provisions at Reykhólar; indeed, some of the wedding-
guests, in their cups, took offence over some imagined slight,
and walked out. But it did not affect the enjoyment of the
others: 'There was now much merriment and good fun,
excellent entertainment and all sorts of games, both dancing,
wrestling and saga-entertainment.'

The mention of 'saga-entertainment' (*sagnaskemmtun*) is
the first recorded reference to what was to become Iceland's
national pastime for many centuries: the reading aloud of
written sagas, as opposed to the casual telling of tales.

The host at the wedding was the owner of Reykhólar, a
priest called Ingimundur Einarsson:

> He was a good poet and a most worthy man in most
> respects . . . He was an excellent scholar, always full of
> sagas and poems. He composed some good poetry him-
> self, for which he was paid when he was abroad . . .
>
> Ingimundur was a man of real quality, a good poet,
> extravagant in taste and temperament and with a great
> capacity for enjoying himself and entertaining others.
> He was highly intelligent and extremely popular.

One of the guests was another popular entertainer, as one
might call him—a local farmer, 'a good saga-man and poet'
called Hrólfur of Skálmarnes.

These were the two men who entertained the wedding-
guests with their own sagas:

Hrólfur of Skálmarnes told a saga about Hröngviður the Viking, and King Olaf the Sailor, and Thráinn the Berserk whose burial mound was robbed by Hrómundur Gripsson, along with a number of verses. This saga was later used to entertain King Sverrir, who said that he enjoyed those sorts of fables best of all; yet there are people who trace their ancestry to Hrómundur Gripsson. Hrólfur had composed this saga himself.

Ingimundur the priest told the saga of Orm the Barra-Poet with a number of verses, as well as a long poem he had composed himself at the end of the saga; and many learned men consider this saga to be true.

Hrómundur Gripsson is said, in later versions of *Land-námabók*, to have been an ancestor of the First Settler, Ingólfur Arnarson; but he is a semi-legendary figure, at best. The fictional saga, or fable, that Hrólfur composed about him is reminiscent of the Legendary Sagas that were to take over from the classical sagas as the main literary product of the fourteenth century. The fact that it was later taken to Norway, and used to entertain King Sverrir (1180–1202), shows how widely this secular saga-entertainment was circulated and appreciated. Later still, around 1400, the saga of Hrómundur Gripsson was converted to verse form (*rímur*) under the title *Griplur*; and from these metrical verses a new prose saga of Hrómundur Gripsson was composed—the saga we have today, one of the large collection of Legendary Sagas.

As for the saga composed by the priest Ingimundur Einarsson, about Orm, the poet of Barra in the Hebrides—that, alas, is now lost, and we have no inkling of what it contained: yet another of the literary products of medieval Iceland that failed to survive.

Such, then, was the literary scene at the end of the twelfth century, at the dawn of the golden age of saga-writing: a robust blend of legend and learning, of fact and fantasy, of history and story, of literary endeavour and family pride, of pagan past and Christian present. It was out of this unique background of sagas as serious popular entertainment that the towering masterpieces of the thirteenth century were created.

CHAPTER 14

Snorri Sturluson

Hann var maður vitur og margfróður, höfðingi mikill og slægvitur . . . Hann samsetti Eddu og margar aðrar fræði-bækur, íslenzkar sögur.

He was an intelligent and very erudite man, a great chieftain, and crafty . . . He composed the Edda *and many other books of learning, Icelandic sagas.*

(*Annals of Oddi*)

Hardly any of the saga writers are known by name, for they never signed their work. But there is one author whose name is very well known to us, a man who towers over the first half of the thirteenth century: Snorri Sturluson of Reykholt, in Borgarfjörður—poet, politician, scholar, statesman, saga-writer and saga-maker, the man who gave the world his monumental history of the kings of Norway in *Heimskringla*, his encyclopaedia of Norse mythology in the *Prose Edda* and, in all probability, *Egils Saga* as well.

Snorri Sturluson lived in an age as lawless and violent as any that had gone before, and the name of his family, the Sturlungs (Descendants of Sturla), has become synonymous with that period: the Sturlung Age, a time when the unique parliamentary commonwealth established at the Althing in 930 disintegrated in a welter of savage power-struggles between half a dozen ruling families, and Iceland was drawn irresistibly into the ambit of the Norwegian crown again, in 1262. Snorri Sturluson was himself one of the leading protagonists in that sorry story.

His own life reads like that of a saga hero, full of promise and early fulfilment but ending in tragedy. His lineage was impeccable. On his father's side he was descended from influential chieftains like Snorri *goði* of Helgafell; on his mother's side he was descended from the great Icelandic Viking-poet, Egill Skallagrímsson of Borg, the hero of *Egils Saga*. He himself was born at Hvammur in Skeggjadalur, the Settlement home of Auður the Deep-Minded (see Ch 4), where there is now a basalt memorial stone hewn by the sculptor Steinthór Sigurðsson to celebrate the connection. It was as if he had been born straight into the Saga Age, two centuries after it was over.

Snorri was born in 1179. His father, Sturla (Hvamm-Sturla), was a ruthless and ambitious chieftain, fierce and unrelenting in temper. Conflict came naturally to him; and it was this appetite for conflict that gave his youngest son, Snorri, an opportunity for educational advancement that changed the course of his life. Hvamm-Sturla became involved in a vicious quarrel over an inheritance for which there seemed no resolution. The case was put to arbitration by the most important chieftain in the country, the powerful and cultivated Jón Loftsson of Oddi (see Ch 11). As part of his adjudication, and in order to placate the implacable Hvamm-Sturla, Jón Loftsson offered to act as foster-father to his son Snorri, who was then only two years old.

Growing up at Oddi, Snorri came into intimate contact with the cultural history of Iceland at its best. Jón Loftsson was the grandson of the first Icelandic historian, Sæmundur the Learned (see Ch 12); he was also the grandson of King Magnus Bare-Legs of Norway, and had been fostered in Norway and attended many state occasions there. So young Snorri Sturluson was reared on a diet of learning and scholarship, with particular reference to the royal courts of Scandinavia, and had free access to all the saga and historical literature that had been produced in Iceland during the twelfth century.

After Jón Loftsson's death in 1197, Snorri threw himself into the pursuit of power and position. Through a carefully-arranged marriage he acquired the estate of Borg—not because of any sentimental dynastic concern for his ancestor Egill Skallagrímsson but because his bride was a wealthy heiress. A few years later, in 1206, he left his wife and two children at Borg and moved some forty kilometres inland to the estate of Reykholt, which he acquired by agreeing to look after the elderly couple who owned it. Reykholt was to be his home for the rest of his life. He kept a succession of concubines there, by whom he fathered several illegitimate children.

From his base in Reykholt, Snorri quickly pushed himself into the forefront of national life. He was amassing considerable wealth and power, and soon owned vast estates all over the country and the chieftaincies that went with them. His life became an intricate pattern of shifting alliances and friendships, and he became Law-Speaker of the Althing in 1215 at the age of thirty-six. He was the quintessential Renaissance man, displaying all the contradictory characteristics of the Renaissance and of the family traits he had inherited: ambition, pride, cunning, love of power, ruthlessness and artistic creativity.

He went abroad for the first time in 1218, and became the friend of kings and great courtiers like Duke Skuli of Norway, regent and uncle of the fourteen-year-old King Hakon Hakonsson—Hakon the Old, as he would later be called. It was the shrewd and wily King Hakon who would eventually succeed in annexing Iceland to the Norwegian throne. Back in Iceland, Snorri plunged into an incredible series of feuds and intrigues, often against members of his own family, cousins and nephews and powerful chieftains who had married and divorced his daughters. The Icelandic republic was racked continuously by these conflicts; all standards of honour and justice were cynically abandoned, pledges broken. The political story of thirteenth-century Iceland became a tragedy of pitched battles, of lawlessness and cruelty and treachery and arson and murder.

Men who greedily sought ever more power courted the support of King Hakon the Old. Snorri Sturluson was no exception. In Norway he had been appointed a gentleman-in-waiting to the king, and had made some sort of agreement to promote the king's interests in Iceland. Whatever it was, he never carried out his side of the bargain, however; indeed, while other chieftains flirted dangerously with the Norwegian throne, Snorri became its enemy. His own position in Iceland was eroded by the determined assaults of another ambitious chieftain, his former son-in-law Gissur Thorvaldsson, who had also become one of King Hakon's protégés and agents. In 1239 Snorri feared so much for his own life that he left Iceland and went back to Norway. But his old friends there were out of favour with King Hakon, and Snorri himself was now *persona non grata* at the court. He left Norway again, without the king's permission; but he was now a spent force in Icelandic politics, little capable of either hindering or helping the king's cause or of thwarting Gissur Thorvaldsson's ambitions to rule Iceland as the king's earl. Gissur, however, was determined to smash the Sturlung power for good, and his excuse came in the form of a letter from King Hakon demanding Snorri's return to Norway, dead or alive. On the night of 23 September 1241, Gissur Thorvaldsson descended on Reykholt with a band of seventy armed men. Snorri was asleep in his bed-closet when they broke into the house. He managed to get down into the cellars and hide there, but his whereabouts were given away by a priest who was promised that Snorri would be unharmed and given safe conduct to Norway. That assurance was cynically ignored: five men went down into the cellar, and there, unarmed and defenceless, Snorri Sturlusson was hacked to death. He was sixty-two years old. It was a brutal and squalid death for Iceland's most distinguished man of letters, but one that was not untypical of the barbarities of the Sturlung Age.

Reykholt
Today, Reykholt is a little farming and educational hamlet, a quiet backwater in a rich green valley edged on both sides with rows of flat-topped hills. The slopes are clothed with dwarf birch trees, the floor of the valley steams lazily with plumes of vapour from sporadic hotsprings.

On a grassy plaza in front of the modern school building stands an imposing statue of Snorri Sturluson by the distinguished Norwegian sculptor, Gustav Vigeland; it was a gift from the Norwegian nation, and was unveiled in 1947 by King (then Crown Prince) Olav of Norway. This was Norway's tribute to the genius of the man who had rescued its history through his *Heimskringla*.

In a hollow behind the school building lies the most remarkable archaeological monument in Iceland—a circular stone-lined pool called *Snorralaug*, Snorri's Bath. It is constructed of hewn blocks of stone (silica sinter), and is nearly four metres in diameter; it is filled with piping hot water led through an underground stone conduit from a hotspring called Skrifla about a hundred metres away, and in the old days the temperature of the water could be altered by the addition of cold water from a brook that is now dried up. The water supply was controlled by means of a stone slab slotted into the conduit. The bath lies in a basin sheltered from the northerly winds by the low hillock on which the farm-buildings of Reykholt have always been built. In the old days it was probably roofed over, so that it could be used at any time of the year. The bath was carefully restored by the National Museum in 1959; an underground passage leading from the farmhouse to the pool was also found, and part of this passage was excavated and restored at the same time.

Although there is no absolute proof, it is believed that this bathing-pool was actually built by Snorri Sturluson himself. Certainly, there was such a pool there in Snorri's time. In *Íslendinga Saga*, the chronicle of the last decades of the commonwealth written by Snorri's nephew, the historian Sturla Thórðarson, we are given a vivid glimpse of the pool in use in Snorri's time, in the year 1228:

> One evening, Snorri was sitting in the pool and the conversation was all about chieftains. Someone said that there was no other chieftain like Snorri, and that no other chieftain could rival him because of the strength of his marriage-alliances. Snorri agreed that his in-laws were by no means inconsiderable men . . .

Sturla Thórðarson also gives us another brief glimpse of

Reykholt in the winter of 1230–31. There had been an exceptional lull in the general hostilities that summer, and Snorri Sturluson, who had been appointed Law-Speaker again, had not even bothered to go to the Althing. He had made peace with another turbulent nephew, Sturla Sighvatsson, who had been recklessly tilting at his position:

> Things now began to go better between Snorri and Sturla. Sturla spent a long time at Reykholt and paid much attention to having copies made of the saga-books that Snorri had written.

It is regrettable that the author of *Íslendinga Saga* did not give any further information about the 'saga-books' that Snorri had composed at Reykholt. Yet the two titles that we can be absolutely certain about—the *Prose Edda* and *Heimskringla*—would in themselves by considered sufficient of a life's work for anyone, never mind a man so immersed in politics and trouble as Snorri Sturluson was for most of his life.

Snorri's *Prose Edda* is a remarkable work. It is not a saga, as such. It consists of three separate sections. The first, which is called *Gylfaginning* (*The Deluding of Gylfi*), is a broad summary of Norse mythology, using the stories found in the original *Poetic Edda* to present a coherent account of the gods of the pagan past. The narrative framework is provided by a legendary Swedish king called Gylfi, who travels to the home of the gods (Ásgarður) to ask questions about their origins and learn from their wisdom. The second section is called *Skáldskaparmál* (*Language of Poetry*); here the central character is Bragi, the god of poetry, who explains the origins and mechanics of poetic inspiration. This section is a handbook for poets, designed to teach the traditional techniques of the *skáld*, or court poet, and to explain the pagan and mythological allusions found in skaldic poetry. The third section is a *tour de force* of Snorri's own technical virtuosity as a poet. It is called *Háttatal* (*List of Metres*), and consists of a poem of 102 stanzas to illustrate the different and highly complex metres of court poetry. This poem had originally

been composed in honour of King Hakon Hakonsson and
Duke Skuli as a thank-you for their hospitality during Snorri's
first visit to Norway in 1218–20.

Heimskringla (*The Orb of the World*) is a very different
work, a work of prodigious scope and scale, a complete
history of Norway from prehistoric times down to 1177, told
in a series of biographical sagas of all the kings who had
occupied the throne of Norway. It is not so much a straight
history as a great portrait gallery of individual monarchs
depicted with immense skill and authority. Snorri Sturluson
saw history as a continual flow of events which he explained in
terms of individual personalities and their aspirations and
achievements and failures, their virtues and faults. It may not
be 'history' in the modern sense of the term, but it is certainly
magnificent. To the writing of *Heimskringla* Snorri brought
not only his outstanding literary ability but also his deep
insight and experience as a protagonist in the power-struggles
of his own times; his attitudes to kingship had been forged in
the bitter fires of personal suffering from his own contacts
with the ruthlessness of crowned might.

Borg in Borgarfjörður: Egils Saga
The church and parsonage of Borg ('Burg') stand quietly
below the craggy outcrop of rock that gave the site its name,
looking out over the busy little town of Borgarnes. In front of
them there is a new commemorative sculpture fashioned by
Ásmundur Sveinsson in typical monumental abstract style.
Borg was the Settlement home of Skallagrímur Kveld-Úlfs-
son, who had been guided to the spot by his father's coffin
(see Ch 3); it was from Borg that he exploited all the natural
resources of the district of Mýrar, both by land and sea (see
Ch 1), and built up his standing in the community as a
prosperous and powerful chieftain. His son was Egill Skallagrímsson, the eponymous hero of *Egils Saga*; and it is one of
his descendants, Snorri Sturluson, who owned Borg at the
beginning of the thirteenth century, who is generally believed
to have written *Egils Saga*.

Egill Skallagrímsson is the most remarkable and compelling character in all the Icelandic sagas. He was a great, hulking crag of a man, larger than life and twice as ugly. He was a man of violence and violent contrasts, a demonic, greedy, ruthless Viking warrior with an extraordinary genius for poetry, a man of volcanic rages and merciless brutality who was still capable of deep and abiding love, a miserly, spiteful man who was also touched with a sublime nobility of soul. *Egils Saga* is an epic in every way, and its hero is worthy of it. The saga tells the story of four generations of the Men of Mýrar, and covers an enormous canvas, from 850 to the end of the tenth century. It gives a panoramic view of the whole Viking world, from the Scandinavian countries to Britain and Iceland. It is unbelievably rich in characters and events, yet it is totally dominated by the unforgettable presence of Egill Skallagrímsson, the greatest warrior-poet of the Viking Age.

The saga tells how Egill's father and grandfather were hounded from Norway for defying King Harald Fine-Hair. Egill himself later went to Norway to seek his fame and fortune there, and try to recover family property; but he in turn fell foul of royal authority in the person of Harald Fine-Hair's eldest son, King Eirik Blood-Axe (*blóðöxi*), and his imperious consort, Queen Gunnhild. In a flurry of violent raids on royal estates, Egill killed many of the king's men, one of the king's sons and one of Queen Gunnhild's brothers, and then left Norway, an outlaw. This theme of the commoner versus the king runs right through the saga and gives it an extra dimension of profundity, a Shakespearian grandeur— and was no doubt given point and edge by Snorri Sturluson's own experience of the reality of royal power.

Some years later, in 948, Egill Skallagrímsson faced his royal foes again when Eirik Blood-Axe had become king of Viking York. This time, Egill was at the king's mercy. To save his own life, Egill composed a eulogy to the king, known as the *Head-Ransom* (*Höfuðlausn*), which so impressed Eirik that he let Egill go unscathed: the poet's pen had overcome the royal axe.

In the year 957, Egill Skallagrímsson retired as a professional Viking adventurer and returned home to Iceland after many years abroad. And now the other side of Egill appeared: the family man. He had married a woman he loved deeply—Ásgerður, the widow of his brother who had been killed fighting at the Battle of Brunanburh, in England, in 937. Now he settled down at Borg with his family, the old Viking come home to his haven at last at the age of forty-seven. His eldest daughter, Thorgerður, 'a fine-looking woman, very tall, intelligent and proud, but usually rather quiet', married Ólafur the Peacock; and their eldest son was Kjartan Ólafsson, the tragic hero of *Laxdæla Saga* (see Ch 15). For Egill Skallagrímsson, all was set fair for a contented and fulfilled old age.

But all too soon, personal tragedy struck. In the year 961, one of Egill's three sons died. But worse was to come. That same autumn his eldest son, Böðvar, only seventeen years old and his father's favourite, was drowned in a freak storm just off Borgarnes. With a heavy heart, Egill rode off to look for his body, and found it lying on the shore down at Einarsnes. He lifted it on to his horse and carried his dead son to the funeral mound in which his father, Skallagrímur, had been buried. He opened the mound and laid Böðvar in it beside the bones of his grandfather, then closed the mound again.

In Borgarnes there is an old burial mound in the little park in the middle of the town. Tradition has it that this was Skallagrímur's, where Böðvar was laid to rest. On a wall beside the mound there is a memorial plaque carved in high relief by the Danish artist Anne Marie Brodersen, wife of the composer Carl Nielsen, at the turn of the century and presented to Iceland by her children in 1963. It depicts the old warrior carrying his dead boy home on his horse, and I always find it immensely affecting.

After burying his son, Egill returned home to Borg and locked himself in his bed-closet. He spoke to no one, and none dared speak to him. He would not eat nor drink. For two days and nights he fasted there, alone, in agony and silence. Early on the morning of the third day, his wife Ásgerður sent word to Hjarðarholt, asking Thorgerður to come at once; she knew how much Egill loved his daughter—this hard man who had never shown a glimmer of compassion for his foes. Thorgerður rode all night from Hjarðarholt, arriving at Borg early in the morning. She loudly refused all offers of breakfast, saying that she had come to starve herself to death beside her father:

> She went to the bed-closet. 'Open up, father', she called out. 'I want us to go the same road together.'
>
> Egill unbolted the shutter. Thorgerður climbed inside and locked the door behind her, and lay down on the other bed there.
>
> Then Egill spoke, 'You do well, my daughter, in wanting to keep company with your father. You have shown me great love. How could I hope to go on living with a sorrow such as this?'
>
> They were silent for a while. Then Egill said, 'What is going on, daughter? Are you chewing something?'
>
> 'I am chewing seaweed,' she replied, 'because I believe it will make me feel worse than ever. Otherwise I might live too long.'
>
> 'Is it bad for one?' asked Egill.
>
> 'Terrible,' she replied. 'Would you like to try some?'
>
> 'What's the use?' said Egill.
>
> A little later she called out and asked for something to drink, some water. Then Egill said, 'That is what happens when you eat seaweed, it makes you all the more thirsty.'
>
> 'Would you like a drink, father?' she said.
>
> He took hold of the horn, and drank great draughts. Then Thorgerður cried out, 'We've been tricked! It's milk!' At that, Egill bit off a huge chunk of the horn, as big as his teeth could take, and threw the horn down.
>
> Thorgerður said, 'What are we going to do now? Now that this plan of ours has failed? My own choice, father, would be for us to keep going a little bit longer; then you could compose a funeral-ode for Böðvar, and I shall

carve the poem in runes on a log. After that we can die if we want to . . .'

The psychology worked. Egill said there was little hope of his composing a poem, even if he made the effort—but at least he agreed to try:

> As the poem progressed, Egill began to get his spirits back; and when it was completed he tried it out before Ásgerður and Thorgerður and the people of the household. Then he got up out of bed and took his place on the high-seat. He called the poem *Sonatorrek* [*On the Loss of Sons*]. After that, Egill held a funeral-feast for his sons, according to custom.

Sonatorrek is Egill Skallagrímsson's greatest poem—some would say the greatest poem in Viking literature. It is a profound and agonized exploration of the nature of faith and grief. Egill was a worshipper of Óðinn, the aristocratic god of princes and warriors, but also the patron god of poetry. He rails fiercely against the god in whom he had trusted, the god who had betrayed him by taking his sons; but in the end he finds consolation, for it was the gift of poetry which makes the loss bearable. By expressing his grief, Egill can master it. The god of the spear had hurt him; now the god of poetry healed him. How well Thorgerður had understood her father!

In the closing chapters of the saga, we meet Egill in his senility, a blind and deaf old man warming himself at the fire and being scolded by sharp-tongued kitchenmaids. By now he was living as a pensioner in the home of his stepdaughter at Mosfell, near Reykjavík. The old baleful spirit still flickered, however. When he was in his eighties, he expressed a desire to go to the Althing once again. His stepdaughter asked him why he wanted to go:

> 'I'll tell you what I have in mind,' he replied. 'I want to take with me the two chests of English silver that King Æthelstan of England gave me. I want to have them carried to the Law-Rock when the crowd there is at its biggest, and then I'm going to throw the silver all over

the place. I'll be very surprised if the people share it out evenly. I bet there will be a bit of shoving and kicking. Maybe in the end the whole Althing will start fighting.'

They would not let him go, of course. Egill sulked, 'and there was an ugly look about him', for he hated to be crossed. But he had the last laugh on them, after all. While the others were at the Althing, he summoned a couple of slaves one night, loaded the chests of silver on to his horse, and went off into the dark. Next morning he was found blundering about, trailing the horse behind him, but neither the silver nor the slaves were ever seen again.

Egill Skallagrímsson died around the year 990, before Christianity came to Iceland. But it seems that his stepdaughter later had his bones moved into the church that was built nearby at a spot called Hrísbrú. When this church was dismantled about a hundred years later and moved closer to Mosfell itself, human bones were found under the altar that were much bigger than other men's bones. A priest called Skafti Thórarinsson picked up the skull, which was assumed to be Egill's, and put it on the wall of the churchyard:

> The skull was exceptionally large, and quite astonishingly heavy. It was ridged all over like a scallop-shell. Skafti wanted to find out just how thick it was, so he picked up a heavy axe and swung it with one hand as hard as he could, and hit the skull with the back of the axe, trying to break it. But the blow neither cracked nor dented the skull; it merely turned white, and from that one can see that this skull would hardly have been affected by the blows of lesser men while it still had skin and flesh on it. Egill's bones were re-interred on the edge of the graveyard at Mosfell.

Today, a handsome modern church with a spiky copper spire stands on the site of the old church. It is a private-enterprise church, built by a local land owner and financed by revenues from the hot water that is pumped from Mosfell District to Reykjavík for its municipal central heating system.

Egill's buried silver has never been found; but at Mosfell, where the old pagan's bones were laid to rest in consecrated ground, the hot water under the ground is buried treasure enough.

CHAPTER 15

Laxdæla Saga

Þá mælti Guðrún, 'Þeim var ek verst, er ek unna mest.'

Then Guðrún said, 'I was worst to the one I loved the most.'

(*Laxdæla Saga*)

Of all the major Icelandic sagas, *Laxdæla Saga* has always been the most widely popular, and understandably so. It is essentially a romantic work: romantic in style, romantic in taste, and romantic in theme. It is a romance that is deeply shadowed by tragedy. The culmination of the saga is a love triangle that goes terribly wrong, as love triangles usually do, when the heroine of the saga, the beautiful and imperious Guðrún, who is married to her lover's best friend against her will, forces her reluctant husband to kill her former lover and forfeit his own life thereby. It is a drama of passion, of pride and jealousy and injured love, a drama dominated throughout by demanding women of iron will and tempestuous desires. In their forceful presence the men of the saga, however heroically presented, pale almost into insignificance. They are not the prime movers of action and event; they are the moved.

Laxdæla Saga is a long, leisurely, apparently rambling dynastic family chronicle. It covers a broad canvas of seven generations for 150 years, from the Settlement of Iceland to the Conversion. The pace of the narrative is slow and deceptively serene as the author unfolds the story in a series of brilliantly visualized episodes that lay the foundations for the culminating tragedy. It was written around the year 1245, and the name of the author is unknown; but in *Laxdæla Saga* he has created one of the epic historical novels of European literature.

The matriarch of the family whose fortunes are followed in the saga was the indomitable Auður the Deep-Minded (who is known as Unnur in *Laxdæla Saga*), the pioneer settler of the Dales who made her home at Hvammur in Skeggjadalur (see Ch 4). When she died, she bequeathed the estate of Hvammur to her grandson, Ólafur *feilan*, and Hvammur is shunted into a siding, as it were, while the narrative concentrates on another branch of Auður's prolific posterity: the House of Höskuldur.

The House of Höskuldur

One of the well-born Norwegian chieftains who had accompanied Auður the Deep-Minded through all her trials and tribulations in Scotland and the settlement in Iceland, was a man called Kollur. She rewarded him with the hand of her granddaughter, Thorgerður, in marriage, and granted him the whole of Laxárdalur (Salmon River Dale) in the Dales district, as a result of which he became known as Dala-Kollur. Dala-Kollur and Thorgerður had a son called Höskuldur who inherited the estate in Laxárdalur; he became a great chieftain, and the name of the family home came to be known as Höskuldsstaðir.

The farm of Höskuldsstaðir stands today where it has always stood, a little way up the long valley of Laxárdalur overlooking the salmon-rich waters of the River Laxá. At the mouth of the river is a bustling little township called Búðardalur, whose name goes right back to saga times: it was there, according to *Laxdæla Saga*, that Höskuldur Dala-Kollsson built a boat-shed for his ocean-going cargo-ship, and some temporary booths (*búðir*)—hence the name.

Höskuldur was an enterprising, ambitious man, ever anxious to improve his standing and prestige. To that end he married the daughter of a wealthy farmer up north. His bride, Jórunn, was considered an excellent match financially but turned out to be a hard-tempered woman, sharp-tongued and steely-minded. They had four children, one of whom, Hallgerður (nicknamed Longlegs), would become a central character in *Njáls Saga* as the unforgiving wife of Gunnar of

Hlíðarendi (see Ch 16). Their elder son, Thorleikur, also turned out to be 'of rather mixed character'.

Despite the litter of children, the marriage of Höskuldur Dala-Kollsson and Jórunn was a loveless one, and Höskuldur was no doubt glad to have the opportunity of spending winters abroad trading in Norway, where he cut a great dash at the court of King Hakon the Good (933–61). On one of these visits, ostensibly made to purchase timber in order to rebuild Höskuldsstaðir, he also bought himself a concubine —a beautiful slave-girl who cost him a fortune, despite the fact that she was, apparently, deaf and dumb.

Back home in Iceland, Jórunn was noticeably unenthusiastic about this addition to the household, especially when the girl bore Höskuldur a son, Ólafur, a peerlessly handsome child whom Höskuldur came to love dearly. The identity of the slave-girl remained a mystery, however, for she never spoke a word. But early one summer's morning, when the boy was two years old and talking and running about like a four-year-old, the concubine's secret was revealed— and we can still stand at the very spot where it happened, down by the stream at the bottom of the homefield at Höskuldsstaðir and out of sight of the house itself:

> It so happened early one morning that Höskuldur was out and about seeing to his farm; it was a beautiful day, and the dawn sun was shining brightly. He heard the sound of voices, and went down to the stream at the foot of the sloping homefield. There he saw two people he knew well—his son Ólafur, and the boy's mother. He realized now that she was not speechless after all, for she was chattering busily to the child. Höskuldur went down to them and asked her what her name was, and told her that there was no point in concealing it any longer. She agreed, and they sat down on the slope of the homefield.
>
> 'If you want to know my name,' she said, 'I am called Melkorka.'
>
> Höskuldur asked her about her family.
>
> 'My father is called Myrkjartan, and he is a king in

Ireland,' she said. 'I was taken captive and sold into
slavery when I was fifteen years old.'

Höskuldur said she had kept silent for far too long over
such a noble lineage. He went back to the house and told
Jórunn what he had discovered while he was out. Jórunn
said she had no way of knowing if the woman was telling
the truth, and that anyway she had little liking for
mystery folk; and they discussed it no further.

What a delightfully revealing cameo it is, that idyllic scene
in the sunlit dell down by the stream. All of Höskuldur's
vanity and social aspirations are revealed in his pleasure at the
disclosure of his illegitimate son's royal lineage—and his
inability to understand why this revelation should leave his
wife Jórunn even colder than before.

Young Ólafur turned out to be a paragon amongst men, as
befitted the son of a princess of the Irish royal line, and his
proud father nicknamed him Ólafur *pái*—Ólafur the Peacock. When he grew to manhood he made a triumphant
voyage abroad. In Ireland his grandfather, King Myrkjartan,
acknowledged his birth and fêted him and flattered him, and
even offered to make him heir to his throne, but Ólafur
courteously declined and returned to Iceland in a blaze of
glory. There, Höskuldur achieved for Ólafur an ambitious
dynastic marriage into the family of the great warrior-poet
Egill Skallagrímsson of Borg, of *Egils Saga* fame. Egill's
daughter, the proud and aloof Thorgerður, at first refused to
marry a mere concubine's son, thinking the match beneath
her dignity, but was dazzled and swept off her feet when
Ólafur the Peacock turned up to woo her in person. Ólafur
now bought the land across the river Laxá facing Höskuldsstaðir, and built for himself and his bride an imposing manor
farm which he named Hjarðarholt (see Ch 8).

At Hjarðarholt, Ólafur the Peacock and Thorgerður
reared a large brood of children, of whom much the most
outstanding was their eldest son, Kjartan, named after his
royal grandfather Myrkjartan. But there was another youngster growing up in the household who would play a crucial

part in the culminating tragedy of *Laxdæla Saga*. His name was Bolli, the son of Ólafur's half-brother, Thorleikur Dala-Kollsson, he of the 'rather mixed character'. As Höskuldur's legitimate son and heir, Thorleikur had become soured by his father's obvious predilection for his illegitimate son by Melkorka, and no doubt jealous of his glittering success; so to staunch the ill-feeling, Ólafur the Peacock magnanimously offered to foster Thorleikur's son Bolli when Thorleikur had to go abroad—magnanimous, because it was the convention in Iceland that fostering implied a lesser status than that of the fostered. The two cousins, Kjartan Ólafsson and Bolli Thorleiksson, became foster-brothers and grew up together at Hjarðarholt, devoted and inseparable friends, two young men of exceptional prowess and accomplishments. But of the two, Kjartan always had the slight edge over Bolli in whatever they did.

With these two brilliant young men, the House of Höskuldur reached its fullest flower, and the scene was set for the tragic love triangle that is the romantic core of *Laxdæla Saga*.

Guðrún Ósvífursdóttir

Round the corner to the east of Skeggjadalur lies the long sheltered valley of Sælingsdalur; and in Sælingsdalur we move centre-stage to the eye of the passionate, emotional storm that brought grief and destruction to the House of Höskuldur.

The scenario opens with the entry of the other main dynastic line from Ketill Flatnose: the descendants of Auður the Deep-Minded's brother, Björn the Easterner, who had settled at Bjarnarhöfn on Snæfellsnes (see Ch 4). Björn's great-grandson, Ósvífur Helgason, had settled at Laugar (Hotsprings) in Sælingsdalur, where he became a great chieftain and sage, with a quiverful of strong, formidable sons, the Ósvífurssons. But it was his daughter, Guðrún Ósvífursdóttir, who attracted most attention:

> Guðrún was the most beautiful woman in Iceland at that time, and also the most intelligent. Guðrún Ósvífursdót-

tir was a woman of such courtliness that whatever finery other women wore, they seemed like mere trinkets beside hers. She was the shrewdest and best-spoken of all women; and she had a generous disposition.

Guðrún was married twice early in her youth. The first marriage ended in divorce, the second in tragic death. By the year 995 she was a young widow, still in her early twenties and still much the most desirable match in the whole district. And it was now that she met the two cousins from Hjarðarholt, her distant kinsmen Kjartan Ólafsson and his foster-brother Bolli.

The manor farm of Laugar in Sælingsdalur was a magnet for young people from far and wide, not just because of Guðrún's spectacular beauty but also because Laugar, as its name implies, had a bathing-pool fed by natural hotsprings that bubbled up from the side of the hill above the site of the farm. There is no sign of the pool today, but the hotsprings supply hot water for the swimming-pool of the Domestic Science School that stands there now; and in 1956, archaeologists who examined the site found traces of an ancient stone conduit under the scree that covers the slopes from some forgotten rock-fall.

Kjartan and Bolli started frequenting the bathing-pool at Laugar every weekend. They both fell in love with Guðrún; but it was Kjartan whom Guðrún preferred, and everyone assumed that they would marry. Kjartan was eager to go abroad first to seek his fame and fortune; Guðrún wanted to go with him, but Kjartan told her that her place was at home in Sælingsdalur for the time being, and asked Guðrún to wait for him in Iceland for three years as his betrothed. Guðrún was piqued by Kjartan's high-handed decision, as she saw it, and refused to commit herself, and they parted rather coolly. None the less it was generally expected that they would marry when Kjartan came home after three years.

So Kjartan went off to Norway with the ever-faithful Bolli at his side. They sailed straight into trouble, for this was the time when King Olaf Tryggvason of Norway was putting strong political pressure on Iceland to accept Christianity (see Ch 9). The king was soon won over by Kjartan's outstanding accomplishments; but now Bolli's submerged resentment of his more brilliant cousin broke surface—especially when Kjartan started spending time in the company of King Olaf's sister, the princess Ingibjorg. When King Olaf exerted more pressure on Iceland by taking hostage the sons of leading chieftains in the year 1000 or 999, just before the Conversion, Kjartan Ólafsson was one of those held at the king's pleasure; Bolli was not.

At the end of the three years, Bolli returned to Iceland on his own. When Guðrún asked about Kjartan, Bolli replied:

> 'There is excellent news to tell of him, for he is at the court of King Olaf enjoying more prestige there than any other man. But it would not surprise me if we in this country were to see little of him for the next few years.'
>
> Guðrún then asked if there were any particular reason for that, apart from the friendship between Kjartan and the king. So Bolli told her of the rumours about the attachment between Kjartan and the king's sister, Ingibjorg, and said he was inclined to think that the king would rather give Ingibjorg to him in marriage than let Kjartan go, if it came to that.
>
> Guðrún said that this was good news—'for Kjartan can only be truly fulfilled if he wins a good wife.' With that she dropped the subject abruptly and walked away, her face deeply flushed . . .

Bolli himself now asked for Guðrún's hand in marriage; and eventually Guðrún, under pressure from her father and brothers, and grieved by Kjartan's apparent perfidy, agreed to marry Bolli, but much against her will. 'There was little love in the marriage on Guðrún's part,' says the saga.

In the following year, Kjartan returned to Iceland after all. When he heard that Guðrún was now married to his foster-brother he showed no outward sign of emotion; instead, he allowed himself to be persuaded to marry, almost casually, a

sweet young girl called Hrefna, the sister of his sailing
partner—just to spite Guðrún, it seems. When the foster-
brothers met socially, Kjartan insisted on his wife being given
precedence over Guðrún. The jealousies and resentments
inherent in this strained situation soon erupted into the open.
Deliberate snubs were repaid by calculated rudeness. Precious heirlooms were stolen. And Kjartan gave vent to his
suppressed rage by besieging Bolli and Guðrún in their home
for three days and denying them access to the outdoor privy.

This final humiliation was more than Guðrún's pride could
bear. She might still have harboured love for Kjartan, but
honour would not allow her to stand by while her husband,
and she, were subjected to public shame and disgrace. So she
gave Bolli a simple but devastating ultimatum: he must either
go and kill Kjartan, or never share her bed again. And Bolli,
with terrible reluctance, realized that he had no choice at all.
So when Kjartan was reported to be riding down the valley of
Svínadalur nearby, careless of his safety, Bolli and Guðrún's
brothers, the Ósvífurssons, went out to lay an ambush.

According to *Laxdæla Saga* there were two witnesses to the
ensuing encounter, a shepherd and his boy. So cunningly is
the story told that we can stand today at their vantage point
and watch the drama unfolding in our mind's eye. We can see
Kjartan with only two companions come riding down the old
bridle path which still shows up against the slope of the
hillside on the other side of the valley. We can see the
ambushers lurking behind the great boulder in the ravine
called Hafragil, where Bolli secretly tried to signal a last-
minute warning to Kjartan by lying on the rock in full view of
any approaching rider, until his brothers-in-law pulled him
down out of sight. We can see Kjartan making his heroic last
defence until exhaustion sets in. And we can see Bolli,
goaded into action by the taunts of his brothers-in-law, and
Kjartan's taunting too, moving numbly forward to deal
Kjartan his deathblow.

Bolli then rode home to Laugar, and Guðrún went out
to meet him. She asked him what time it was. Bolli said it

was around mid-day. The Guðrún said, 'Morning tasks are often mixed: I have spun yarn for twelve ells of cloth, and you have killed Kjartan.'

Bolli replied, 'This luckless deed will live long enough in my mind without you reminding me of it.'

'I do not think it luckless,' said Guðrún. 'It seems to me that you had more prestige in the year that Kjartan was in Norway than now, when he has ridden roughshod over you ever since he came back to Iceland. But above all, what I like best is the thought that Hrefna will not go laughing to bed tonight.'

Then Bolli said, in sudden fury, 'I doubt if she will turn any paler at the news than you, and I suspect that you would have been less dismayed if I had been left lying on the battlefield and Kjartan had lived to tell the tale.'

Guðrún now saw how angry Bolli was, and said, 'Do not say such things, for I am deeply grateful to you for what you have done. I now know for certain that you will do anything to please me.'

Ólafur the Peacock strove desperately to reach an honourable settlement that would heal the awful breach that had opened in his family, and for three years, until his own death, he managed to secure an uneasy peace. But once his moderating influence was gone, there was no holding back the bloodvengeance that the crime demanded. Kjartan's mother, Thorgerður, the daughter of the old Viking Egill Skallagrímsson, summoned her sons to go riding with her to Sælingsdalur. When they were in the valley, opposite Bolli's home, she asked her sons who lived there:

'You know that, mother,' they replied.

Thorgerður snorted. 'Yes, I certainly know that!' she said. 'I know that Bolli lives here, your brother's killer. And you are remarkably unlike your noble kinsmen if you do not want to avenge such a brother as Kjartan was. Your grandfather, Egill Skallagrímsson, would never have behaved like this. It is cruel to have such craven sons; and I for one believe that it would have suited you better to be your father's daughters and be married off . . .'

The Ólafssons now planned their revenge. They knew that Bolli and Guðrún were staying at a summer shieling far up at the head of the valley, supervising the dairy-work and haymaking. They enlisted the help of a warrior called Helgi Harðbeinsson, and set out on their expedition of vengeance. Their mother, Thorgerður, insisted on going too: 'For I know you well enough, my sons, to know that you will need spurring on.'

Up at the shieling, Bolli and Guðrún had sent the farm-workers about their work early that morning and gone back to bed; Guðrún was pregnant. Suddenly they heard a number of men approaching, and they both knew what that presaged. Bolli insisted that Guðrún should leave the shieling, and she went down to the stream to do some washing. Meanwhile Bolli prepared himself to meet his fate, while the men outside argued about who should have the dubious privilege of bursting through the door first.

Near the top of the valley, a few yards from the stream, there are several low grass-grown hummocks among the heather, rather difficult to discern at first. For centuries the spot has been known as *Bollatóttir*—Bolli's Ruins. They are the remains of an old building, measuring some five metres by three, with an opening facing south down the valley. Local tradition insists that they are the remains of the shieling in which Bolli met his death, and the site fits perfectly the topography of the place as it is described in the saga. It is easy to envisage the drama of the scene, to see the door through which the first man came surging, only to have his skull cleft in two by Bolli. Then Helgi Harðbeinsson came in wielding a wicked iron-bound spear with which he impaled Bolli against the far wall. As the Ólafssons hesitated, their mother, Thorgerður, urged them to finish the task, and one of Kjartan's brothers sprang forward and decapitated Bolli with his axe: 'May your hands prosper,' said Thorgerður, and added that Guðrún would now have some red hairs to comb for Bolli.

And Guðrún? She finished her washing, and then calmly talked to her husband's killers, to fix their names and faces in her memory until such time as her unborn son would be ready to wreak vengeance in return.

Guðrún at Helgafell

After Bolli's death, Guðrún could not bear to stay on in Sælingsdalur. So she asked her lifelong friend, Snorri the Priest of Helgafell, to exchange homes with her; and in the year 1008 Snorri *goði* moved to Sælingsdalur, and Guðrún moved to Helgafell on Snæfellsnes.

Soon afterwards, Guðrún married for a fourth time. Her new husband was a great chieftain called Thorkell Eyjólfsson and in him, we feel, she found at last a big enough man to match her own mettlesome spirit. Meanwhile, Guðrún and Snorri laid complex plans to achieve vengeance for Bolli; and when the son she had been carrying when Bolli died—Bolli Bollason—reached the age of manhood at twelve years old, he encompassed the death of Helgi Harðbeinsson, thus fulfilling the demands of the blood-feud. Later, Bolli Bollason married Thórdís, the daughter of Snorri the Priest; she was a descendant of Ólafur *feilan* of Hvammur.

In the year 1026, Thorkell Eyjólfsson drowned at sea on his way back from a trip to Norway to purchase timber to rebuild the church at Helgafell; his son by Guðrún, Gellir Thorkelsson, became the grandfather of Iceland's first vernacular historian, Ari the Learned.

And now Guðrún, after her passion-racked life, turned to religion for her consolation; she became a nun, and Iceland's first anchoress:

> Guðrún became a deeply religious woman, and was the first woman in Iceland to learn the Psalter. She would spend long hours in the church at night saying prayers.

Towards the end of her days, when she was very old and blind, her son Bolli Bollason came to visit her in her hermitage at Helgafell. He was curious about the great enigma in his mother's life, her feelings about the love triangle in which she had been trapped, and he asked her a pointed and searching question: 'Will you tell me something, mother, that I am very curious to know? Which man did you love the most?'

Guðrún replied with an objective assessment of the merits and demerits of each of her four husbands. But in Icelandic, the word for 'husband' and 'man' is the same, and Bolli refused to be deflected:

'I understand clearly what you are telling me about the qualities of your *husbands*; but you have not yet told me which *man* you loved the most. There is no need to conceal it any longer.'

'You are pressing me very hard, my son,' said Guðrún. 'But if I must tell someone, then I would rather tell it to you.'

Bolli begged her to do so.

Then Guðrún said, 'I was worst to the one I loved the most.'

It was one of those laconic, cryptic responses so characteristic of the sagas; and for the life of me I am still not sure which man she meant—whether it was her former lover, Kjartan, whom she had had killed out of a passionate mixture of jealousy and affronted pride, or her husband, Bolli, who had reluctantly killed his cousin and foster-brother at her ferocious behest and forfeited his own life thereby. It was Guðrún's secret, a profound secret of human behaviour, a secret that she took with her to her grave at Helgafell.

Just outside the present churchyard at Helgafell, but in an area that was once part of the old churchyard, there lies a long, raised grave-mound, just over three metres in length. Curiously, it is aligned not east and west as was the normal custom with Christian graves, but north/south. This grave is traditionally associated with Guðrún Ósvífursdóttir, and has a modern headstone to that effect. It was excavated in 1897 by the English artist W. G. Collingwood and an Icelandic scholar, Dr Jón Stefánsson. They reported that the mound had been carefully lined with stones on all sides. There was a thick layer of charcoal, and underneath that, a layer of decayed bone. Some very small teeth were found at the north end, and the remains of a skull. The grave had already been disturbed in antiquity, and all that was found in it apart from the bones were some traces of iron rust, a pebble, and a small stone with several highly polished and gleaming facets—an amulet, perhaps.

Is it Guðrún's grave? Or someone else's? It probably does not matter very much; but romantics dearly want to be able to associate it with the last resting-place of this remarkable saga heroine, lovely and imperious, as fierce in hatred as she was in love, this passionate woman who finally made her peace with life and her God in the little church at Helgafell.

There is a further clue, or coincidence at least, to intrigue the curious. In the churchyard at Borg, in Borgarfjörður, the home of Egill Skallagrímsson, there is another grave-mound that stands out from the rest because it, too, is orientated north and south, like the grave at Helgafell. According to *Laxdæla Saga*, Kjartan was buried at Borg because there was no other church in the Dales at that time, two or three years after the Conversion. It is tempting to think that this exceptional grave at Borg might be the resting-place of Kjartan Ólafsson—a match for the grave at Helgafell in which the woman he had loved is thought to lie buried. The grave had a headstone with runic lettering on it. Wishful thinking in the past had deciphered it as 'Here rests Kjartan Ólafsson'; but sober modern scholarship insists that it simply reads 'Here rests Hallur Hranason'.

It makes no difference, really. It only illustrates the power of the saga, that men should always have longed to find tangible proofs of its enduring truth.

CHAPTER 16

Njáls Saga

'Hefir hverr til síns ágætis nökkut,' segir Gunnar, 'ok skal þik þessa eigi lengi biðja.

'To each his own way of earning fame,' said Gunnar. 'You shall not be asked again.'

(*Njáls Saga*)

Njáls Saga is the greatest and the most cherished of all the Icelandic sagas. It was written around 1280 by an unknown author, a mighty masterpiece that towers over the saga landscape, an epic in every sense of the term.

The landscape of *Njáls Saga*—the *Njála* country, as it is familiarly called—lies on the southern coastal plains, bounded by the River Rangá to the west and the powerful waters of the River Markarfljót to the east, and the slopes of Fljótshlíð to the north. This is the heartland of the action of the saga, for it contains the homes of the two major protagonists, the peerless hero Gunnar of Hlíðarendi and the farmer-sage Njáll of Bergthórshvoll.

At the core of the drama is Njáll himself: Njáll Thorgeirsson, the kindly, thoughtful farmer who is burned alive in his home with his violent sons by a confederacy of enemies in the year 1011. His young friend and protégé is Gunnar Hámundarson, a man of outstanding prowess and accomplishments, who is also done to death by a band of enemies after a heroic lone defence in his home in the year 990. The two tragedies are inextricably linked by bonds of friendship and feud; and they give the author material for a profound and moving exploration of the deepest motives of human behaviour and morality, of heroism and headstrong courage,

Borg at Borgarnes: the home of Egill Skallagrímsson, eponymous hero of *Egils Saga,* and also, for a time, of his descendant, Snorri Sturluson, the historian and probable author of the saga.

Snorri's Pool at Reykholt: the open-air pool, filled from a natural hotspring, was built in the thirteenth century by Snorri Sturluson. In the background, the underground passage that led to the cellar of his home.

of love and loyalty, of cowardice and treachery, of faith and fate. It is written with extraordinary sureness and skill, a mastery of language and event, and an exceptional visual talent that brings vividly to life the places that we can visit to this day, and relive the highly charged events that took place there a thousand years ago.

Njáls Saga is written in the form of a trilogy. The first part tells the story of Gunnar of Hlíðarendi; the central part concerns the events leading up to the Burning of Njáll; and the final section deals with the protracted vengeance exacted by Njáll's son-in-law, Kári Sölmundarson, and the final reconciliation. The three are interwoven into an immense tapestry of humanity in action, a drama of mounting intensity that overwhelms all those involved in it.

In the centre of the gathering storm stands the slight figure of Njáll Thorgeirsson of Bergthórshvoll:

> Njáll was wealthy and handsome, but he had one peculiarity, in that he could not grow a beard.
>
> He was so skilled in law that no one was considered his equal. He was a wise and prescient man. His advice was sound and benevolent, and always turned out well for those who followed it. He was a gentle man of great integrity; he remembered the past and discerned the future, and solved the problems of any man who came to him for help.
>
> His wife was called Bergthóra . . . She was an exceptional and courageous woman, but rather harsh-natured.

Yet Njáll is not a saint, despite the bland description with which he is introduced in the saga. He is a complex and even ambiguous man, a man of peace and goodwill and good intentions who was none the less blinded by loyalty to his own family. With his wisdom and foresight he struggles to control events which are ultimately uncontrollable because they are pre-ordained, not by some impersonal supernatural force of destiny but by the predispositions and propensities of human beings themselves.

Gunnar of Hlíðarendi

It is impossible to summarize the 'plot' of *Njáls Saga* in a few brief pages. But one can experience some of the highlights and give them coherence in terms of the places that still stand in the *Njála* landscape.

The saga opens, oddly enough, in the middle of another saga, in the farmstead of Höskuldsstaðir in *Laxdæla Saga*, the home of Höskuldur Dala-Kollsson (see Ch 15). The occasion was a family feast where Höskuldur was entertaining his half-brother, Hrútur Herjólfsson. As they sat together at table, Höskuldur's daughter Hallgerður was playing on the floor beside some other girls:

> She was a tall, beautiful child with long silken hair that hung down to her waist . . .
> Höskuldur said to Hrútur, 'What do you think of her? Don't you think she is beautiful?'
> Hrútur made no reply. Höskuldur repeated the question. Then Hrútur said, 'The child is beautiful enough, and many will suffer for her beauty; but I cannot imagine how thief's eyes have come into our kin.'

With that flashing, ominous reference to her 'thief's eyes' we are introduced to the tempestuous, selfish and unstable Hallgerður, who will later play a significant part in the downfall of her husband, Gunnar of Hlíðarendi.

Hrútur Herjólfsson is one of the early characters in *Njáls Saga* whose actions will have incalculably dire consequences on the lives of others later on. He was betrothed to a young lady called Unnur, the daughter of an eminent chieftain who lived at the manor farm of Völlur, high in the Rangriver Plains. Hrútur decided to delay the marriage in order to go to Norway to collect an inheritance; but in Norway, in order to improve his position at court, he allowed himself to be seduced by the nymphomaniac Queen Mother of Norway, Gunnhild, the widow of Eirik Blood-Axe (see Ch 14). When he left Norway to claim his bride, the baleful Gunnhild laid a curse on him that prevented him from consummating his marriage to Unnur. Unnur thereupon divorced him; her father tried to claim the dowry back, but Hrútur, his pride insulted, refused to give it back and challenged her father to a duel instead, which the old man wisely declined. Unnur, demoralized by the failure of her marriage, squandered the estate of Völlur that she inherited on her father's death, and in order to get her dowry back from Hrútur, she turned for help to her cousin, Gunnar of Hlíðarendi:

> He was a tall, powerful man, outstandingly skilful with weapons. He could strike or throw with either hand, and his sword-strokes were so fast that he seemed to be brandishing three swords at once. He was excellent at archery, and his arrows never missed their mark. He could jump more than his own height in full armour, and just as far backwards as forwards. He could swim like a seal. There was no sport at which anyone could even attempt to compete with him. It has been said that there has never been his equal.

Gunnar went to see his friend, Njáll of Bergthórshvoll, for advice on how to tackle the problem, and recovered the money by turning the tables on Hrútur and confronting him with a challenge to a duel that he declined. Unnur turned out to be a weak and shallow woman; much against Gunnar's pressing advice, she married a vicious, spiteful man called Valgarður the Grey. Unnur's gratitude to Gunnar turned sour, and her son, Mörður Valgarðsson, was brought up to hate Gunnar of Hlíðarendi and his friends with ferocious malevolence. Mörður, smooth-talking, handsome and plausible, is the only deliberately evil agent in the saga, as malignant as Iago, consumed with envy and coldly dedicated to the downfall of others. It is Mörður's machinations that release the destructive forces that overwhelm first Gunnar of Hlíðarendi and then the sons of Njáll.

After his victory over Hrútur, Gunnar went abroad to win fame and fortune as a Viking adventurer. He returned home in a blaze of glory; and at the Althing that summer, basking in the sunshine of celebrity and wealth, he met the ravishingly

beautiful Hallgerður Long-Legs (see Ch 7). Volatile, passionate and ruthless, Hallgerður had been married twice by then,
and widowed twice; both of her husbands had had occasion to
slap her face, and had been done to death by her foster-father
for their pains.

Gunnar and Hallgerður fell in love there and then and were
betrothed on the spot, much to the dismay of Njáll, who
foresaw nothing but trouble from the match. Hallgerður and
Bergthóra, Njáll's large-tempered wife, immediately started
a quarrel that led to a deadly feud of killing and counter-
killing of each other's slaves and workmen. Each time, Njáll
and Gunnar paid the appropriate compensation for the
crimes, and their friendship remained unimpaired; but one of
the men killed had been the foster-father of Njáll's three
warrior sons, and present at his killing had been Gunnar's
kinsman and Hallgerður's son-in-law, the vain and showy
Thráinn Sigfússon. It was something the Njálssons would
never forget or forgive. For the time being, they contented
themselves by striking down the men who had actually done
the killing; it is the first time we see the three brothers in
action—Helgi, Grímur, and the eldest son, the huge and
demonic Skarp-Héðinn.

Hallgerður continued to make trouble for Gunnar. When a
churlish farmer called Otkell refused to sell provisions to
Gunnar one time, Hallgerður sent a slave to steal the food
from him. When Gunnar realized what Hallgerður had done,
he slapped her on the face. Otkell refused to accept a
handsome offer of compensation, and ultimately so
exasperated Gunnar's pride that Gunnar killed him in a fury.
Gunnar's fame and prowess became a provocation to all men
of turbulence; against his will he found himself being continu-
ally drawn into battle. Njáll, faithful to his friend despite the
enmity between their wives, tried desperately to ward off the
worst and protect him from the consequences of his killings.
But Mörður Valgarðsson, scheming tirelessly in the background, was always twisting events to confound men of good
faith and ruthlessly using other men's lives to bring about
Gunnar's downfall. The violence erupted spectacularly when

Gunnar and his brother Kolskeggur were ambushed one day on the banks of the River Rangá by a band of men led by Otkell's son, Thorgeir. Gunnar fought with such ferocity that Thorgeir and several others were killed. In the ensuing lawsuits, Njáll managed to negotiate a settlement that involved paying compensation; but for the sake of peace in the district, Gunnar and Kolskeggur were also sentenced to a three-year outlawry. It was hoped that this would give tempers a chance to cool down.

Gunnar seemed to accept the sentence with good grace. But when the day came to go into exile, he changed his mind, to everyone's dismay:

> Gunnar sent his own and Kolskeggur's goods down to the ship. When everything was on board, and the ship was almost ready to sail, Gunnar rode to Bergthórshvoll and other places to thank all those who had given him support.
>
> Early next morning he made ready to ride to the ship, and told all his people that he was going abroad for ever. Everyone was saddened at the news, but hoped that some day he would return. When he was ready to leave he embraced them all one by one. The whole household came out to see him off. With a thrust of his halberd he vaulted into the saddle, and rode away with Kolskeggur.
>
> They rode down towards Markarfljót. Just then Gunnar's horse stumbled, and he leapt from the saddle. He happened to glance up towards his home and the slopes of Hlíðarendi.
>
> 'How lovely the slopes are,' he said, 'more lovely than they have ever seemed to me before, golden cornfields and new-mown hay. I am going back home, and I will not go away.'

The site of Gunnar's Hlíðarendi was in a hollow on the hillside at the eastern end of Fljótshlíð, the long low range of hills that stretches towards the Markarfljót. Today there is a neat little group of white-painted farm buildings there, and a handsomely restored country church. From Hlíðarendi we can look out over the sweeping vista of the low-lying Land-Isles, the marshy plains that stretch southwards to the edge of the sea; in the far distance we can just make out the hillock on which Bergthórshvoll still stands. To the east, beyond the Markarfljót, looms the glittering ice-cap of Eyjafjallajökull. It was across this broad expanse that Gunnar and his brother set off on their journey to exile; and it was somewhere down there that Gunnar's horse stumbled, and Gunnar looked back at the sloping fields and meadows of his home and made his sudden, impulsive decision, knowing that he was putting his life in jeopardy by breaking the sentence of the court. From now on he would be an outlaw, 'not to be aided nor abetted, not to be fed nor forwarded nor ferried', his life forfeit to any who wanted to take it. Everyone knew what the inevitable outcome would be—not least Gunnar himself.

Next autumn a confederacy of enemies gathered, determined on a showdown. The motive spirit was Mörður Valgarðsson, as usual; but the leader was an eminent chieftain called Gissur Teitsson, Gissur the White of Skálholt, who would lead the Christian party at the Conversion of Iceland only ten years later (see Ch 10). One evening they surrounded the house at Hlíðarendi while Gunnar was alone at home with his wife, Hallgerður, and his old mother, Rannveig. They lured his dog away from the house and killed it; as it died it gave a dreadful howl, which wakened Gunnar inside the house. As his enemies attacked, he fought them off with his bow and arrows; then an assailant managed to get close enough to slash through his bowstring. Gunnar now knew that unless he could repair his bow quickly, he was doomed:

> He said to Hallgerður, 'Let me have two locks of your hair, and help my mother plait them into a bowstring for me.'
>
> 'Does anything depend on it?' asked Hallgerður.
>
> 'My life depends on it,' said Gunnar, 'for they will never overcome me as long as I can use my bow.'
>
> 'In that case,' said Hallgerður, 'I shall now remind you

of the time you once slapped me on the face. I do not care in the least how long you manage to hold out.'

'To each his own way of earning fame,' said Gunnar. 'You shall not be asked again.'

Rannveig said, 'You are an evil woman, and your shame will long be remembered.'

Gunnar defended himself with great courage, and wounded eight more so severely that many of them barely lived. He kept on fighting until exhaustion brought him to his knees. His enemies then dealt him many terrible wounds, but even then he got away from them and held them at bay for a long time. But in the end they killed him.

Njáll of Bergthórshvoll

Gunnar's death was avenged in blood by his young son, Högni, with the help of the eldest of the Njálssons, Skarp-Héðinn, for whom Gunnar had always been a hero to look up to. Njáll's younger sons, Helgi and Grímur, went off on a light-hearted Viking jaunt abroad, but found themselves embroiled in trouble as a result of the folly of Thráinn Sigfússon, Hallgerður's son-in-law. The smouldering hostility flared up anew. Back in Iceland, accompanied by their brother-in-law, Kári, a footloose Hebridean Viking who had come to their assistance, the Njálssons resolved to try conclusions with Thráinn.

On the west bank of the Markarfljót a sudden hill, a miniature mountain called Dímon, rears steep and stark, seventy-eight metres high, out of the lowlands of the Land-Isles. In *Njáls Saga* it is called Rauðaskriður (Red Scree). It used to be wooded, and it was there that the first killing of a slave took place in the murderous tit-for-tat between Berg-thóra and Hallgerður; today its rugged flanks are green with mossy grass. It was high on the slopes of Dímon that Skarp-Héðinn and his brothers lay in wait for Thráinn Sigfússon and his friends early one bright winter's morning when the Markarfljót was flowing fast between banks of ice. Njáll saw his sons setting off at dawn, having been wakened by the bump of an axe against a wooden panel:

> Skarp-Héðinn was in the lead, dressed in a blue jacket and carrying a round shield, with his axe hoisted on his shoulder. Next to him was Kári, wearing a silk jacket and a gilded helmet; there was a lion painted on his shield. Behind him walked Helgi, wearing a red tunic and a helmet, and carrying a red shield decorated with a hart. They all wore coloured clothing.

Thráinn and his men came into sight on the other side of the river. There was an ice-bridge across it, which they were expecting to cross. But they saw shields glinting in the morning sunshine on the flanks of Dímon, and guessed it might be an ambush, so they changed course and stayed on the far side of the bridge. There seemed little to fear, so Thráinn took off his cloak and helmet. The Njálssons would have to come at them across the river in a frontal attack, and they were outnumbered. But that did not stop them. They scrambled down the side of Dímon and started running hard towards the bridge. Just then, Skarp-Héðinn's shoe-thong broke, and he stopped to tie it as the others ran on ahead:

> They turned down towards the ice-bridge, running as fast as they could. Skarp-Héðinn jumped up as soon as he had tied his shoe, and hoisted his axe. He raced down straight towards the river, which was too deep to be forded anywhere along that stretch. A huge sheet of ice had formed a low hump on the other side of the channel. It was as smooth as glass, and Thráinn and his men had stopped on the middle of this hump. Skarp-Héðinn made a leap and cleared the channel between the ice-banks, steadied himself, and at once went into a slide: the ice was glassy-smooth, and he skimmed along as fast as a bird.
>
> Thráinn was then about to put on his helmet. Skarp-Héðinn came swooping down on him and swung at him with his axe. The axe crashed down on his head and split

it down to the jaw-bone, spilling the back teeth on to the ice. It all happened so quickly that no one had time to land a blow on Skarp-Héðinn as he skimmed past at great speed. Tjörvi threw a shield into his path, but Skarp-Héðinn cleared it with a jump without losing balance and slid to the other end of the sheet-ice.

Kári and the others came running up.

'That was man's work,' said Kári.

'Now it's your turn,' said Skarp-Héðinn.

The long grudge against Thráinn Sigfússon had been repaid, with interest. But the hatreds had been revived. Once again Njáll tried to avert the doom he foresaw by adopting as his own foster-son Thráinn's orphaned son, Höskuldur. He grew up in Njáll's household, a gentle and lovable boy. By binding the boy into his family, Njáll hoped to ligature a potentially lethal blood-feud against his sons. So he gave the boy all his love, and did everything in his power to advance him; he got him a chieftaincy, and arranged a good marriage for him with a woman called Hildigunnur, the proud and haughty niece of a powerful chieftain from the east of Iceland, Flosi Thórðarson of Svínafell. But the more he did for the saintly young Höskuldur, the more his own sons began to resent him. Christianity had come to Iceland, but it made little difference to people's behaviour. Now Mörður Valgarðsson stepped in again. He sensed that underneath the veneer of close friendship between Höskuldur and the Njáls-sons there were hidden tensions that he could exploit to bring about the ruin of Njáll and his family. He began to court the Njálssons' friendship, much to Njáll's dismay, playing on their jealousy of the young chieftain so favoured by their father. He found the Njálssons all too ready to believe ill of Höskuldur, and to believe that he was planning to kill them in revenge for his dead father. Mörður urged them to get their blow in first, and they, with agonizing credulity, fell for his scheming. That night they made their way to the farm of Ossabær nearby, where Höskuldur and Hildigunnur lived, and waited behind a fence:

Höskuldur woke up early that morning. He dressed and put on the cloak that Flosi had given him. With a seed-basket in one hand and a sword in the other he went out to his cornfield and started to sow.

Skarp-Héðinn had agreed with the others that they should all strike him. Now he jumped up from behind the fence. Höskuldur saw him and started to move away, but Skarp-Héðinn ran up to him and said, 'Don't bother to run away!'

With that he struck. The blow fell on Höskuldur's head. Höskuldur sank to his knees. 'May God help me and forgive you all,' he said.

They all rushed at him and cut him down.

The killing was so horrifying, so pointless, that the whole country was shocked. But there was Njáll to consider. Such was his standing and prestige that many chieftains were prepared to lean over backwards to try to reach an honourable settlement that would not involve further bloodshed—even Flosi Thórðarson of Svínafell. But on his way from the east of Iceland to the Althing where the case would be heard, Flosi had to pass the farm of Ossabær where his niece, Hildigunnur, was waiting for him with a special welcome:

'What redress will you get me?' she asked. 'How much help will you give me?'

'I shall press your claims to the full extent of the law,' said Flosi, 'or else conclude a settlement which in the eyes of all good men will satisfy every demand of honour.'

Hildigunnur said, 'Höskuldur would have avenged you with blood if he were in your place now . . .'

She walked from the room and unlocked a chest. She took out the cloak, the gift from Flosi, which Höskuldur had been wearing when he was killed, and in which she had preserved all his blood. She came back with the cloak and went up to Flosi without a word; Flosi had finished eating and the table had been cleared. She threw the cloak about his shoulders, and the clotted blood rained down all over him.

'This is the cloak you gave to Höskuldur, Flosi,' she said, 'and now I give it back to you. He was wearing it when he was killed. I call upon God and all good men to witness that I charge you in the name of all the powers of your Christ, and in the name of your courage and your manhood, to avenge every one of the wounds that marked his body—or be an object of contempt to all men.'

Flosi threw off the cloak and flung it back into her arms. 'Monster!' he cried. 'You want us to take the course which will turn out the worst for all of us. Cold are the counsels of women!'

Flosi was now under intolerable pressure to exact a blood-revenge. Desperately, Njáll went round all his old friends and acquaintances at the Althing, seeking their support in the lawsuit; but wherever he went, Skarp-Héðinn followed, sardonically undermining all his father's pleas for help. Yet somehow, a peace settlement was arranged. Njáll agreed to pay an unheard-of sum of money in compensation for Höskuldur's life, and Flosi was persuaded to accept it. Njáll got all the money together and piled it on the floor of the *Lögrétta* (Court of Legislature); and as a grace-gift, an extra to cement the agreement, he laid on top of it a beautifully embroidered silk cloak as a personal gift for Flosi. Now Flosi approached the *Lögrétta*, stiff-legged, bristling and touchy; and suddenly the reader knows that something is going to go terribly wrong.

Flosi entered the Court of Legislature to look at the money, and said, 'This is a great sum of good money, and handsomely paid, as was to be expected.'

Then he picked up the cloak and asked whose contribution that might be. No one answered him. Again he waved the cloak and asked who had given it, and laughed; but still no one answered. Then he said, 'Does none of you really know who owned this garment? Or does none of you dare to tell me?'

'Who do you think gave it?' asked Skarp-Héðinn.

'If you want to know,' said Flosi, 'I will tell you what I think. I think it was your father who gave it, "Old Beardless", for few can tell just by looking at him whether he is a man or a woman.'

'It is wrong to mock him in his old age,' said Skarp-Héðinn, 'and no real man has ever done that before. You can be sure that he is a man, for he has fathered sons on his wife; and we have let few of our kinsmen lie unavenged at our doors.'

He snatched the cloak away and tossed a pair of blue drawers at Flosi, saying that he would have greater need of them than a cloak.

'Why should I need them more?' asked Flosi.

'You certainly will if you are, as I have heard, the mistress of the troll of Svínafell who uses you as a woman every ninth night.'

Then Flosi kicked the pile of money and said he would not take a penny of it; he said they would take no other compensation for Höskuldur than blood-vengeance . . .

Flosi's taunts about Njáll were bad enough. But Skarp-Héðinn's crudely obscene insult, implying every sort of perversion, was unforgivable. It was as if Skarp-Héðinn had deliberately set out to destroy the fragile, precarious settlement that had been painstakingly agreed. From now on there was no going back, and events moved inexorably towards their terrible end.

The Burning at Bergthórshvoll

At 6 p.m. in the evening of Monday, 20 August in the year 1011, a warlike band of men, a hundred strong, gathered at the roots of the mountain Thríhyrning, north of the Land-Isles, under the leadership of Flosi Thórðarson. It was their intention to deal once and for all with the sons of Njáll. And now they set off riding down across the broad plains of the Land-Isles, heading south for Bergthórshvoll.

The farmhouse of Bergthórshvoll has always been perched

on a low swelling mound standing proud of the plain, just a hump of land divided into three distinct hillocks. Today there is an air of shabbiness about it all. Yet one can stand outside the farmhouse and visualize with total clarity the scene on that dramatic evening; every telling detail is described in the saga, as vividly as in a film scenario.

For several weeks, ever since the abortive peace-meeting at the Althing, the air in the southlands had been charged with tension: ominous, doom-laden. Nerves had been at full stretch as people waited for the inevitable showdown between Flosi and the Njálssons. Kári Sölmundarson told his father-in-law that he would be staying on at Berthórshvoll that summer instead of going to his own home: 'Your sons and I shall stand or fall together.' On the day itself, Njáll's younger sons had been away on a visit to a farm just along the coast, where their children were in fosterage. They had not planned to return that night; but they heard some vagrant beggarwomen gossiping about the unusual amount of movement they had seen in the district that day: 'One might say that everyone is on the go these days.' And with that, Grímur and Helgi had hastened back to Bergthórshvoll. A senile old woman called Sæunn who had been with the family all her life was found by Skarp-Héðinn outside the house, whacking furiously at a pile of chickweed: 'This chickweed will be used as the kindling when they burn Njáll and my foster-child Bergthóra inside the house.' And that afternoon, Bergthóra said, 'You are all to choose your favourite food tonight, for this is the last time I shall be serving a meal for my household.'

In the gathering twilight, Flosi and his men came riding fast across the Land-Isles, each leading two fresh horses. They thought they might catch the household unawares. But at Bergthórshvoll they found the Njálssons and Kári and all their farmhands ranged in front of the house, a formidable crew of thirty men, armed to the teeth and ready for a fight. Flosi, faced with this uncompromising show of strength, halted. Watching them, Njáll now made a strange suggestion. Perhaps he had had enough of all the violence and bloodshed, the vicious circle of vengeance and counter-vengeance.

Whatever the reason, he asked his turbulent sons, hard men all of them, not to try to defend the house from outside but to go indoors, where he said they would be safer. It was a suicidal request, for inside the house they would be trapped, and dreadfully vulnerable to fire. Njáll knew it, his sons knew it, Flosi knew it. And yet the Njálssons agreed, because they wanted to grant the old man his last request:

> 'Let us do as our father wishes,' said Helgi. 'That will be best for us all.'
> 'I am not so sure of that,' said Skarp-Héðinn, 'for he is now a doomed man. But still, I do not mind pleasing my father by burning with him in the house, for I am not afraid of dying.'

They went indoors. 'Now they are doomed,' said Flosi. He and his men surrounded the house and attacked the doors vigorously. But they could make no headway, and his own men started suffering heavy losses. Flosi began to realize that if he was going to get the better of the Njálssons, he had no choice but to resort to fire:

> 'We must set fire to the house and burn them to death, which is a grave responsibility before God, since we are Christian men ourselves. But that is what we must do.'

They kindled a fire with the chickweed they found lying around, and soon the whole house was ablaze. Flosi allowed all the women and children to leave; then he stepped up to the door and called Njáll and Bergthóra to come out and speak to him, offering them a chance of leaving the burning house:

> 'I have no wish to go outside,' said Njáll, 'for I am an old man now and ill-equipped to avenge my sons; and I do not want to live in shame.'
> Flosi said to Bergthóra, 'You come out, Bergthóra, for under no circumstances do I want you to burn.'
> Bergthóra replied, 'I was given to Njáll in marriage young, and I promised him that we would share the same fate.'

Then they both went back inside the house. 'What shall we do now?' asked Bergthóra. 'Let us go to our bed,' said Njáll, 'and lie down.'

Only Kári survived from that terrible night; when the roof collapsed he managed to jump out from a burning wall, and dodged away under cover of the smoke. All the rest perished. At dawn, as the flames still sputtered, flaring up and dying down, the dead were found. Skarp-Héðinn, warrior to the last, had been trapped by a falling rafter against a wall:

> He had held himself upright against the wall; his legs were almost burnt off below the knee, but the rest of him was unburnt. He had bitten hard on his lip. His eyes were open but not swollen. He had driven his axe into the gable with such violence that half the full depth of the blade was buried in the wall, and the metal had not softened . . .

It is such a vivid and compelling scene, the Burning at Bergthórshvoll—such drama, such implicit terror, such lurid tragedy: the sullen roar of flames fanned by an easterly wind, the spiteful hiss of flying sparks, the choking sobs and screams, the anguished courage of the doomed; and then, come the dawn, the eerie smoking silence in the fitful aftermath of storm. Naturally, people have wanted to know if there was any proof of the event. Was it true? Or was it pure, spell-binding fiction?

There have been two major archaeological excavations conducted at Bergthórshvoll, in 1927–8 and more significantly in 1951–2. These excavations proved conclusively that a fire had taken place at Bergthórshvoll, and carbon-14 tests showed that it took place during the Saga Age, at about the time indicated by the saga itself and by the Icelandic Annals. There was ample evidence of destruction by fire of some outhouses—a drying-oven (*sofnhús*) and a large cow-byre for thirty head of cattle. Not much ash was found on the site of the farmhouse itself, but over the centuries houses had been built one after another on the same site, and little ash could be expected to have remained.

Kári Sölmundarson

The Burning is the climax, though not the culmination, of *Njáls Saga*. Kári Sölmundarson had escaped, and inside the blazing house he had promised to avenge Skarp-Héðinn if he happened to survive. Both he and Flosi Thórðarson gathered allies from all over the country for a massive trial of strength at the legal proceedings that ensued at the Althing. After a lengthy and dramatic court-room battle, a legal blunder allowed the Burners a loophole to get off scot-free. At that, the friends of Kári rushed to arms, and a pitched battle broke out. When peace was eventually restored and a proper settlement agreed, Kári refused to be party to any agreement, thus leaving himself free to undertake the blood-vengeance he had promised Skarp-Héðinn. One by one he tracked the Burners down, pursuing them relentlessly far beyond Iceland's borders. Flosi made no attempt to retaliate as the Burners were killed off, one after the other. Eventually, Kári's blood-lust was satisfied. The two men were reconciled, and to symbolize the end of the blood-feud, Kári was given the hand in marriage of Flosi's niece, Hildigunnur, the widow of murdered Höskuldur. All passion was spent; the evil forces aroused by envy and greed and brutality had exhausted themselves.

'And there I end the Saga of the Burning of Njáll.'

Njáls Saga was written at the end of an era: the culmination of the golden age of saga-writing, and the end of the Icelandic commonwealth. The author had seen the high ideals of the founding fathers of the nation being traduced by the self-seeking power-struggles of the chieftains of the Sturlung Age. He had seen the social fabric of the nation crumble and disintegrate, he had seen Iceland's independence mortgaged to the Norwegian crown only a few years before he began to write his masterpiece.

His profound knowledge of human nature had surely been

deepened by the traumatic events he had witnessed in his own lifetime; and his telling of the story of Njáll and the Burning must have been profoundly affected by his awareness of men's infinite capacity for destructiveness. He used the past to illuminate for all eternity the present, in a way that only the greatest writers can. He elevated this story of early Iceland to a peak of sublime achievement that nothing could surpass.

And there I end the Iceland Saga.

BOOKS FOR FURTHER READING

There is a vast literature, in many different languages. This list is limited to books in English. Many of them are now out of print, but should be available through good libraries.

General history

Bárðarson, Hjálmar R., *Iceland, a portrait of its land and people*, Reykjavík, 1982
Gjerset, Knut, *History of Iceland*, New York, 1924
Hood, John C. F., *Icelandic Church Saga*, London, 1946
Jensen, Elisabeth, *Iceland: Old–New Republic*, New York, 1954
Kristjánsson, Jónas, *Icelandic Sagas and Manuscripts*, Saga Publishing Co., Reykjavík, 1970
Magnusson, Magnus, *Iceland* (photographs by John Chang McCurdy), Almenna Bókafélagið, Reykjavík, 1979
Magnússon, Sigurður A., *Northern Sphinx: Iceland and the Icelanders from the Settlement to the Present*, Snæbjörn Jónsson & Co., Reykjavík, 1984
Njarðvík, Njörður P., *Birth of a Nation*, Iceland Review History Series, Reykjavík, 1978
Turville-Petre, Gabriel, *Origins of Icelandic Literature*, OUP, 1953
Wilson, David (ed.), *The Northern World*, London, 1980

Saga translations

A Pageant of Old Scandinavia, Henry Goddard Leach (ed.), American-Scandinavian Foundation, New York, 1946
Arrow-Odd: A Medieval Novel, (trs.) Paul Edwards & Hermann Pálsson, University of London Press, 1970
A Tale of Icelanders, (trs.) Alan Boucher, Iceland Review, Reykjavík, 1980

Egil's Saga. (trs.) Hermann Pálsson & Paul Edwards, Penguin Classics, 1976

Eirik the Red and other Icelandic Sagas, (trs.) Gwyn Jones, World's Classics, 1961

Eyrbyggja Saga, (trs.) Hermann Pálsson & Paul Edwards, New Saga Library, Edinburgh, 1973

Four Icelandic Sagas, (trs.) Gwyn Jones, New York, 1935

Gautrek's Saga and other Medieval Tales, (trs.) Hermann Pálsson & Paul Edwards, University of London Press, 1968

Göngu-Hrolfs Saga, (trs.) Hermann Pálsson & Paul Edwards, Canongate, 1980

Grettir's Saga, (trs.) Denton Fox & Hermann Pálsson, University of Toronto Press, 1974

Heimskringla, (trs.) Lee M. Hollander, University of Texas Press, 1944

Hrafnkel's Saga and other Icelandic stories, (trs.) Hermann Pálsson, Penguin Classics, 1970

Hrolf Gautreksson, a Viking Romance, (trs.) Hermann Pálsson & Paul Edwards, Southside, Edinburgh, 1972

Íslendingabók (trs.) Halldór Hermannsson, Ithaca, 1930 (*Islandica*)

King Harald's Saga, (trs.) Magnus Magnusson & Hermann Pálsson, Penguin Classics, 1966

Laxdæla Saga, (trs.) Magnus Magnusson & Hermann Pálsson, Penguin Classics, 1969

Njal's Saga, (trs.) Magnus Magnusson & Hermann Pálsson, Penguin Classics, 1960

Origines Islandicae I–II, (trs.) Gudbrand Vigfusson & F. York Powell, Oxford, 1905

Orkneyinga Saga, (trs.) Hermann Pálsson & Paul Edwards, Hogarth Press, 1978

Seven Viking Romances, (trs.) Hermann Pálsson & Paul Edwards, Penguin Classics, 1970

Sturlunga Saga I–II, (trs.) Gudbrand Vigfusson, Oxford 1878

Tales from the Eastfirths, (trs.) Alan Boucher, Iceland Review, Reykjavík, 1981

The Book of Settlements, (trs.) Hermann Pálsson & Paul Edwards, University of Manitoba Press, 1972

The Conferates and Hen-Thorir, (trs.) Hermann Pálsson, Southside, Edinburgh, 1975

The First Grammatical Treatise, (trs.) Einar Haugen, Longmans, 1972

The Northmen Talk, (trs.) Jacqueline Simpson, London 1965

The Prose Edda of Snorri Sturluson, (trs.) Jean I. Young, Cambridge, 1973

The Saga Library I–VI, (trs.) William Morris & Eiríkur Magnússon, London, 1891–1905

The Saga of Gisli, (trs.) George Johnston, London, 1965

The Saga of Gunnlaug Serpent-Tongue, (trs.) Randolph Quirk, Edinburgh, 1957

The Saga of Hallfred the Troublesome Scald, (trs.) Alan Boucher, Iceland Review, Reykjavík, 1981

The Saga of Hord and the Holm-Dwellers, (trs.) Alan Boucher, Iceland Review, Reykjavík, 1983

The Saga of King Heidrek the Wise, (trs.) Christopher Tolkien, Edinburgh, 1960

The Saga of the Jomsvikings, (trs.) N. F. Blake, Edinburgh, 1962

The Saga of the Volsungs, (trs.) R. G. Finch, Edinburgh, 1965

The Sagas of Kormák and the Sworn Brothers, (trs.) Lee M. Hollander, New York, 1949

The Vatnsdalers' Saga, (trs.) Gwyn Jones, Princeton University Press, 1944

The Vinland Sagas, (trs.) Magnus Magnusson & Hermann Pálsson, Penguin Classics, 1965

Three Icelandic Sagas, (trs.) M. H. Scargill & Margaret Schlauch, New York, 1950

Víga-Glúm's Saga & the Story of Ögmund Dyatt, (trs.) Lee M. Hollander, New York, 1972

ACKNOWLEDGEMENTS

In this book I have drawn on the works of many scholars, both Icelandic and non-Icelandic, to help me present an up-to-date assessment of the Icelandic sagas and their place in the Iceland Saga. In particular I am indebted to my friends Dr Jónas Kristjánsson, Professor Hermann Pálsson, and the late Professor Björn Thorsteinsson, all of whom have done much to guide and influence my thinking over the years. This book is written very much from an Icelandic point of view; but it is a pleasure to acknowledge the tremendous contribution that scholars in Britain and the United States have made to Icelandic studies in general and this book in particular.

The translations in this book are, nominally, my own; but I have made free use of the work of other translators where I found I could not better their efforts. I have also taken the liberty of amending my own earlier translations (in collaboration with Hermann Pálsson) in the Penguin Classics series, especially in the use of Icelandic rather than Anglicised proper names.

The publishers wish to thank Gretar Eiriksson for permission to reproduce the photograph of Helgafell, and Mats Wibe Lund for permission to reproduce the rest of the photographs in this book.

INDEX

Vitazgjafi (sacred cornfield), 97–8
volcanoes, volcanic eruptions, 2,
   3–5, 26, 58–9, 73–4, 119, 141–2
Völlur, farm, 216, 217
Völsunga Saga, 21–2

Völuspá (*Sybil's Prophecy*), 23

Wagner, Richard, 23
Westmann Islands
   (Vestmannæyjar), 4, 40, 137,138